Virtual Voyages CINEMA AND TRAVEL

JEFFREY RUOFF, EDITOR

Duke University Press   Durham and London   2006

© 2006 DUKE UNIVERSITY PRESS

All rights reserved

Printed in the United States of America

on acid-free paper ∞

Designed by C. H. Westmoreland

Typeset in Janson and Frutiger

by Tseng Information Systems, Inc.

Library of Congress Cataloging-in-Publication Data

Virtual voyages : cinema and travel /

Jeffrey Ruoff, editor.

p. cm.

Includes bibliographical references and index.

ISBN 0-8223-3701-0 (cloth : alk. paper)

ISBN 0-8223-3713-4 (pbk. : alk. paper)

1. Travelogues (Motion pictures, television, etc.)

—History and criticism. I. Ruoff, Jeffrey

PN1995.9.T73V57 2006

791.43′62—dc22   2005026240

A Jean Rouch et Jay Ruby

LES MAÎTRES FOUS

I ALWAYS THINK OF DOCUMENTARY

AS HAVING CERTAIN FUNDAMENTAL CHAPTERS.

THE FIRST CHAPTER IS OF COURSE THE TRAVELOGUE.

—JOHN GRIERSON

CONTENTS

ACKNOWLEDGMENTS

||||||||||||||||||||||||||||||||||||||||||||||||||||||||||||||||||||||||||||||||||||||||||||||||||||||||||||||||||||||||||||||||

The ethnographic filmmaker Jean Rouch introduced me to anthropology, in both its written and visual forms, when I was an undergraduate studying abroad in Paris. Most memorable was his course at l'Ecole Pratique des Hautes Etudes en Sciences Sociales on "*La cinématographie des rites funéraires,*" in which we watched, among other films, his extraordinary Sigui saga on the Dogon of Mali. Later, as an MFA student at Temple University, I was fortunate to study with Jay Ruby, who shared his passion for ethnographic film and photography. Sadly, Jean Rouch passed away on 18 February 2004, in a car accident in Niger, as I was editing this volume. I dedicate this anthology to Jean and Jay because it grows out of interests that they sparked and nourished.

More recently, I was privileged to team-teach a course with the anthropologist David Napier, "Film and Anthropological Representation," an experience which inspired me to continue working in interdisciplinary endeavors. David made numerous suggestions to the proposal for this anthology, as did Glenn Altschuler and Lauren Rabinovitz, for which I am thankful. I am grateful to the manuscript reviewers who supported the publication of this work, while making useful suggestions for its improvement, including the now no longer anonymous Richard Chalfen, Bill Nichols, and Lucien Taylor. My thanks to Paul Hockings, the editor-in-chief of *Visual Anthropology*, for the opportunity to guest-edit issue 15, no. 1, "Travelogues and Travel Films," and for encouraging me to publish an expanded version in book form. My gratitude goes also to Nina Graybill, Esq., for legal assistance with this project.

My colleagues in the Department of Film and Television Studies at Dartmouth College—Mark Williams, Bill Phillips, Amy Lawrence, Mary Desjardins, David Ehrlich, and Jim Brown—have created and maintained a wonderful place to teach and do research. My thanks to Cheryl Coutermarsh, our academic coordinator, for forwarding my mail to Paris and many other favors, large and small. I would like to acknowledge my students, too numerous to mention individually, whose comments on anthropology, representation, and travel have contributed to this work. Otmar Foelsche and Susan Bibeau of the Humanities Computing Center gave the kind of timely advice that makes scholarship not only feasible but enjoyable. I am also indebted to John DeSantis, the film studies bibliographer at Baker-Berry Library, for his assistance acquiring videos and manuscripts. Jane Carroll, Assistant Dean of the Faculty, has been quick to assist my search for funds to do research, which I greatly appreciate.

In 1997–98, the National Endowment for the Humanities awarded me a year-long research fellowship which enabled me to begin my work on travelogues. My thanks also to the Walter and Constance Burke Foundation, the John Sloan Dickey Center for International Understanding, the Nelson A. Rockefeller Center for the Social Sciences, and the Marion and Jasper Whiting Foundation for generous research funds. Additional thanks to the Dickey Center for a grant to bring four scholars to Dartmouth to discuss their contributions to this anthology. Chris Wohlforth, the Dickey Associate for Program Development, provided much assistance in the planning of this event as did the Assistant Director, Margot de l'Etoile. At this workshop, Paula Amad, Peter Bloom, Alison Griffiths, and Lauren Rabinovitz made important contributions to the overall approach of this book in addition to sharing their individual essays. Funds left over from this workshop also helped acquire some of the illustrations used in this anthology.

Lenore Grenoble, the Associate Dean of the Faculty at Dartmouth, granted funds to support the publication of this book, for which I am most appreciative. Mme Frédérique LeBris, archivist at the Musée Albert-Kahn in Paris, provided the illustration featured in the chapter on Kahn and helped me get permission to reprint it here. M. Jean-Michel Berrier, director of Connaissance du Monde, graciously accorded me an interview and granted permission to use several stills from French travelogues in this anthology. I am grateful to Genoa Caldwell, who generously provided the Burton Holmes illustrations that appear in a number of essays. My thanks to Roland Cosandey for providing photographs to illustrate Tom Gunning's essay and to Jan-Hein Bal of the Nederlands Filmmuseum for frame enlargements from *By Aeroplane to Pygmyland* for use in my introduction.

During my research on travelogues I have been invited to lecture at the University of Iowa, the University of Chicago, Reed College, the Smithsonian Institution, Northwestern University, San Francisco State University, the University of California-Santa Cruz, the University of Southern California, the University of California-Irvine, Indiana University-Bloomington, and Evergreen State College. For an invitation to speak about travelogues at a colloquium on "Voyage et cinéma" at the University of Provence, I am beholden to professors Jean-Luc Lioult and René Gardies. To faculty and students at all these institutions, my thanks for their thoughtful responses.

My editor at Duke, Ken Wissoker, and editorial assistants Christine Dahlin and Courtney Berger provided outstanding help throughout the whole process of publication. The references in this volume to Duke University Press books attest to Ken Wissoker's long-standing contribution to related topics. My thanks to the contributors to this volume for completing their work brilliantly, and on time, making my work as editor as pleasurable as possible. I learned a lot and I regret that praise is the only compensation I can offer the individual contributors. I am grateful to Helen Reiff for proofing and indexing this volume with her usual dexterity and wit. A special thanks to Glennis Gold and our daughter Natalie Gold for accompanying me on research trips to France and for "keeping me company," as Natalie likes to say, at home in Vermont.

"'The Whole World within Reach': Travel Images without Borders" by Tom Gunning originally appeared in *Cinéma sans frontières/Images Across Borders*, ed. Roland Cosandey and François Albera, Lausanne: Editions Payot, 1995. It is reprinted here with the permission of Tom Gunning. Lauren Rabinovitz's "From *Hale's Tours* to *Star Tours*: Virtual Voyages and the Delirium of the Hyper-Real" first appeared in *Iris* vol. 25 in 1998. It is reprinted here with the permission of *Iris*. Earlier versions of the following four chapters appeared in *Visual Anthropology* 15, no. 1 (January-March 2002), and are reprinted here with permission from Taylor & Francis: "Homemade Travelogues: *Autosonntag*—A Film Safari in the Swiss Alps," Alexandra Schneider; "Hollywood and the Attractions of the Travelogue," Dana Benelli; "'The Last of the Great (Foot-Slogging) Explorers': Lewis Cotlow and the Ethnographic Imaginary in Popular Travel Film," Amy J. Staples; and "Show and Tell: The 16mm Travel Lecture Film," Jeffrey Ruoff. An earlier version of "Show and Tell: The

16mm Travel Lecture Film" appeared in *CineAction* 47 in 1998 and it is reprinted here with the permission of *CineAction*.

Peter J. Bloom retains the copyright for his essay "Trans-Saharan Automotive Cinema: Citroën-, Renault-, and Peugeot-Sponsored Documentary Interwar Crossing Films."

The Filmic Fourth Dimension

CINEMA AS AUDIOVISUAL VEHICLE

JEFFREY RUOFF

||||||||||||||||||||||||||||||||||||||||||||||||||||||||||||||||||||||||||||||||||||||||||||||||||||||||||||||||||||||||||||||||||

The cinema is a machine for constructing relations of space and time; the exploration of the world through images and sounds of travel has always been one of its principal features. This anthology focuses on the travelogue film, a form that dominated the early cinema period from 1895 to 1905, played an important role in the consolidation of documentary and ethnographic film in the second and third decades of the twentieth century, flourished in the post–World War II era of 16mm distribution, and continues to this day in IMAX theaters as well as a host of nontheatrical venues. The travelogue is certainly the "first chapter" of the history of documentary, as John Grierson suggests (Sussex 1975: 29), but it is also manifest in avant-garde cinema, home movies, and fiction films. For generations, audiences around the globe have viewed other cultures through fictional and nonfictional travel imagery. The travelogue returns the cinema to its vocation as a machine for knowing the world, the visionary device that the documentary filmmaker Dziga Vertov imagined in 1924, "the microscope and the telescope of time" (1984: 41). Theorizing the cinema as a machine for travel returns us to questions about the basic cinematic apparatus but without the essentialist assumptions that guided earlier approaches in film studies. Instead, *Virtual Voyages* proposes historically grounded approaches that illuminate our understanding of the medium by seizing different instances in its use and reception over the past one hundred years.

Why Travelogues?

Travelogues are not to be celebrated simply because they are a fascinating, neglected form. Travelogues matter because they are an intrinsic form of cinema, consonant with common parlances such as the *traveling* shot and *motion* pictures. Regardless of the multiple ways of dating the origins of cinema, the travelogue played a fundamental role in its conception and earliest configurations. The travelogue often involves a live component, embracing experiential and performative dimensions of the cinematic experience that challenge our conceptions of the medium. Frequently episodic, travelogue narration offers an alternative to hegemonic narrative forms in both the documentary and the feature fiction film. Moreover, industrialized forms of representation (photography, the illustrated daily newspaper, movies) arose together with industrialized modes of transportation (the steamship, the train, the automobile), and these diverse components of our modern world intersect precisely in travel, tourism, and colonialism; in the vortex of these forces lies the travelogue. The goal of this volume is to understand representations of travel in the history of cinema and to share these investigations with scholars and students in a variety of disciplines, including film studies, cultural studies, anthropology, sociology, geography, and history.

The Travelogue as Education

The live illustrated travel lecture is one of the pre-cinematic forms that influenced the basic vocabulary of motion pictures. Charles Musser and X. Theodore Barber have done pioneering work on individual travel lecturers (Musser 1984; Barber 1993).[1] They demonstrated the play between education and pleasure in travelogues, a feature that Richard Altick refers to as "rational amusement" in his magisterial study of British public entertainment from 1600 to 1851, *The Shows of London* (1978: 3). Of the art of the eighteenth-century panorama (a scene depicted on a moving cylindrical canvas), Altick notes that viewers could count on being "edified, never corrupted" (184). From nineteenth-century American magic lantern travel lectures (Barber 1993: 69), through the twentieth-century travelogue film, and even in today's IMAX movies, the educational justification for travelogues—whatever its actual merits—often draws to

1 A full house for an evening of Holmes's travelogues at Orchestra Hall in Chicago. Courtesy of the Burton Holmes Collection, Seattle, Wash.

theaters audiences who are otherwise alienated from fiction film: "The travel lecture emerged [at the outset of the twentieth century] as the antithesis of the dominant film industry. The one appealed to a small elite seeking education and entertainment, the other to a mass audience seeking amusement" (Musser and Nelson 1991: 181–82). Early-twentieth-century travelogue presenters such as Lyman Howe and Burton Holmes distinguished their presentations by appeals to those for whom simple entertainment was not sufficient rationale for motion picture attendance (Figure 1). Rick Altman's dissection of the term "illustrated lecture" (see his essay in this volume), together with his discussion of the Chautauqua circuit, further indicates how the form combines education with ornament.

Most travelogues fly under the rubric of instruction. As such, they participate in what Bill Nichols, in his discussion of documentary representation, has referred to as the instrumental "discourses of sobriety" (1991: 3). The educational impulse of the travelogue is one of its defining characteristics, even when it is a pretext for other, less edifying, pleasures. This feature allows Sony Classics to aggressively market such IMAX movies as

Across the Sea of Time (1996) to high school teachers, when its principal highlights include purely sensational 3D experiences: a helicopter flyby, a phantom subway ride, and a Coney Island roller-coaster romp. Producers and distributors understand that the educational stamp carries cultural capital that may be exploited for other purposes, as was the case with the sex-ed *Aufklärungsfilme* screened in Weimar Germany after World War I, described by the German film historian Lotte Eisner as "supposedly devoted to sex-instruction but treating straightforward brothel stories in pseudo-scientific fashion" (1973: 309).

As Paul Fussell notes in his pioneering study *Abroad: British Literary Traveling between the Wars*: "Before the development of tourism, travel was conceived to be like study, and its fruits were considered to be the adornment of the mind and the formation of the judgment" (1980: 39). The promise of instructional entertainment still holds sway in the domain of the travelogue. The French organization Connaissance du Monde, which celebrated its sixtieth anniversary in 2003, claims at its website to be "the most important organization of filmed lectures in the world."[2] The live performance I attended at the Cinéma Renoir in Aix-en-Provence, *Québec, je t'aime*, was showing in alternation with *The Matrix Revolutions* (2003), to mutually exclusive audiences, confirming that travelogue viewers are still looking for movies that offer something other than the current diet of sex, violence, and special effects available in commercial fiction films (Figure 2). Many cinematic travelogues traffic in the classificatory tendency Ali Behdad finds in nineteenth-century Western tourist guides about the Orient "systematic bodies of encyclopedic knowledge that provided the traveler with information on everything" (1994: 39). Here we are in the realm of what the director Luis Buñuel, recalling his own schooling, called "useless facts" (1984: 3).[3] This educational impulse is further echoed in the many tours sponsored by American universities and other nonprofit organizations such as the National Geographic Society. While writing this introduction, I received a brochure from Smithsonian Journeys, "The Best in Educational Travel." Appropriately enough, one of the tours goes to the "tiny mountain village of Telluride for the thirty-first Telluride Film Festival," an event programmed by my Dartmouth colleague Bill Pence. Even in our age of mass tourism, *pace* Fussell, connections between travel and education persist.

As archaic as live travelogue lectures might appear today, they are curiously similar to our practices as teachers and scholars, relying heavily on face-to-face encounters, whether in classrooms, lecture halls, seminars,

2 Poster for the 2003–2004 season of Connaissance du Monde at the Cinéma Renoir in Aix-en-Provence, France. Courtesy of Photo Hall BICC, copyright Photo Hall BICC.

or conferences. Indeed, the "show and tell" mode of lecturing as well as "studying abroad" remain staples of liberal arts education. The performative dimension of live narration also appears in alternative cinema modes; presentations of home movies typically include in-person narration, often by the filmmaker (Ruoff 1992b: 295; Chalfen 1987). The presence of the filmmaker/artist has similarly been a significant dimension of experimental film exhibition, at least since Maya Deren's activities in the late 1940s (Rabinovitz 1991: 49-91). Indeed, *Cross-Cultural Filmmaking: A Handbook for Making Documentary and Ethnographic Films and Videos* cites the filmmaker Trinh Minh-ha's advice for independent producers: "Once your film is released you may have to travel with it" (Barbash and Taylor 1997: 460). Trinh further mentions firsthand encounters with the public as a constitutive feature of independent film, a contention that surely deserves additional analysis. Beyond such alternative cinemas, movie festival audiences, such as those at Telluride, also take for granted the in-person appearances of directors and stars, accompanying their films. Touring with *Reservoir Dogs* (1992), Quentin Tarantino reportedly "did more than four hundred interviews and travelled something approaching sixty thousand miles" (Clarkson 1995: 178). In all these instances, the presence of the filmmaker turns the director into a star and the movie into a performative event (Altman 1990: 2-4), which should force us to rethink our infatuation with films as texts.

Tourism, Transportation, and Representation

According to the travelogue producer Thayer Soule, the lecturer Burton Holmes "did more to start people traveling than anyone except Henry Ford" (1997: 14). While this claim is impossible to substantiate, there is an obvious link between the armchair traveler—whose virtual experience of travel may come from a movie instead of a book—and the traveler who physically moves through time and space. Furthermore, movies of all kinds encourage travel. For example, tourism is among the most important industries in Tunisia, as it is, incidentally, where I live in Vermont. *The Rough Guide to Tunisia* is just one of many that lists the feature fiction films shot on location there. Luke Skywalker's desert planet home Tatooine is named after the Tunisian town of Tataouine and a number of the sets of *Star Wars* (1977) and its prequels may be visited in towns and dunes in the south. Tunisian travel agencies offer organized tours for aficionados that include travel to Matmata to visit the Hotel Sidi Driss, where "you can sit down to a meal in the exact spot Luke had dinner with his aunt and uncle" (Jacobs and Morris 2001: 319).[4] Obviously, travelers who seek the locations where their favorite films were shot have clear precursors in those who follow in the footsteps of their favorite authors (Matos 1992: 219). As is the case with ride films such as *Star Tours* (see Lauren Rabinovitz's essay in this volume), tourism inspired by movies gives viewers the chance to revisit experiences and landscapes already mediated by the cinema.

Just as the printing press ushered in a new era of written travel accounts (Coltman 1989: 6–7), so the advent of motion pictures has contributed to an explosion of travelogues in the modern era. The undocumented trip is, apparently, not worth taking. Tellingly, in H. G. Wells's *The Time Machine*, the Time Traveler regrets not having taken a picture of the Underworld during his expedition to the future ([1895] 1995: 49). The admonition of eco-conscious travel guidebooks such as the *Rough Guide* series—"Take only photographs, leave only footprints"—suggests that images and conscientious image makers leave the original terrain more or less intact. It remains to be seen whether or not this constitutes appropriation in the strong sense of the term. On the other hand, we have Burton Holmes's proprietary claim that "to travel is to possess the world," from his mid-twentieth-century autobiography, immodestly titled *The World Is Mine* (1953: ix), a comment that manifestly links knowledge with ownership for the Euro-American male adventurer/filmmaker (Griffiths 2002: 203–27).

While much work has been done linking the development of the train to new modes of vision associated with film (Kirby 1997), comparatively little has appeared on the relations between the automobile and the cinema, despite the historical coincidence of their development. When the Ford Motor Company introduced the Model T in 1908, the automobile was on the way to becoming a standard feature of the American landscape, just as movies were consolidating in nickelodeons (Figure 3). Automobiles freed travelers from the standardization of railroad timetables and established routes, breaking the railways' monopoly on cross-country tourism. While the train resembles classical Hollywood narration moving toward its fixed destination, the automobile stands for the episodic travelogue, where detours beckon just around the bend. In *Americans on the Road*, Warren Belasco notes: "Like another recent invention, the motion picture, the automobile offered unprecedented experi-

3 In preparation for his 1927 trip across the United States, Kiyooka Eiichi takes apart and reassembles his Model T Ford's engine. Courtesy of Jeffrey Ruoff.

ences of time, space, and movement" [1979: 17]. Nor were these changes limited to the United States; enamored of the new machines of image and sound recording, the Soviet futurist-turned-constructivist Vertov asked, in his 1923 manifesto "Kinoks: A Revolution," "How can one not admire the automobile?" (1984: 20). Indeed, the separate histories of transportation and representation need to be brought together, for there are parallels as well as divergences in the experiences offered by ocean liners, trains, airplanes, automobiles, and moving pictures (see Tom Gunning's essay in this volume). In this respect, we should theorize the cinema as a mode of transportation and the automobile as a mode of representation.

As I have argued elsewhere (1991: 246), travelogues celebrate new means of transportation as much, if not more than, the new lands and views they afford. This is often the case, as Peter Bloom, Tom Gunning, Jennifer Peterson, and Lauren Rabinovitz show in this anthology, because transport companies promote the use of motion pictures in advertising, travel, and tourism. My 1991 case study of amateur motion pictures, "Forty Days across America: Kiyooka Eiichi's 1927 Travelogues," demonstrates the centrality of the automobile in the evolving landscape of early-twentieth-century America; indeed, here the Model T Ford is the star (247). As another example, in By Aeroplane to Pygmyland, Stir-

ling New Guinea Expedition (1927), an ethnographic travelogue produced by Matthew W. Stirling and the Smithsonian Institution, despite the on-camera presence of the expedition leaders, the American-made Yackey BRL-12 airplane is the star (Figure 4). The film trumpets its first flight into the interior of New Guinea, offering "bird of paradise" views of the expedition encampment and surrounding countryside. The top-billing of the plane is subsequently eclipsed by the arrival of the "Pygmies" in the final segment; the title perfectly captures this split focus. Of course, as Hamid Naficy (in this volume) remarks of the conclusion to *Grass: A Nation's Battle for Life* (1925) and Alexandra Schneider (in this volume) notes of amateur film safaris generally, the finished motion picture proper is the latent star. *By Aeroplane to Pygmyland* is the trophy brought back that documents the heralded departure, the flirtation with danger, the ultimate triumph, and the successful return of its male heroes, Stirling and cameraman Richard K. Peck (Figure 5).

In contrast to classical Hollywood films, the cinematic apparatus is frequently displayed and appreciated in travelogues. With IMAX, the technology is the star. The format itself is on display; it is the main attraction. As Alison Griffiths suggests in this volume of *Everest* (1998), IMAX's most celebrated work to date, the format stands in for its colossal subject. I first attended an OMNIMAX screening at the Oregon Museum of Science and Industry in Portland. After we entered the theater and took our seats, a live master of ceremonies introduced us to the machine. Individual aspects were highlighted; if I recall correctly, the bass speakers received a prominent billing. Inevitably, IMAX films themselves are upstaged by the device, just as artworks exhibited at the Guggenheim Museum are often overshadowed by the assertiveness of Frank Lloyd Wright's building. So, *contra* director Jean-Jacques Annaud, who said that IMAX must "tell stories or die" (Grimes 1994), the format appears likely to do neither; Annaud's own failed foray *Wings of Courage* (1995), the first dramatic IMAX-3D film, provides perhaps the most compelling evidence of this. Comments by Roger Ebert in his review of *Wings of Courage* capture the purely descriptive nonnarrative appeal of the format: "There are a few straight dramatic scenes—in a nightclub, in the airline headquarters and with the wife at home—and they're so detailed and realistic, they're almost distracting. There's so much in each scene to look at that I found it hard to focus on the characters because I was checking out other details" (1996). Given the travelogue's affinity for exploring time and space, I would sooner say that IMAX must travel or die.

4 Stirling's American-made Yackey BRL-12 airplane is the featured star of the ethnographic travelogue *By Aeroplane to Pygmyland* (1927). Courtesy of the Nederlands Filmmuseum. Copyright P. I. C. for the Smithsonian Institution.
5 Cameraman Richard K. Peck films *By Aeroplane to Pygmyland* (1927) on location in New Guinea. Note the feathers in his hat and the pistol holstered to his right hip. Courtesy of the Nederlands Filmmuseum. Copyright P. I. C. for the Smithsonian Institution.

Episodic Narrative

Generally speaking, the travelogue is an open form; essayistic, it often brings together scenes without regard for plot or narrative progression. During the hegemonic period of the studio system, the travelogue kept alive the loose narrative aspects of the picaresque in movies. Episodic narration offers an alternative to both the linear cause-and-effect structure of classical Hollywood cinema and the problem-solution approach of Griersonian documentary. The episodic narrative—such as Roberto Rossellini's *Viaggio in Italia* (*Voyage to Italy*, 1953) or Chris Marker's *Sans soleil* (*Sunless*, 1983)—does not subordinate time and place to the regime of plot or story nor are its elements typically yoked to an argument. Description thrives. In his 1846 literary travelogue *Narrative of a Four Months' Residence Among the Natives of the Marquesas Islands; or, A Peep at Polynesian Life*, Herman Melville gives a nice summary of this approach: "Sadly discursive as I have already been, I must still further entreat the reader's patience, as I am about to string together, without any attempt at order, a few odds and ends of things not hitherto mentioned" ([1846] 1986: 301). William S. Burroughs described the episodic narrative more recently, and more prosaically, as "one god-damned thing after another" (Choukri 1973: book jacket).

It is precisely the free combination of exposition, narrative, and comment that one finds in the most accomplished cinematic travelogues such as Ross McElwee's *Sherman's March: A Meditation on the Possibilities of Romantic Love in the South in an Era of Nuclear Weapons Proliferation* (1985). Frequently autobiographical, the first-person episodic narrative leaves room for detours and digressions. *Sherman's March*, which retraces General Sherman's military campaign during the American Civil War, plays with the persona of the male adventurer of classic Western fiction from *The Odyssey* onward, highlighting the voyeurism of most narrative fiction film with its explicit display of women's bodies (Fischer 1998: 335-38).[5] McElwee's spoken narration recalls the ironic voice-over commentary of Stanley Kubrick's *Barry Lyndon* (1975) and the many self-conscious narrators of the British novel, including those of William Thackeray and other authors who address their "dear readers." The rambling subtitle of McElwee's movie is further indication of his roving, discursive approach. As Fussell suggests of British travel writing between the wars, though his comment could be applied more broadly to the travelogues of a McElwee or a Marker: "The genre is a device for getting published essays" (1980: 204).

Travel in Fiction Films

Although *Virtual Voyages* has only one essay on feature fiction films, the travel dimension in fiction should not be underestimated. Travel and movement are central to fiction film, with the journey among its most common narrative tropes, particularly stories of men who voyage forth and the women they leave behind (De Lauretis 1984: 110), as in Kenji Mizoguchi's *Ugetsu monogatari* (*Ugetsu*, 1953). But to say that all cinema is travel cinema blurs distinctions that have yet to be adequately described and analyzed. Clearly, films of exile and immigration such as Ousmane Sembene's *La noire de* (*Black Girl*, 1966) and Michael Winterbottom's *In This World* (2003) invoke travel experiences directly. Picaresque road movies such as Monte Hellman's *Two-Lane Blacktop* (1971) are widespread in new American cinema while science fiction films such as Paul Verhoeven's *Total Recall* (1990) explore their own versions of virtual travel. The space ballet in Kubrick's *2001: A Space Odyssey* (1968) provides a non-narrative display before the later total implosion of story in the penultimate "Stargate Corridor" travel sequence.

Furthermore, directors who reject classical narratives and conventional storytelling—such as Wim Wenders (*Alice in den Städten* [*Alice in the Cities*, 1974]; *Bis ans Ende der Welt* [*Until the End of the World*, 1991]; *Lisbon Story*, 1994) and Jim Jarmusch (*Mystery Train*, 1989; *Night on Earth*, 1991; *Dead Man*, 1995)—have consistently returned to a ground-zero travelogue aesthetic as a means of reinventing the cinema. Think of the almost four-minute tracking shot following Nanni Moretti's scooter to the monument to director Pier Paolo Pasolini outside Rome, in Moretti's episodic *Caro diario* (*Dear Diary*, 1994). The Moroccan director Mohamed Abderrahman Tazi described the appeal of the travel narrative for the making of his first feature, *Ibn al-Sabil* (*The Big Trip*, 1981): "I was tempted by the genre—the road film, with a series of encounters all tied together by one main character; a film with movement; a film that traveled, that would free me from the restrictions of unity of place, that would allow me to use images to express the countryside" (Dwyer 2004: 110).

Additionally, the travelogue itself played a role, however subordinate, in the standard Hollywood exhibition package, particularly during the era of the double bill. While recent work on animation has illuminated the place of cartoons in the diet of American audiences in the studio era (Smoodin 1993), our understanding of the documentary short subjects shown before Hollywood features (newsreels, travelogues, etc.) is woefully inadequate and has scarcely advanced since Raymond Fielding's pioneering efforts in *The American Newsreel, 1911–1967* (1972) and *The March of Time, 1935–1951* (1978). During the classical Hollywood era, a montage of attractions persisted in this juxtaposition of shorts and features. How did travelogues inflect the reception of the feature films that they preceded? I particularly regret the absence of scholarship on James Fitzpatrick's celebrated MGM series *Traveltalks: The Voice of the Globe* and later *Vistavision Visits* with Paramount, produced and shown in American movie theaters between 1930 and 1954. Perhaps too familiar to deserve comment from the first generation of film historians, Fitzpatrick's films are now virtually unknown. Not unlike Frank Capra's now canonical *Why We Fight* series, produced by the U.S. government during World War II, Fitzpatrick's travelogues provided a stock set of images and concepts about the world abroad at a time when hardly any international films were available to American audiences and when comparatively few Americans could travel to Ceylon, Argentina, or Japan, to name just a few of Fitzpatrick's destinations.

Similarly, while the boom of research on early cinema has been tremendously productive, the rediscovery of the diversity of early film has flattened our understanding of other eras. One gains the erroneous impression, for example, that the travelogue faded from view after a brief period of primacy in the first decades of cinema, once the rise of narrative eclipsed the naïve satisfactions of movement in distant views. In this anthology, Dana Benelli shows that travel imagery provides a means for 1930s Hollywood cinema to incorporate the earlier cinema of attractions alongside the constraints of classical narrative. In addition, many silent films distributed with intertitles in the 1920s were also exhibited by live lecturers, as Hamid Naficy (in this volume) notes occurred with *Grass*, though previous historians have largely ignored the persistence of such live film presentations. One would never know from mainstream film histories that Burton Holmes's 1945–46 season, in which he lectured to half a million people, was among his most lucrative (Wallace [1947] 1977: 12). Although Genoa Caldwell edited a gorgeous album in 1977 on Holmes, the doyen of twentieth-century travelogue lecturers, his vast oeuvre remains scandalously overlooked.[6] It is equally symptomatic of the myopia of the field that next to nothing has been written of the IMAX extravaganza *To Fly* (1976), a film that the Smithsonian Institution claims has been seen by more Americans—now estimated at over 100 million—than any other motion picture.[7]

Travelogues in Time: Films and Filmmakers

To incorporate the travelogue into film studies, the field must recognize the heterogeneity of its objects of study. For the past several decades, the written history of photography has tried to embrace all the manifestations of the photographic medium: art, fashion, journalism, advertising, documentary, family snapshots, and so forth (Rosenblum 1984), while our general histories of motion pictures continue to privilege a distinct minority of feature fiction films, particularly Hollywood movies, and, at best, some documentary and avant-garde alternatives. They pass in silence over generations of home movie footage, not to mention other amateur films, industrials, educational movies, scientific films, and the like. *Virtual Voyages* addresses this gap, tracing the intersection of technology and ideology in representations of travel in a wide variety of cinematic forms, while recovering important but forgotten figures and films. The essays included here draw on extensive, and impressive, primary research on, among other forms, independent documentaries, illustrated lecture films, IMAX movies, ethnographic films, amateur movies, and Hollywood features. They examine the role of travel imagery in the narrative economy of the cinema while simultaneously considering how travel films construct cultural realities.[8] In this volume, we move beyond debates about cinematic realism, and facile ideological denunciations of the reality effect, to a nuanced appreciation that films and their makers, and especially travelogue filmmakers, actively produce the worlds they represent.[9]

Virtual Voyages represents a unique contribution to the literature of film studies, but it should also appeal to a general educated book-reading audience. It is deliberately broad and ecumenical, encompassing travelogue films from many eras of the now more than one-hundred-year history of the cinema and drawing examples from films produced in North Africa, France, Vietnam, the United States, Iran, and Switzerland, among other countries. In the first section of the book, "Traveling Machines: Space, Time, Difference," introductory essays by Tom Gunning and

Lauren Rabinovitz survey travel imagery in the nineteenth and twentieth centuries respectively. While Gunning describes new modes of vision incorporated in an array of travel images and the growing nineteenth- and twentieth-century desire to grasp the world itself as a picture, Rabinovitz looks on representations of travel as sensation and draws a suggestive parallel between the multiplicities of early cinema and our own experimental digital moment. On the one hand, travelogues may fulfill a desire for knowledge, vision, and contemplation of the world; in this context we might rephrase Burton Holmes's comment about travel as "to know is to possess the world." On the other hand, travelogues may simply indulge viewers in the thrill of movement, the visceral shriek of cinematic turbulence, without any appeal to conceptual knowledge. Gunning makes apparent the manifest colonial and imperial perspectives embodied in many early travel films, and their desire to possess the world, but his readings remain sensitive to contradictory, and oppositional, forces. In lieu of appeals to a desire to take possession of the world through representation, Rabinovitz's ride films "privilege the sensational" (Williams 1995: 142), a typical feature of genres of bodily excess; the flyover that provokes the sensation of falling is the money shot in IMAX movies as well as ride films. Readers should note, however, that Rabinovitz delineates a mode of cinema spectatorship that extends work on body genres in a new direction. Following this two-hundred-year overview, Rick Altman, in another leading example in his ongoing rediscovery of the heterogeneity of early movie exhibition (2004b), argues for the importance of the lecturer in silent cinema and for the centrality of live presentations in our understanding of travelogue films. Altman advocates a film history that highlights performances rather than movies. Together with that of Musser and Barber, the seminal work of Gunning, Rabinovitz, and Altman has had a marked influence on the younger scholars whose contributions follow.

The next section, "Travelogues and Silent Cinema," explores a range of travel films from the first three decades of motion pictures when genres and modes of production were consolidating. In her essay on early travelogues about the western United States, Jennifer Peterson examines pictorial conventions that encouraged immigration and transformed the rugged frontier into natural playgrounds for tourists. Her work provides a suggestive comparison for research on the western genre that has virtually always focused on fiction films. While Peterson considers the role of nonfiction in the myth of the American frontier, Paula Amad looks at a little-known utopian alternative to commercial cinema in France. Of the remarkable French banker and philanthropist Albert Kahn, the focus of Amad's essay, we can truly say that the world was his oyster. Kahn's world tour in 1908–9, together with his vast fortune, laid the groundwork for his *Archives of the Planet*, a unique collection of films shot all over the globe. In a nuanced and richly documented essay, Amad explores the ambivalent culture of travel in Kahn's archival oeuvre, particularly in relation to French colonies.

A family resemblance exists between travelogues and ethnographic films, especially during the colonial era, as Hamid Naficy suggests in his analysis of the American film *Grass*, produced by Famous Players-Lasky Corporation and shot on location in Turkey, Syria, Iraq, and Iran. Naficy is a widely published authority on diasporic media (2001) whose work has also been influential on the younger scholars featured in this anthology. While Cooper's and Schoedsack's *Grass* is a canonical work in the history of cinema, the story of its making and reception has never been researched and told with such attention to gender and race as Naficy offers here. Continuing the emphasis on the ideological significance of border crossings and colonialism, Peter Bloom explores the nexus of transportation—new experimental vehicles, new highways—and motion pictures in 1920s French nonfiction shot in North Africa. Once again, thanks to the involvement of major automobile manufacturers, the motor car prevails on the screen, in this instance drawing the map of colonial rule. Alexandra Schneider, exploring the prevalence of travel imagery in what are commonly referred to as "home movies" or "family films," shows that the colonizing gaze also appears in films produced within national borders. Schneider provides a close analysis of a 1930s Swiss amateur film of a weekend trip that brings back images of rural families as trophies of urban tourists. Where Gunning celebrates flight from the colonialist gaze, Schneider emphasizes how the participatory mode of home movies sustains an uneasy exchange between filmmaker and subjects.

The travelogue played a role in the consolidation of visual anthropology, in particular in the construction of images of supposedly remote peoples, as several subsequent essays note. The final section of the anthology, "Travelogues in the Sound Era," carries our knowledge of travelogues from the 1930s into the present day. Dana Benelli explores the role of exotic travel imagery in 1930s Hollywood cinema. He suggests that our understanding of the norms of classical cinema should be redefined to include the ways in which spectacular travel footage diverts and even interrupts classical narration. Important for understanding the relationship between fiction and nonfiction in classical Hollywood, Benelli's thesis reminds us how modes of address vary at the level of the feature fiction film proper. While rehearsing anthropology's love/hate relationship with amateur voyagers and popular travel accounts, Amy Staples rediscovers the films of the once celebrated but now forgotten explorer-adventurer Lewis Cotlow—Claude Lévi-Strauss's shadow in the Amazon in the 1940s—as an example of the ethnographic imaginary of mid-century America, a site of multiple, conflicting discourses. As Cotlow's best-known film *Jungle Headhunters* (1950) was produced and distributed by RKO, Staples's essay extends Benelli's comments about the hybridity of classical Hollywood into the postwar era.

The concluding essays return to a number of questions and topics raised in the essays on early cinema. My contribution, which resonates most fully with Rick Altman's emphasis on live performances, looks at the American 16mm illustrated lecture industry at the end of the twentieth century; I argue that the live travelogue, with its educational and encyclopedic tendencies on display, is the prototypical travel film experience. Alison Griffiths considers the panoramic possibilities of IMAX through a general discussion of large-format visual media as well as detailed readings of several IMAX travelogues. Revisiting some of the topics Rabinovitz embraces in her discussion of ride films, Griffiths shows how recent IMAX features combine old and new media in movies that simultaneously indulge educational aspirations and offer roller-coaster thrills.

The Filmic Fourth Dimension

There are really four dimensions, three which we call the three planes of Space, and a fourth, Time.—H. G. Wells, *The Time Machine*, 1895

Neither a genre nor a mode, the travelogue surfaces in all forms of cinema —avant-garde, popular fiction, home movies, art cinema, documentaries, IMAX.[10] As such, its study breaks down parochialisms in film scholarship in which the feature fiction film and its many alternatives are theorized as distinct practices. Description and analysis of noncanonical forms such as the travelogue should raise new questions that can be asked of other movies. If travelogues need a definition, then I would accept Jennifer Peterson's: "nonfiction films that take place as their primary subject"

(1998: 2). Space *and* time are the subjects of the travelogue; indeed travel rhetoric frequently combines, or collapses, the two. As Fussell notes: "One travels to experience the past, and travel thus is an adventure in time as well as distance" (1980: 210). Holmes puts it more literally: "To go to Egypt is to go back to the beginning of human history" (Caldwell 1977: 147). Of course, time travel is a fiction, but one that many travelogues indulge. Several scholars have noted the historical coincidence of the 1895 publication of Wells's *The Time Machine* and the first public screening of the Lumières' cinematograph in Paris (Friedberg 1993; Rony 1996). Indeed, if cinema is, as Rabinovitz suggests, the paradigmatic vision machine of modernism, it could be argued that the motion picture medium as a whole responds to the desire for time travel expressed in Wells's dystopia. Cinema may not be "objectivity in time," as André Bazin put it ([1945] 1967: 14-15), but it is a medium of space in time; travel has been the way filmmakers have explored this nexus. If, in the new physics heralded by Wells, space and time are one, then cinema is the art of travel.

In 2004, the Explorers Club in New York City celebrated its one-hundreth anniversary. Appropriately enough, given the historical importance of the lecturer in travelogue films, the mountaineer George Leigh Mallory uttered his famous justification for climbing Mount Everest—"Because it's there"—during his 1923 New York City lecture tour to raise money for his next expedition (*New York Times* 1923). As Mallory's tour suggests, travel takes place in a symbiotic relationship with its representation. The financing of many large-scale trips, including the expedition that produced *By Aeroplane to Pygmyland*, depends on pre-sales of photographs and films, so without the promise of publicity, there is no trip to speak of, no travel without representation. While travel writing has lately come under intense scrutiny (Kowalewski 1992; Kaplan 1996; Siegel 2004), very little has been written about the travelogue film experience, where the educational and performative dimensions of cinema are frequently paramount. Attendant at the birth of the cinema, the episodic, descriptive, informative travelogue film, despite critical neglect, has remained as durable as Everest. Further, as the essays here demonstrate, technologies of travel and technologies of representation intersect in travel cinema, a feature that deserves additional consideration. As Michael Renov notes in *Theorizing Documentary*, the feature fiction film is no longer "the king's highway of filmic expression" (1993: 1). By taking this detour through the travelogue, film studies acknowledges new hybrid forms, new modes of production and reception, and new kinds of spectators. While this anthology expands the agenda of visual studies to bring into view a vast body of overlooked films, more importantly *Virtual Voyages: Cinema and Travel* returns us to basic temporal and spatial dimensions of the cinema as audiovisual vehicle, a machine that finds its raison d'être in movement through space and time.

Notes

For detailed comments on this introduction, I am indebted to Rick Altman, Paula Amad, Alison Griffiths, Richard Horwitz, and, especially, Lauren Rabinovitz.

1. The references that appear at the end of *Virtual Voyages: Cinema and Travel* provide a good cumulative guide to research on related topics. Readers interested in archives of travel films should consult "A Resource Guide to Travel Film Repositories" (Njoku 2002). Although the travelogue is a staple of motion pictures, its importance is not reflected in film studies; there is no body of literature on the travelogue per se to survey here. While sporadic chapters of interest have appeared in Anne Friedberg's *Window Shopping: Cinema and the Postmodern* (1993), Fatimah Rony's *The Third Eye: Race, Cinema, and Ethnographic Spectacle* (1996), Lynne Kirby's *Parallel Tracks: The Railroad and Silent Cinema* (1997), Cynthia Erb's *Tracking King Kong: A Hollywood Icon in World Culture* (1998), and Alison Griffiths's *Wondrous Difference: Cinema, Anthropology, and Turn-of-the-Century Visual Culture* (2002), there is only one book in print on the subject, Charles Musser's and Carol Nelson's *High-Class Moving Pictures: Lyman H. Howe and the Forgotten Era of Traveling Exhibition* (1991).

2. http//www.connaissancedumonde.com/htm/mot.htm, accessed 12 April 2004. For an early discussion of the screenings of Connaissance du Monde at the celebrated Salle Pleyel in Paris in the 1940s, see Pierre LeProhon's *L'Exotisme et le cinéma* (1945: 98–100).

3. Buñuel's demonic travelogue *Land without Bread* (1937), which tracks the exotic other deep into the heart of darkest Catholic Spain, is a parody of the educational pretenses of the form, particularly in its subversion of the authoritative voiceover (Ruoff 1998a: 51). Parody is a good indication of the ubiquitousness of any genre; for a written spoof of safari film expeditions, see Chappell's *Through the Alimentary Canal with Gun and Camera: A Fascinating Trip to the Interior* (1930).

4. For websites with GPS maps and photographs of Tunisian locations in the *Star Wars* series, see http://home.tiscali.be/mark.dermul/tatooine2003/index.htm and http://www.toysrgus.com/travel/tunisia.html.

5. For a study of how several feminist documentary filmmakers inflect and reinvent the typically male scenario of the American road movie, see Joyce Hammond's "Difference and the I/Eye of the Beholder: Revisioning America through Travelogues" (2002).

6. See Rick Altman's *Silent Film Sound* (2004) for a fresh appraisal of Holmes's technique as a lecturer. In a resurrection worthy of Paul Auster's novel of silent film scholarship *The Book of Illusions* (2002), two hundred reels of rare 35mm footage shot by Burton Holmes from 1899 to the late 1930s, long believed lost, were found in 2004 in an abandoned storage unit in Los Angeles. Genoa Caldwell, archivist of the Burton Holmes Collection and editor of *Burton Holmes: The Man Who Photographed the World*, is currently involved in their restoration and preservation. This remarkable discovery should move forward the long overdue academic assessment of Holmes's work and place in film history. There is also a fascinating website devoted to the work of Burton Holmes, www.burtonholmes.org, which provides a good basis for additional research on this pivotal figure.

7. Regarding travelogues, the efforts of film archivists, as evidenced in such works as the DVD sets *Treasures from American Film Archives: 50 Preserved Films* (Simmon 2000) and *More Treasures from American Film Archives, 1894– 1931* (Simmon 2004), have probably been in advance of the research of film scholars and historians. Rick Prelinger's archive of 48,000 "ephemeral films," founded in 1983 and acquired in 2002 by the Library of Congress, is exemplary. Similarly, archivists at the Nederlands Filmmuseum sponsored several workshops in the mid-1990s that brought together scholars and early nonfiction films, resulting in pioneering, though little circulated, publications on documentary before Flaherty—*Nonfiction from the Teens* (Hertogs and de Klerk 1994) and *Uncharted Territory: Essays on Early Nonfiction Film* (Hertogs and de Klerk 1997)—in which travelogues were prominently featured. The Orphan Film Symposium, with its focus on movies that have fallen by the wayside of film history, parallels in a number of ways the work of this anthology. Four of the contributors to *Virtual Voyages* gave presentations at the Orphan Film Symposium "On Location: Place and Region in Forgotten Films" in 2004.

8. Although this is the first book on travelogues, many of the contributors to this volume are working on book-length manuscripts of which these chapters form individual sections. So, we can look forward to forthcoming studies by Lauren Rabinovitz on immersive spectacles; Alison Griffiths on

panoramas, museums, and interactive media; Dana Benelli on jungles and landscapes in 1930s Hollywood cinema; and Peter Bloom on French nonfiction film of the colonial era, to mention only a few. This anthology also features the work of such new scholars as Amy Staples, whose 2002 dissertation on postwar ethnographic safari films explores connections, and contradictions, among ethnography, documentary, and commercial cinema, as well as Alexandra Schneider, whose 2001 dissertation on Swiss home movies between the wars (published in German in 2004) covers tourism as one of the two most popular motifs of amateur cinema. In addition, Jennifer Peterson and Paula Amad drew on untapped primary resources in European archives for their recent dissertations on early cinema. When published, each will make a significant contribution to our understanding of the varying modalities of nonfiction in the silent era, now recognized as much more complex than our current histories suggest.

9. Given the wealth of travelogue forms in cinema, I decided to limit the focus of this anthology to the film medium. Although Lindsay Powell's essay on travel programs on Japanese television appeared in the special issue of *Visual Anthropology* that I guest-edited on "Travelogues and Travel Films," it is not included here because of this anthology's focus on cinema. See Powell 2002. Television is a vast travel machine in its own right—from *The Undersea World of Jacques Cousteau* (1966–1973) to the Discovery Channel (1986–present) to *Full Circle with Michael Palin* (1997), with televised LA freeway car chases and the ubiquitous "We take you now to Baghdad" TV news rhetoric in the mix. The field of media studies dearly needs an account of the extraordinary diversity of travel material on television, and several recent studies of the parallel world of nature programs have opened up this fascinating terrain: Gregg Mitman's *Reel Nature: America's Romance with Wildlife on Film* (1999) and Derek Bouse's *Wildlife Films* (2000).

10. Time and space did not permit an anticipated chapter on travel in avant-garde cinema to be published here, an unfortunate limitation because the episodic, descriptive, nonnarrative form of the travelogue appeals to many experimental filmmakers. Just a few examples are Howard Guttenplan's single-frame renditions of his strolls across Europe in *Eastern European Diary '72* (1974), Peter Rose's *The Man Who Could Not See Far Enough* (1981) with its extraordinary climactic ascent of the Golden Gate Bridge, Babette Mangolte's exploration of the western landscape in *The Sky on Location* (1983), and Leighton Pierce's sketches of small-town Iowa life in *On the Road Going Through* (1987) and *You Can Drive the Big Rigs* (1989). Scott MacDonald's *The Garden in the Machine: A Field Guide to Independent Films about Place* (2001) demonstrates the importance of space, place, and travel in avant-garde film.

I

Traveling Machines

SPACE, TIME, DIFFERENCE

"The Whole World Within Reach"

TRAVEL IMAGES WITHOUT BORDERS

TOM GUNNING

|||||||||||||||||||||||||||||||||||||||||||||||||||||||||||||||||||||||||||||||||||||||||||||||||||||||||||||||||||||||||||

What clearer example can we have of films that cross national boundaries than those devoted to portraying (to use a term often found in early
film catalogues) "foreign views" and travel? However, we must approach
such films with caution. "Foreign views" portray not only a distant site
but also a particular point of view, one from outside the land viewed. My
purpose will be to explore this tourist viewpoint as embodied in early
travel films, to examine the forms this viewpoint takes, and the discourse
that surrounded it, and to understand its place within a peculiarly modern experience in which the role of images has taken on a new dimension.
I believe that early travel films display a mode of perception which may
give a new sense to the phrase "images without borders."

As Charles Musser has demonstrated in a pioneering and penetrating essay, the travel genre was "one of the most popular and developed"
genres in early film (1984: 47). In terms of pure numbers of productions
it could rank with any other form of filmmaking until about 1906. And as
Musser and others have shown, it is perhaps the genre of early film that is
most clearly prepared for by pre-cinematic practice (Musser 1984, 1990;
Musser and Nelson 1991; Kirby 1989). Musser's careful research into the
pre-cinematic lantern slide illustrated travel lectures of John L. Stoddard
and Burton Holmes establishes that the travel film grew directly out of
this form. In fact, one would be hard pressed to make a definitive separation between the two, since travel lecturers like Burton Holmes adopted
motion pictures as a natural extension of the lantern slides he was already
using and, soon after the invention of cinema, simply introduced them
into his lectures, interspersing moving and still images (Figure 1). Travel
films became absorbed so smoothly into the travel lecture that the older

1 A marquee announces Holmes's first season in London in 1904. Courtesy
of the Burton Holmes Collection, Seattle, Wash.

practices of lecture and explanation adapted to the new technology without a major adjustment.

   However, travel films share with other forms of early cinema an enormous range of exhibition contexts. While serving as illustration for a lecture may be their most privileged mode (and one with enough status and
popularity to permanently influence the way travel films were made and
understood), such films were also shown as brief segments in a variety
format of mixed genres (in the earliest years of exhibition), projected in
special theaters designed as railway cars or other means of transportation (e.g., The Hale's Tours in 1905–06), or as multi-shot films known
as "scenics" formed a part of many nickelodeon programs (from 1907 or
so on). Further, as Musser has pointed out, elements of the travel genre
were adopted early on by fiction films (1984: 57), with travel providing
the background for fictional action, resulting in a narrativization of the
genre that persists to this day (Wim Wenders's *Until the End of the World*
providing the most recent and interesting example).

   But a thorough understanding of the travel film must go beyond the
travel lecture as its source and place it within an extensive industry of
travel images that arose in the nineteenth century. In an age of mechanical
reproduction, photographs of distant places and countries probably were
surpassed only by portraits as the most commonly reproduced images
(Fabian and Adam 1983). The travel lecture provided perhaps the most

public way of consuming these transnational images, but travel images were also displayed in the stereoscope with its illusion of three dimensions. The contrasting modes of these two forms make the importance of travel imagery in each more striking: from an audience in darkness in a public space watching a large bright image under the control of the lecturer, to a single individual seated in her own home holding the apparatus in her hand, determining the order and length of each view and absorbed in an illusion of depth and recession. Yet both lantern and stereoscope were means of appropriating some distant place through an image, of seeming to be somewhere else by being absorbed in a "view." They attest to what Lynne Kirby has called a "touristic consciousness, a fascination exerted by foreign images that was fed by a number of different technologies" (1989: 59).

Along with the stereoscope and the magic lantern image, the postcard became by the turn of the century a major form of travel imagery (travel photographers such as William Henry Jackson or Eadweard Muybridge usually worked in all three forms). The mode of reception contrasts with both stereoscope and lecture, since the postcard also functioned as *evidence* of travel, sent by a tourist en route back to friends and relatives who had not made the journey. Observers at the turn of the century described hordes of tourists ascending the Rigi in Switzerland and then rushing to buy postcards and immediately sitting down and writing home (Fabian and Adam 1983: 339).[1] The postcard seemed to function not only as a souvenir of the journey but as its goal and purpose. This obsession with documenting one's trip by an image brings me to the core of the issue that I believe the travel genre poses for modern perception and use of images. In the modern era the very concept of travel becomes intricately bound up with the production of images. The image becomes our way of structuring a journey and even provides a substitute for it. Travel becomes a means of appropriating the world through images (Figure 2).

The postcard shows that modern travel images cannot be understood without placing them in a larger context of the development of mass tourism. A Biograph catalogue from 1902 understood this and informed potential film buyers: "It will be noted also that the foreign subjects include most of the places visited and admired by tourists" (Musser 1985: 130). Images of foreign lands took on a more tangible quality when audiences knew it was possible to travel to them, even if they did not undertake the journey themselves. And this sense of the accessibility of foreign lands forms a cornerstone of the modern worldview in which technology can

2 *Vues d'Espagne en cartes postales* (Views of Spain from Post-cards). Pathé Frères, 1907, Pathé Catalogue N. 1805. Joye Collection. National Film and Television Archive, London.

render every distant thing somehow available to us. The creation of Cook Tours in the middle of the nineteenth century was more than a systematic approach to making the process of traveling more rational and convenient. It had a symbiotic relation to the development of modern means of transportation (the railway and steamship, especially) (Feifer 1985: 166–68). The new systems of transportation made tourism possible and the extension of tourism then allowed further development of transportation systems.

As the development of industrial capitalism made areas of the world more accessible, travel became more economical in term of finances, as well as energy, to a larger number of people. The production of travel images was essential to this new travel industry. A travel lecture illustrated by lantern slides or motion pictures served as not only an ersatz for actual travel for those lacking finances or energy but a stimulant and preparation for those who had the means. One wanted to travel partly because one had already seen images of distant places. And one went to travel lectures to make sure what one should see. But travel images did more than incite journeys. As the postcard shows, they were also the end products of the journey, the proof one had been there, and the means by which one reflected on one's experience. This became even more true with the introduction of the Kodak "Brownie" camera, which made every tourist a travel photographer, and, eventually, the perfection of celluloid slides, which converted family gatherings into travel lectures. In other words, we should not simply think of travel images as substitutes designed for those who cannot travel (although they can play that role). Rather, during the modern era images penetrate deeply into the process of travel itself, structuring our experience of the journey.

The turn of the century saw a striking diversity of ways in which travel images were consumed by spectators, from devices that could be held in the hand and enjoyed at home to formal and public exhibitions. The largest and most grandiose representations of travel extended beyond travel lectures to more cumbersome forms of spectacle. The idea of making the world available in the form of a spectacle stretches back to the panorama of the end of the eighteenth century and to the world expositions of the latter part of the nineteenth. Besides bringing together the consumer products and technological marvels of the developed nations, the world expositions always provided attractions which plunged spectators into exotic environments. The Eskimo villages of the 1901 Pan American Exposition, the Cambodian temple of the Paris 1900 Exhibition, Little Egypt's hoochie-coochie dance at the 1893 Chicago World's Fair all presented traditional cultures within a simulacrum of their real environment, designed to give gawkers the illusion of having traveled there. These expositions were explicit hymns to the colonial expansions of the industrialized nations. They provide searing illustrations of spectacle as appropriation, as the traditions and inhabitants of the unindustrialized world were posed for the contemplation of citizens of the modern world.

It is no coincidence that such expositions also staged elaborate presentations of travel films in exhibition environments that simulated the travel experience, from the Cinéorama of the Paris Exhibition of 1900 (which simulated balloon flight by projecting motion pictures panoramically to an audience seated in a mock-up of a balloon's gondola), to the Hale's Tours, which projected moving landscape films to spectators seated in a train-car screening room. But these forms of cinematic simulation were often side by side with pre-cinematic forms of travel simulation. As Emmanuelle Toulet has shown in her exemplary research on the Paris 1900 Exposition, the Cinéorama competed (and unsuccessfully, for it proved inoperable) with such pre-cinematic means of conveying a journey as the Maréorama, in which a tilting deck, a seabrine-infused ventilation system, and moving canvas panoramas gave spectators the illusion of a sea voyage; or the Trans-Siberian Panorama, in which viewers sat in train cars as a moving painted panorama of landscapes along the Trans-Siberian route unfurled beyond their windows; or the Stéréorama, which presented an unfolding panorama of a sea voyage along the coast of Algeria (Toulet 1991). Such elaborate apparatuses demonstrate the link between cinematic travel imagery and the introduction of the panorama and diorama earlier in the nineteenth century. Travel images (views of natural wonders or famous cities) supplied the most frequent subjects of panoramas and dioramas from the end of the eighteenth century into the modern era.

All of this indicates that the production of foreign views, of images crossing borders, in early cinema must be placed in a larger context, one which extends from the travel lecture to the postcard industry to world fair exhibits. But as soon as this horizon is constructed, the larger social and technological forces behind these phenomena loom: the tourist industry, the development of modern transportation, the expansion of colonialism. However, this connection involves more than traditional historical arguments of causes and influence. I would claim that rather than simply acting as underlying causes of this industry of travel images, a base to this superstructure, these forces are clearly visible within these images. In other words, travel images are more than an effect; they supply essential tools in the creation of a modern worldview underlying all these transformations. One cannot understand modernity without penetrating its passion for images. Images fascinate modern consciousness obsessively, and this modern sense of images comes from a belief that images can somehow deliver what they portray. Image as appropriation dominates the modern image-making industry, and travel images provide a unique perspective onto this modern phenomenon. Lynne Kirby has pointed out that the epigraph to Burton Holmes's memoir reads: "to travel is to possess the world" (1989: 112).

If early cinema plays a crucial role in the ideological analysis of the cinematic apparatus, it is less because it represents an age of innocence than a sort of naiveté in which elements that later become camouflaged are frankly displayed. For instance, the link between foreign views and colonialism needs no deconstructive analysis to be demonstrated. A straight reading of American film catalogues from the turn of the century suffices. The travel views that Edison and Biograph marketed directly paralleled the colonial wars of the period. Views of Cuba and the Philippines ap-

peared along with films of the Spanish-American War and were catego-
rized as war films. For instance, in 1902 the Biograph Company released
a brief film called *Aguinaldo's Navy*. The film consists of a view of Philippine native canoes on a river, but the title evokes the name of the leader of
Philippine resistance to U. S. occupation. Clearly the Biograph Company
wanted to attract audience curiosity to a rather bland actuality film. But
the title also makes a mocking colonialist joke which equates the ability to
photograph this image with U. S. dominance over the native people. Our
technology (our navy, certainly, but in some sense our cinema as well)
can overwhelm these simple people, the film proclaims.

Travel curiosity intersected with the interest in colonial wars in a number of locales, and the genres of travel and war pictures often intersected
in the catalogues of early American manufacturers. The Biograph catalogue proclaims that the camera followed the flag in these instances. "In
every case our operators worked under the direct patronage and with
the most perfect co-operation of the respective Governments involved"
(Musser 1985: 138). The Biograph Company marketed a view of the Taku
road in China by stressing that this street scene was taken "under the
occupation of the city by allied forces" after the Boxer Rebellion. Likewise, Edison in 1901 announced their films of China by informing potential exhibitors that "people will eagerly appreciate any pictures that relate to the localities in which the war in China was prosecuted" (Musser
1985: 91).

The connection between early American travel films and the transportation industry is proudly displayed in early film catalogues. There
is no real dividing line between travel films and railway films in this
period, and both are prominent genre headings in catalogues. In the
Edison catalogue, railway views are offered under the name of the railways involved: Denver and Rio Grande; Mexican International Railway;
Mexican Central Railway; Acheson, Topeka, and Santa Fe; and others
(similarly, Edison offers a series of films under the sponsorship of the
Occidental and Oriental Steamship Company, showing views of Shang-
hai, Hong Kong, Yokohama, Tokyo, Macao, and Hawaii). In all cases the
transportation companies sponsored these films with the specific inten-
tion of encouraging tourism along their routes. The Edison catalogue,
for instance, introduces its series of Denver and Rio Grande films by saying: "Tourists who choose this route are assured of magnificent scenery
and also of the very best of treatments" (Musser 1985: 103). Railways frequently not only encouraged the production of such films but organized

their own tours of travel lectures using motion pictures and lantern slides to increase their tourist patronage (McLuan 1985: 39).

In the United States the Santa Fe Railway exemplifies the circuit between industrial expansion and tourism and the role travel images play in moving consumers over this route. As T. C. McLuan has shown in *Dream Tracks*, in the 1890s the advertising department of the railway sought to overcome bankruptcy by aggressively promoting the line as a tourist route. To accomplish this, the corporation contracted landscape artists to paint scenic images from the great American Southwest, along with picturesque images of Native American life. These images were circulated nationwide on posters, brochures, and calendars (McLuan 1985: 18–33). For the 1915 Pan Pacific Exposition the Santa Fe Railway even constructed its own panorama of the Grand Canyon (Kirby 1989: 61). In addition, photographers such as William Henry Jackson were contracted (and provided with specially equipped photographic railway cars) to produce still photos, lantern slides, and postcards. Eventually motion picture cameramen were also hired who shot not only the southwestern landscape but the line's greatest tourist draw, the Hopi Snake Dance at Walpi Pueblo. Travel images were part and parcel of a modern advertising campaign, as were most of the early railway series filmed by American film companies (the Union Pacific provided the motion picture cameraman Billy Bitzer with his own car, as well) (Bitzer 1973: 25).

We can see clearly, then, that the travel genre in early film occurs within a context of feverish production of views of the world, an obsessive labor to process the world as a series of images and to make those views available as never before through a range of methods: actual tourism, fairground simulations of journeys, projected images, stereographs, or postcards sent through the mail. This consumption of the world through images occurs in the context of industrial and colonial expansion, with war and the railway leading both photographers' and spectators' curiosity into new geographical realms. In short, the travel genre exemplifies what Martin Heidegger has called the "Age of the World Picture":

> Where the world becomes picture, what is, in its entirety, is juxtaposed as that for which man is prepared and which, correspondingly, he therefore intends to bring before himself and have before himself, and consequently, intends in a decisive sense to set in place before himself. Hence, world picture, when understood essentially, does not mean a picture of the world but the world conceived and grasped as picture. ([1962] 1977: 129)

3 *Les Chillouks, tribu d'Afrique centrale* (The Shilluks, a Central African Tribe). Pathé Frères, 1910, director Alfred Machin. Joye Collection. National Film and Television Archive, London.

In other words, for Heidegger the metaphysical (and destructive) nature of modern Western man views the world as something that can be appropriated through becoming a picture. No better illustration of this could be conceived than the travel images of the nineteenth and twentieth centuries. The phrase used by a number of early film companies as their motto, "the whole world within reach," exemplifies this thinking: the world brought close as a picture and appropriated by the viewer.[2] No longer are even the most remote reaches of the planet inaccessible. They can be brought forward and consumed as images (Figure 3). And this form of image consumption is not merely a *faute de mieux*.

Rather than ersatzes, images become our way of possessing the world, or the universe. Does anyone doubt that on the first tourist voyage to the moon, the first stop for tourists will be at the postcard rack to buy images produced by NASA?

But if early cinema travel films arise from a deep context of image making that characterizes the modern world, does the fact that they are *films* add anything unique to the pictures? I believe so. The unique aspect of motion pictures, the representation of movement, supplied a new way the world could be transformed into pictures. But this modern transformation of the picture itself also has its roots in the passion for images of distant places that marks the nineteenth century. The explosion of travel images that I have been tracing also transformed the nature of the picture. Although undoubtedly inspired by traditions of landscape painting and the picturesque, all the devices I have discussed project the idea that there is something insufficient about the simple framed perspectival illusion. Each device tries to supplement this insufficiency in a different manner.

For instance, the panorama constructs its canvases in such a way that the limits of the picture frame seem abolished. In stationary panoramas the circular form of the painting and the arrangement of lighting and architecture (which deemphasized the upper and lower edges) created a sense of an image without borders.[3] In moving panoramas the unfolding canvas, which could never be visible in its entirety at any particular moment, seemed equally to produce an image without a frame. Daguerre's diorama through sheer size also undermined the sense of its border, while illumination from behind the translucent canvas created an uncannily lifelike image that could also transform itself with a change of light, thereby exceeding the illusion allowed by a traditional landscape painting (Gernsheim and Gernsheim 1968: 15-17). Illumination and transformation (through dissolving views) also intensified the visual power of magic lantern imagery. And the stereoscope endowed images with an illusionary depth achieved by the superimposition of two parallax images.

While traditionally these supplements are thought of as attempts at greater realism, it might be more useful to think of them as attempts to overcome the limits of the traditional picture and its frame. As such, they heighten the experience of an image by either giving it a greater visual saliency (illumination, stereoscopy) or a temporal dimension (both forms of panorama; transforming views) since the view cannot be exhausted from one view point. Clearly the cinema combines these traditions, wedding illumination with movement. But I believe all these new forms of travel images also construct a new form of observer, as Jonathan Crary has demonstrated about the stereoscope (1990: 116-36). Interestingly, in all these devices the appropriation through imagery becomes somewhat agonistic as the scale, depth, movement, or brilliant illumination and transformation of the image seems to elude the viewer's grasp as much as it offers itself up to him or her. All these devices in some sense create an image that overwhelms the viewer through change, scale, or intensity, or all three in concert.

Early travel films frequently make use of what they term "panoramic

4 *La vie sur l'Alpe* (Life on the Alps), Eclipse, 1910. Joye Collection. National Film and Television Archive, London.

views." This is an extremely polyvalent term in early cinema. Occasionally it means simply a broad view of a landscape from some "panoramic" point, like a high mountain (Figure 4). But more frequently such films try to recreate either the circular effect of the stationary panorama or the unfolding of a mobile panorama through camera movement. "Circular panorama" generally made use of the panning (the term comes from "panorama") possibilities of the camera tripod; the Edison catalogue offered a number of films under this specific category (Musser 1985: 106–7). Advertising one circular panorama of a Parisian street, the catalogue suggested that a view such as this provided more information about Paris than a dozen street scenes taken under the older method (i.e., with a stationary camera). As well as being the genesis of such arching panning shots, "panorama" was also used to describe films in which the camera was in motion on some vehicle: railway train, trolley car, motor boat, or automobile. The Lumière cameraman Promio claimed he first hit upon the idea of this sort of motion when touring Venice in a gondola. As he recalled twenty-five years later to the film historian G.-Michel Coissac, he reasoned that "if the immobile camera allowed the reproduction of moving objects, then perhaps one could reverse the proposition and film immobile objects with a moving camera" (Coissac 1925: 196).

The popularity of such moving camera shots in early travel cinema can be easily explained. First, they allowed a broader view of the landscape. Second, the actual movement seems to carry the viewer into the image, realizing what Charles Musser has called the "spectator as passenger convention" (1990: 429). It is no accident that one of the later terms for such camera movements would be the "traveling shot." Rather than simply reproducing the view, such films seem to recreate the actual penetration of space that traveling involves. Finally, a moving camera creates a sort of stereoscopic illusion as the varied rates of apparent movement of objects at different distances within the visual field provide another depth cue. Early film catalogues frequently stressed the stereoscopic nature of their moving panorama films. Like the earlier pre-cinematic devices that the word "panorama" links them to, these moving camera films provide a supplement not available in traditional landscape painting. The moving camera's ability to seem to surpass its own frame creates another image, which seems to pass beyond its own borders.

These means of representing travel (both protocinematic and filmic) share what might be called a "sensational" approach; they attempt to increase the power of representation either by addressing more senses (particularly the physical sensation of movement known as kinesthesia) than the traditional painting can or by making vision more intense (through illumination or stereoscopy). The manufacture of sea air in the Maréorama, Daguerre's ringing church bells in the diorama, or the sound of train whistles in the Hale's Tours, along with the kinesthetic experience of pitching boat decks or lurching train cars, are only the most extreme experiments in surpassing the landscape painting. These devices aim at direct physiological stimulation and recall Crary's definition of the modern observer as one whose body plays an acknowledged role in the creation of the illusions s/he observes (1990: 129–36).

The terms that early film catalogues use to make these panoramic travel films attractive to exhibitors contrast sharply with the experience of absorption in the contemplation of nature associated with a traditional landscape painting (although they might be related to the romantic sublime landscape, which pictures nature as an overwhelming force). Again and again descriptions of panoramic travel films emphasize that the camera is not only moving but moving at a high rate of speed. The Biograph catalogue description of the film *A Panoramic View in the Grand Canal* does not invoke the somnolent sway of a gondola but stresses that it was "taken from the front of a rapidly moving launch" (Musser 1985: 138). Likewise, the same catalogue describes *Panoramic View of Siegesallee, Berlin* as "taken from an automobile in rapid motion" and a view of the Battery of New York City as "taken from a rapidly moving tug." As much as stereoscopy or a sense of traveling, these descriptions advertise the sensation of speed. They promote a truly modern perception of landscape, one mediated by technology and speed.

Wolfgang Schivelbusch has supplied an already classic account of the way the view of the landscape from a rapidly moving train became emblematic of modern perception. Revealingly, Schivelbusch calls this new mode of perception "panoramic." Panoramic perception involves a separation between the viewer and the spectacle observed: "Panoramic perception, in contrast to traditional perception, no longer belongs to the same space as the perceived objects: the traveler sees the landscape, objects, etc. *through* the apparatus which moves him through the world" (1979: 66).

As a number of film scholars have pointed out, this description anticipates the mode of film viewing (Doane 1991; Rabinovitz 1990; Musser 1984; Kirby 1989; Gunning 1989). In the case of early panoramic films the "panoramic" effect is doubled as the apparatuses involved include both the means of transportation and the cinema itself. Cinema in early travel film becomes itself a mode of transportation, as works by Giuliana Bruno (1993) and Anne Friedberg (1993) have indicated.

Schivelbusch's study of the railway journey reveals that the new form of travel initially carried with it a deep-rooted anxiety over the possibility of an accident (1979: 118–25). Curiously, while railway companies tried to minimize this anxiety, the descriptions provided for some early train films seem rather to maximize it (and it seems likely that such descriptions found their way into the pattern of travel lecturers using these films). Take, for instance, the Edison 1902 description of the film *Panoramic View of Lower Kicking Horse Canyon* from their *Rocky Mountain Panoramic Railroad* series: "Of all panoramic mountain pictures this is the most thrilling, as the audience imagines while they are being carried along with the picture the train will be toppled over thousands of feet into the valley below." Another panoramic view of the same canyon is advertised in this way: "The train seems to be running into the mountains of rock as each curve is reached and rounded, making the scene exciting from start to finish." Likewise, Edison's description of *Panoramic View of Mt. Tamalpais, Cal.*

proclaims the view from a mountainside train: "This makes the picture most thrilling as one experiences the sensation of momentarily expecting to be hurled into space" (Musser 1985: 168).

What is one to make of these curiously masochistic fantasies so at odds with the usual genteel conception of travel as a form of contemplation?[4] Obviously, the sensation of imminent danger can be offered as pleasurable entertainment because the peril is illusionary, and the spectator can have her thrill while safely seated in a theater. The viewer of travel films is not simply a surrogate of the tourist, seeking the ersatz of the traveler's original experience. The security of the cinema seat can have advantages the tourist never enjoys.

For instance, the mediation of the cinematic apparatus allows viewpoints not available to the tourist. A 1903 Edison description for *Phantom Ride on the Canadian Pacific* points out that the view taken from the front of the train running at high speed is one that "even tourists riding over the line are not privileged to enjoy" (Musser 1985: 309). Further, the cinema protected viewers against the dangers that flesh-and-blood tourists might have to face and even presented these dangers as an additional thrill for the secure spectator. Descriptions of travel films frequently point out the danger or discomfort in which the actual tourists find themselves. A 1903 Edison description of *Tourist Climbing Mt. Blanc* gives this as one of the fascinations of the film: "As the audience views the picture it will be spellbound, momentarily expecting to see the mountain climbers fall into a chasm and be dashed to pieces" (Musser 1985: 292). Such descriptions show that early travel films often participate in the aesthetics of sensation and astonishment so basic to the early cinema of attractions (Gunning 1989). The viewer is not a detached contemplative spectator but a physiologically stimulated observer.

These images in which the audience is "carried along" by both film images and modes of transport seem to act out the aggressive appropriation of space that Heidegger finds implicit in the world picture. But the ambivalence of early cinema asserts itself; this fantasy of appropriation through images is laid bare by such nakedly aggressive visual strategies. And when the image of aggressive appropriation becomes stripped of all camouflage, could a process of demythologization be beginning? When the world comes within one's imagistic grasp so tightly, is squeezing the only option?

These unanswered questions penetrate to the core of cinema's complicity with the most destructive aspects of modern perception, its links to war and colonial expansion and exploitation. But they also raise the issue of the utopian aspects of cinema, an aspect that early cinema also reveals. In Walter Benjamin's utopian conception, cinema overcomes all forms of distance to bring everything closer to its mass audience. For Benjamin (1969) this modern passion for nearness wields a destructive power that is also liberating, a power that smashes older forms of control and ownership of the image.[5] To express this utopian power of cinema, its ability to evade the entrapments of the older static culture, Giuliana Bruno introduces to film study a term coined by the Italian philosopher Mario Perniola, *transito*, which she says cannot be translated into English by a single word. Bruno defines the term "as a wideranging and multi-faceted notion of circulation. Transito connotes many levels of desire as inscribed in both physical and mental movement: it includes passages, traversing, transitions, transitory states, and erotic circulation, and it incorporates a linguistic reference to transit" (1993: 82).

For Bruno transito is a neglected source of cinematic pleasure, one which escapes from the strategies of containment and ideology. History teaches us that utopias provide inspiration only as long as they are situated nowhere, as they remain u-topic. Certainly to find in early cinema and especially early travel films a form that escapes the claims of ideology and entrapments of power and aggression would be the worst sort of deception. However, within these early films one also sees utopian possibilities in which cinema, like these early panoramic films, seems not only to trace the routes of power and appropriation but also to describe a line of escape and flight.

An Edison film shot in the West Indies in 1903 typifies the double nature of these foreign views, these images shot beyond our borders. A single-shot film entitled *Native Woman Washing a Negro Baby in Nassau, B. I.*, it lasts less than a minute. It is typical of a large number of travel films in which the inhabitants of other lands, particularly of less industrialized nations, are treated as curious sights not unlike the landscape.[6] The first part of the film consists of the title action, which the Edison catalogue summarizes in this way: "The baby seems to enjoy the washing until he gets soap in his eyes and begins to cry." The Edison description ends with this expression of slightly mocking and condescending amusement. But the film continues beyond this. Suddenly the camera pivots, making a swift panoramic turn. In a sort of reverse angle we discover that the process of turning the daily life of native people into a spectacle has itself become a spectacle as the camera reveals a group of native children and adults watching the filming. Then, suddenly, this group of witnesses flees, dashing out of the frame, away from the camera's view.

The film says it all, balancing the horror with the escape. On the one hand, it depicts a slice of native life seized and presented as an amusing and possibly even laughable spectacle for the delectation of viewers from another culture and race. But then the frame becomes unstable with movement and the camera discovers another context. The spectacle makers themselves have become a spectacle, the tables turned with the camera's pivot. And, finally, a sublime moment as this witnessing audience refuses to become a spectacle in turn and takes off, escaping the frame and the camera, running off into unimaged space. The film captures and contains, mocks and reduces, but then it responds to its own capacity for motion and also reveals. It shows what possibly no other form of travel representation could represent, the escape of its subject, its pure *transito* and flight.

Notes

1. See also T. C. McLuan's *Dream Tracks: The Railroad and the American Indian*, which describes a 1906 tourist train disembarking in the American Southwest: "About half the tourists jump from the train almost as soon as they stop and run from one place to another in search of souvenir postal cards, flop themselves down in the waiting room or on the brick curb and write feverishly, hunt around for some place to buy stamps and then mail their cards, and then by that time have only a few minutes left to patronize the lunch counter. Meanwhile the greater portion of the other half are taking snapshots of the hotel or station, or are posing against one of the other buildings for someone else's picture. It is as good a circus to watch it" (1985: 37).

2. Méliès Star Film Company adopted the motto "The whole world within reach" when it still intended to produce actualités (Hammond 1974: 30).

3. See the description of the panorama by Quatremère de Quincy from 1832, reprinted in André and André 1987: 173.

4. I believe these early fantasies relate strongly to what Philippe Dubois has examined as the devouring and terroristic aspect of the close-up in early cinema, which he relates to the movement of the train toward the camera in Lumière's *L'Entrée d'un Train en Gare de La Ciotat* (Dubois 1984–1985).

5. The most insightful commentary on Benjamin's relation to cinema is Hansen 1987.

6. For instance, a Biograph 1902 film catalogue advertised the film *Home Life of a Hungarian Family* thus: "Nothing more novel than this picture could be shown to an American audience. The view was taken in the doorway of a peasant's hovel" (Musser 1985: 138). See also the Selig Polyscope catalogue's description of *Solomon Island Dance*: "A wild and jerky dance which has the cannibalistic touch in every step" (Musser 1985: 89).

From *Hale's Tours* to *Star Tours*

VIRTUAL VOYAGES, TRAVEL RIDE FILMS, AND

THE DELIRIUM OF THE HYPER-REAL

LAUREN RABINOVITZ

||||||||||||||||||||||||||||||||||||||||||||||||||||||||||||||||||||||||||||||||||||||||||||||||||||||||||||||||||||||||||||

From their beginning, movies played a key role in accustoming audiences to sensory overloaded, hyper-real spectacles. Early cinema was always a spectacular "event" generally comprising movies, music, live ambient sounds, magic lantern slides, spoken accompaniment, and sometimes even theatrical acts. More pointedly, *Hale's Tours and Scenes of the World* and other amusement park "movie rides" coordinated sounds, motion pictures, and mechanical movement to reproduce the realism of train travel and to offer virtual travel to remote areas that the railroad had recently opened up for tourism in the United States, Canada, and Europe (Rabinovitz 2001).[1] *Hale's Tours* was composed of one, two, or even three theater cars that each seated seventy-two "passengers." Using rear screen projection in many cases so that the projector was not seen, the movies shown out the front end of the otherwise closed car generally offered a filmed point of view from the front or rear of a moving train, producing the illusion of movement into or away from a scene while mechanical apparatus and levers simultaneously vibrated, rocked, and tilted the car. Other effects enhanced the sensation of travel: steam whistles tooted, the sound of clattering wheels was heard. The first travel ride films simulated railroad or auto travel in order to foreground the body itself as a site for sensory experience. They articulated a seemingly contradictory process for the spectator: they attempted to dematerialize the subject's body through its extension into the cinematic field while they repeatedly emphasized the corporeality of the body and the physical delirium of the senses.

When they ceased early in the second decade of the twentieth century,

Hale's Tours went "underground" as travel ride films were absorbed into narrative cinema (a complication beyond the scope of this essay) but re-emerged during World War II in military training simulations.[2] In post-war world's fairs and amusement parks, *Hale's Tours*–like rides reappeared in new motion-simulation rides like *Trip to the Moon* (Disneyland, 1955) and *Impressions of Speed* (Brussels' International Exposition, 1958). These formats relied on widescreen uses of forward motion and objects flashing by at the margins in order to enlarge the spectator's cognitive immersion in the spectacle. In the 1970s, this type of travel format became more fully systematic when IMAX Corporation introduced a giant film image several stories high and movies that deploy a *Hale's Tours*–like vocabulary of high camera angles and movements that create vertiginous bodily orientations in a format dominated by documentary and travelogue. Together with modern motion simulation rides, they resuscitate a complex simulated travel machine that we need to examine more closely in order to understand its phantasmagoric pleasures and function for reveling in the physicality of one's own body.

Travel ride films foreground the bodily pleasures of the cinematic experience, pleasures already inherent in cinema itself and important in such bodily-oriented genres as pornography, action adventure, horror, and melodrama. But ride films carefully coordinate the spectator's physical and cognitive sensations, whereas one might argue that the standard Hollywood approach involves substantial conflict between various cognitive cues. Across the history of cinema, ride films best represent an experience unaccounted for by theories of cinema spectatorship that have generally represented moviegoing as a passive experience where spectators are increasingly drawn *out* of their bodies and into the screen.

Back to the Body: The Nostalgia of Ride Films

At both the beginning of cinema and now ostensibly at the "end" of cinema, travel ride films responded to dramatic technological shifts that questioned prior epistemological relations between the subject and visualization. Cinema challenged experiential norms for knowledge because (as an improved photographic technology) it ideally intensified perception through a focalization and autonomization of sight. Computer technologies (already diffused into motion pictures) today threaten our acquired understanding of the photographic/cinematic domain. Their threat stems less from their ability to simulate a photograph and thus achieve an indexical representation that actually has no basis in reality than from their tendency to undermine the subject's ability to determine whether or not the representation has a real-world referent.

Hale's Tours responded to the newness of cinema's autonomization of vision and the process of its normalization by grafting the process itself onto a bodily sensation of motion and coordinating it with synchronized sound effects; it retained the experiential across the site of the body. Almost one hundred years later, modern motion simulation rides similarly compensate for the loss of visual faith in the image's indexical properties by articulating certitude at the level of the subject's bodily experience. Ride films provide a conservative, even nostalgic function as they accustom spectators to new technologies: they maintain a definition of knowledge rooted in the "familiar" terrain of the body.

The idea of embodiment itself is a well-known feature of the liberal subject and central to understanding cinema's origins not as the mechanical inventions of its apparatus but as the historically conditioned subjectivity of the movie audience. As the art historian Jonathan Crary argues, the beginning of modernism is not so much a radical affront to the past but is rather a consequence of shifting regimes of vision and perception put into place in Enlightenment liberalism (1999). Crary contends that nineteenth-century visual culture was founded on the collapse of classical subject-object duality and on the admittance of sensory activity that severs perception from any necessary relationship to an exterior world. Furthermore, Crary's claim that at the historical moment in which visual perception is relocated as *fully embodied*—the period in the nineteenth century in which a series of photographic practices replaced the cultural importance of the camera obscura—the way was paved for the historical emergence of autonomous vision understood as a corporealization of sensation.

Crary writes the body back into the field of signification while simultaneously arguing for a historical rupture in the fixed model of classical spectatorship. Within his newly admitted historical context for cinema's subjects, cinema depended on reconciling bodily experience (and cognitive understanding) with the ascendancy of vision as the privileged self-sufficient source of perceptual knowledge. In other words, if cinema is—as so many have claimed—the paradigmatic Vision Machine of modernism, it achieves this only by hyperbolizing vision in relationship to an embodied perceptual spectatorship. Rather than categorize cinema as a disembodied fantasy that has been the dominant strategy within both theories of cinematic realism and psychoanalytic spectatorship, I argue that cinema attempts to effect and promise embodiment as a prophylactic against a world of continuing disembodiment. Indeed, this is the model against which *all* cinema should be read (as promising embodiment in relationship to disembodiment): cinema represents a complex interplay between embodied forms of subjectivity and arguments for disembodiment.

I propose a model of cinema that shifts from a technologically determinist cinema as an ongoing effort for improved cinematic realism. Ride films are not just about what is being depicted—the *sight* of the destination—but are bound to how they reveal the capacity of the apparatus for summoning novel points of view, for extending the panoptic gaze, and for eliciting perceptually felt wonder at the apparatus. Ride films always present their subjects as a cinema-of-novelty display: they transform the landscape into pure spectacle. Conquering space not only with the gaze, such spectacles foreground the body itself as a site for sensory experience within a three-dimensionally contained space. They coordinate the cinematic images with a range of other cues: visual and auditory effects may emanate from different points in the auditorium; atmospheric or environmental stimuli may affect skin responses and sensations; and there are efforts to produce kinesthesia (or actual movement).

The degree to which these movies have been historically successful at these attempts may be exemplified by a continuous, unintended side effect. The historian Raymond Fielding has suggested that *Hale's Tours* incited nausea in some of its participants (1983: 129). Furthermore, attendants regularly warn audiences at the beginning of today's motion simulation rides: "If you start to feel nauseous, simply close your eyes." Travel ride films thus invoke the physical delirium of the senses, sometimes so much so that they overdo it. But what is most important is the degree to which all these examples bind vision to a wider range of sensory affect.

Across the century, ride films articulate a seemingly contradictory process for the spectator: they attempt to dematerialize the subject's body through its visual extension into the cinematic field while they emphasize the spectator's body itself as the center of an environment of action and excitement. They have to sensationalize and smooth over the gaps between the in-the-body experience (affect) and the out-of-the-body sense of panoptic projection. Previous discussions, however, about the "participation effect" and sense of immersion associated with wraparound

screens, interactive hypertexts, and virtual reality attend only to an out-
of-body immersion in the diegesis (Belton 1992; Sobchack 1995). What
is more important are the multiplicity of effects *on* the body—not only
the sharp images and loud sounds of the movie but the overall physical
sensations as well as the actual wind effects, laser lights, cold fog, motion shocks, and animatron-actors in the auditorium. In addition, theater spaces are frequently punctuated by the screams and shouts of audience members. Like their "cousins"—IMAX, Cinerama, virtual reality,
and other immersion cinemas—travel ride films work for the sensation of
physical immersion in the visual field while they bombard the senses with
a variety of over-the-top stimuli (Rabinovitz 2004). Their promise of an
embodied spectatorship seemingly celebrates a heightened interactivity,
although such resistance to a pure passive gaze may not generate a truly
active spectator. Instead, these films simply require that we frame the history of moviegoing differently, as a spectatorship of sensory fascination,
a *jouissance* instead of distraction.

Ride Films as a History of Cinema:
Film as "Reality Itself"

There are numerous speculations about the conceptual origins of *Hale's
Tours* in which the American entrepreneur-promoter George C. Hale
is alternately influenced by moving panoramas, his previous experience
staging theatrical spectacles about firefighting, a 360-degree motion picture show at the 1900 Paris Exposition (Cinéorama, which burned down
after two nights), or Lyman Howe's illustrated lecture travelogues. What
is known is that Hale first introduced *Hale's Tours and Scenes of the World* at
the 1904 Louisiana Purchase Exposition in St. Louis. His success led to a
more permanent installation for the 1905 season at the Kansas City Electric Park. With his partner Fred Gifford, Hale took out two patents for
his "illusion railroad ride."[3] By the end of the 1906 summer season, there
were more than five hundred installations at amusement parks and store-
front theaters in all major U.S. and Canadian cities as well as in capitals
of Europe (*The Billboard* 1906b: 20). They offered subjective point-of-
view journeys to scenic spots in the United States and Canada (including
Niagara Falls, the Catskills, the Rocky Mountains, northern California,
the Black Hills, and the Yukon), to foreign lands that were especially remote or pre-industrial (China, Ceylon, Japan, Samoa, the Fiji Islands),

and even to urban centers via trolley or subway (*Views and Films Index* 1907; *Biograph Bulletin* 1906). *Hale's Tours* was highly successful, often among a park's biggest moneymaker concessions.[4] Even *The Billboard* reported that *Hale's Tours* "raised the standard of attractions" at amusement parks and was enjoying "great popularity" (1906c: 24). They began to disappear around 1909 when it is likely that the increased systematization and consolidation of the movie industry made it difficult to obtain new phantom train ride movie products.

Modern motion simulation rides date from 1986, the year that Douglas Trumbull installed *Tour of the Universe* at Toronto's CN Tower. His tourist attraction was a simulated space adventure that featured Trumbull's high-speed Showscan process of 70mm film cinematography and an auditorium outfitted with hydraulic lifts under the seats. It inspired the Disney and Lucasfilm collaboration that resulted the following year in *Star Tours* (eventually installed at Disney theme parks in California, Florida, Tokyo, and Paris), which became the industry model, according to Fitz-Edward Otis, Omni Film International vice president of sales (Kaufman 1993: 27). *Star Tours'* success led Disney to add motion simulation rides to Epcot Center in Orlando (*Body Wars*, 1989) and to its refurbished Disneyland in Anaheim in 1995 (*The Indiana Jones Adventure: Temple of the Forbidden Eye*). Disney's chief theme park competitor, Universal Studios, opened its own Trumbull-designed ride attraction, *Back to the Future — The Ride*, at its parks in 1991. Each of these was designed to show only one film and used the architecture as well as a lobby "pre-show" to activate and advance the narrative.

In 1993, Trumbull's *In Search of the Obelisk* (part of a theatrical trilogy entitled *Secrets of the Luxor Pyramid*) at the Hotel Luxor in Las Vegas may be said to have marked the maturation of modern travel ride films. Designed and installed as part of the hotel's overall concept, it demonstrates the degree to which a motion simulation theater has become a standard feature at many resort-entertainment complexes. *In Search of the Obelisk* relies on the surrounding associations of the hotel's pyramid structure and a video pre-show to launch a fictional rescue mission through time to a lost civilization. The film itself results in a vertiginous diegesis that spins around and upside down so much that it eludes any references to north, east, west, or south. The only on-screen spatial anchor is the narrative's "pilot," who appears in the center on-screen and speaks over his shoulder to the audience-passengers "behind him."

While some travel ride films—like those at Disney parks, the Luxor,

Universal Studios, or other parks like Busch Gardens—are fixed (one film only) so that they can coordinate the setting with the film, most motion simulation rides change films on a regular basis and are thus housed in more generic movie theaters. A handful of companies supplies motion simulation rides to these theaters in shopping malls, hotels, casinos, family entertainment complexes, museums, and zoos or nature parks. Corporate efforts to increasingly integrate the hardware (the projection and seat installation) and software systems (the computer software and movies) led to mergers, buyouts, and trade monopoly lawsuits in recent years.[5]

Thus, the rides depend on computer technologies not simply for the movies' special effects but for software-driven movie products that can simultaneously control and synchronize the hydraulics of the seats. A small sample of popular titles includes *Alpine Race* (Showscan, 1991), *Space Race* (Showscan, 1991), *Devil's Mine Ride* (Showscan, 1993), *Asteroid Adventure* (IMAX RideFilm, 1993), *Robo Cop: The Ride* (Iwerks Entertainment, 1993), *Dino Island* (Iwerks Entertainment, 1995), *Funhouse Express* (IMAX RideFilm, 1995), *Secrets of the Lost Temple* (Iwerks Entertainment, 1997), *Aliens: Ride at the Speed of Fright* (Iwerks Entertainment, 1997), *Glacier Run* (nWave Pictures, 1999), and *Deep Sea: The Ride* (SimEx!Iwerks, 2003). Unlike *Hale's Tours'* emphasis on picturesque travel, topographical landmarks, and tourist travel experiences, modern titles are dominated by fantasy travel that features scenery of outer space, futuristic cities, lost civilizations. But there are also representations of current-day automobile races, train panoramas, and roller-coaster rides. Their goal is to produce both a physical and emotional frenzy, a goal shared by other amusement park thrill rides that combine pleasure and fear.[6]

The realism of ride films is organized through two regimes of textual address—the cinematographic properties of the image and the conventions of narrative. First, the cinematographic image itself foregrounds the subject's visual experience of moving through the environment. Visual cues emphasize fluid temporal movement into a deep field in which the features of the landscape seem to fly toward the viewer. For example, *Hale's Tours* films typically featured the landscape as the train picked up speed so that the items accelerating into the foreground were the object of information. The films employed both editing and camera movements but usually only after presenting an extended shot (often one to two minutes or longer in a seven- to eight-minute film) organized by the locomotion of the camera. The continuous flow of motion delineated the

visual and temporal information within the frame as that of objects rushing toward the camera. The camera was mounted at a slightly tipped angle
in order to show the tracks in the foreground as parallel lines that con-
verge at the horizon, an important indicator of perspectival depth. Tele-
phone poles, bridges, tunnels, and other environmental markers in the
frame functioned as markers of flow according to the lines of perspective. Passing through tunnels affected a particularly dramatic difference
of darkness/light, no image/moving image, and interruption/flow. The
repetition of all these elements contributed to an overall impression that
the perceptual experience of the motion of the camera is a recreation of
the flow of the environment.

Recent rides reproduce this goal in a quite similar manner. They rely on
the same cinematic conventions, in effect persuading spectators to perceive their bodies as hurtling forward through time and space because
they visually perceive a flow of environmental motion toward them while
being physically bumped up and down and tilted forward and backward.
Most often, these visual cues consist of passing vehicles or features of the
landscape represented in foreshortened animation and computer graphic
images (CGI). These cinematic light shows are not only indirect successors to Cinerama and other widescreen special effects but are direct heirs
to Douglas Trumbull's famous seventeen-minute "Stargate Corridor" sequence in *2001: A Space Odyssey* (Stanley Kubrick, 1968) that depicts forward movement in interplanetary space through stroboscopic colored
lights and aerial perspective.

Early industry reporters related apocryphal stories of the sensory delirium produced in persuading the *Hale's Tours* spectator to take the bodily
place of the subject in the camera's absence. These stories are reminiscent of the reception of the earliest Lumière films: "The illusion was so
good that when trolley rides through cities were shown, members of the
audience frequently yelled at pedestrians to get out of the way or be run
down. One demented fellow even kept coming back to the same show,
day after day. Sooner or later, he figured, the engineer would make a mistake and he would get to see a train wreck."[7] The "demented fellow" may
have recognized the delicious terror of *Hale's Tours* better than the reporter since it is precisely the anticipation of disaster that provides the
thrill at the heart of ride films. The *Hale's Tours* reporter only understood
the irony since the ride—like all other ride films—controlled the fact that
disaster would not happen and that the "demented fellow" would always
experience disaster safely. Obviously a fan of *Hale's Tours*, the "demented

fellow" may have been exhibiting less dementia than the delirious effect produced by these rides.

The same expectation dominates today's rides: out-of-control vehicles rule the field. Regardless of whether the vehicle is a race car, airplane, spaceship, submarine, or mine cart, today's narratives depend on a small number of technological and mechanical crises: a bad landing, "something's wrong with our ship," "Oops! Wrong direction!," or an encounter with an evil creature. These may occur singly or in combination. For example, *Star Tours'* interplanetary shuttle trip piloted by *Star Wars'* androids first heads the wrong way, then hides from and narrowly avoids enemy ships, and finally crash lands. *Back to the Future—The Ride* (inspired by the Hollywood film after which it is named) uses the movie's characters and story in order to combine outer-space flight, time travel, the reckless pursuit of a villain, problems with the ship's mechanical systems, and the requisite bumpy ride that frequently and narrowly averts disaster.

The "demented fellow" may well be kin to the modern ride film aficionado, who professes a fondness for repeat rides, for "collecting" ride experiences at different locations, and for the thrill. Another ride film lover, none other than the film critic-distributor-entrepreneur Amos Vogel, said in the 1950s: "The total impression [is] so vivid as to approach the actual experience. The jury is stumped: Has film left behind the 'illusion of art' and become reality itself?" (1958: 175). In a more sophisticated and self-aware response fifty years after the "demented fellow's" ride, Vogel's words demonstrate the enthusiasm with which spectators have greeted ride films as exciting, hyper-real simulations rather than as mere representations.

The Essential Expedition of *Hale's Tours*: A Narration of Tourism

Hale's Tours did not have to maintain a strict cowcatcher point of view to get across its sensations. The emphasis on flow and perspective of travel was frequently broken in order to display dramatic incidents and bits of social mingling between men and women, different classes, farmers and urbanites, train employees and civilians, ordinary citizens and outlaws. Changes of locale occurred abruptly through editing, the camera position was moved, or the perspective from the front or rear of the train was abandoned altogether. When this happened, the film usually expanded its travel format to offer up views of accompanying tourist attractions or stretched the travelogue with comic or dramatic scenes. A 1906 advertisement in *The New York Clipper* for *Hale's Tours* listed five "humorous railway scenes" that could be included in *Hale's Tours* programs. *Trip through the Black Hills* (Selig Polyscope, 1907) covered "the difficulties of trying to dress in a Pullman berth" (Fielding 1983: 128). In addition, the early film classic *The Great Train Robbery* (Edison Manufacturing Company, 1903) played in *Hale's Tours* cars. *Hale's Tours'* latent content assumed a newly commercialized tourism—the traveler made over into a spectator by taking a journey specifically to consume the exotic, whether that was the city for the country "rube," the "primitive" for the westerner, or picturesque nature for the urbanite.

It was not unusual for the films to cut regularly to the interior of a railroad car, producing a "mirror image" of the social space in which the ride film patron was seated. These films were not purely travelogues, then, but were also about the social relations and expectations connected with the experience of travel. They suggest that what was fundamental to the ride film was not merely the sight of the "destination" and the sensation of immersion in it but the *experience*—both physical and social—of being in that place. Thus, *Hale's Tours* commodified the logic of a new experience—the inscription of being a tourist of the world.

For example, *The Hold-Up of the Rocky Mountain Express* (American Mutoscope and Biograph, 1906) switches to the car interior not just once but twice to portray social interactions among the passengers and then a train robbery (Figure 1). *Grand Hotel to Big Indian* (American Mutoscope and Biograph, 1906) is a variant of the same practice. After a similar extended shot of a cowcatcher traveling point of view along the well-known Horseshoe Loop on the New York state Ulster and Delaware Railway, the film cuts to the train interior where men and women are seated on opposite sides of the aisle. The conductor walks through the car while mattes of traveling landscape "flow" through windows on each side. A porter enters and seats a well-dressed man in a place just vacated by another passenger. No sooner has that action been completed than the man who initially vacated his seat returns and wants his seat back. A fight in the aisle ensues, it is broken up, and everyone goes back to his or her seat. The film then cuts back to the cowcatcher point of view (Figure 2). Other such narrative "interruptions" of the continuous flow of locomotion in

1 A series of stills from *The Hold-Up of the Rocky Mountain Express*.
American Mutoscope and Biograph, 1906.

2 A series of stills from *Grand Hotel to Big Indian*.
American Mutoscope and Biograph, 1906.

3 A sequence of stills from *A Trip on the Catskill Mt. Railway.*
American Mutoscope and Biograph, 1906.

these films include a man who cannot get his horse to move off the tracks,
fights on the tracks, or a man and woman kissing when the train emerges
from a tunnel.

Hale's Tours thus offered its customers vicarious long-distance railroad
journeys compressed into ten minutes while it poked fun at tourist travel.
Primarily the domain of the affluent, the famous Pullman railroad car
like the ones depicted in *Hold-Up of the Rocky Mountain Express* and *Grand
Hotel to Big Indian* was advertised as "a steamship on rails" that signified
luxury travel and class status. The railroad trip and the advent of train
tourism, moreover, may be said to have initiated men and women into
their new standing within the system of commodity production, convert-
ing them from private individuals into a mass culture consuming machine, travel, and nature alike (Figure 3). In this regard, *Hale's Tours* supported this process, transforming the status of a mechanical conveyance
into a seemingly limitless commodity of pleasure and excitement.

The Virtual Voyage of Modern Ride Films:
A Narration of Movie Dreams

Narrativization is an equally important marker of realism in the modern simulation rides, although it is employed differently. This is interesting in light of the fact that the shift effected by *Hale's Tours* was a novel one, a way of introducing narrative strategies to the cinema as an institution, whereas narrativization in today's ride films relies on a conservation of what is cinema's dominant strategy. For example, films like *Alpine Race* employ a voice-over narrator who functions as a fellow passenger or conductor-like guide, a cinematic yet off-screen source for locating agency and narrative organization of the visual sensations. *Alpine Race* begins with a heavily accented male voice-over announcing that "he" is the Italian driver of the car and that many people think "he" is a bad driver. His nationality, social position, and sexuality are all signified by sound information. Although he is never visually inscribed, he becomes an important narrative agent of the film as he informs the spectator that, as the driver, he controls the events of the car's forward movements while he offers a running commentary throughout the ensuing wild ride of hairpin turns, spins, near accidents, and dramatic scenery rushing by in the Italian Alps. Not only does the voice announce its control over velocity and turns that are synchronized with the visual information but "he" coordinates a definition of the space as coherent because of the movements through it.

Secrets of the Lost Temple is more complex, relying on both cinematic and genre conventions for building up its narrative. It begins twice, both in the video pre-show outside the auditorium and again on the theater screen. The prologue offers a cinematically conventional exposition—all in third-person point of view—of a teenage boy finding a book on the floor of a mausoleum-like library. Opening the mysterious book, he is transported to another dimension in a blinding flash of light and dematerialization. Certainly, the prologue's purpose is not only to explain the narrative premise but to offer up a figure for identification in the most traditional syntax of Hollywood cinema. At this point, the ride film begins and, as the audience is first lifted by the hydraulics and then dropped, the boy on-screen simultaneously experiences a fall to the floor in front of an "Indiana Jones" adventurer look-alike. The two converse and, as they are about to be whisked away on a raft down the waterways and chutes of the lost temple, the film switches to the boy's subjective point of view. Throughout the rest of their ensuing wild ride, the film steadfastly maintains the boy's point of view as the audience is asked to assume his place. At the conclusion of their journey, the boy finds himself back in the library, and the film reveals this re-entry with a return to a third-person point of view. The shift is synchronized with the grinding to a halt of motion shocks and effects. The movie effects narrative closure through the boy's discovery that he is clutching his hero's battered fedora (an exact duplicate of the one worn by Indiana Jones in the Steven Spielberg movies). He doffs the beloved hat and jauntily departs. But this return to a conventional movie "ending" in the context of the ride film is most jarring in its shattering of a subjective position. The return to a third-person point of view occurs *with* the loss of motion and effects; in this manner, the ride film lingers on a conclusion that overturns subjective dynamism and returns to the stasis of a more traditionally passive spectatorship. It registers the "end" of the delirium of the body in all its immersive cinema state with the dematerialized subject position of "third-person" omniscience. The rupture here can only hold out an affect of disappointment and of an experience of loss. In this regard, today's ride films function differently than did *Hale's Tours*, which worked to inscribe its audiences into an idealized novel position of authoritative invisibility and surveillance. Toward this end, permanent installations improve on ride film experiences like *Secrets of the Lost Temple* by diffusing lines of demarcation between a subjective state of material immersion and a dematerialized gaze and more gradually moving their audiences back and forth between the two.

Star Tours, *Back to the Future — The Ride*, *Body Wars*, and other permanent installations extend the narrative to the social spaces of the building beyond the movie theater. The lobbies outside the movie auditoriums especially carry an important atmospheric weight, providing a preparatory zone for the ride that prefigures the spectatorial processes inside the auditorium. For example, *Star Tours* really begins with one's entrance into the waiting lanes in the lobby, an architectural space whimsically presented as a futuristic space airport. The lobby features a glassed-in control tower visible from the floor in which animatrons of *Star Wars* android characters go about their business. An animatron of the character C3PO greets visitors with a running commentary. Video displays show arrivals and departures to foreign galaxies, a public address system announces rules about futuristic "no parking zones" that parody current airport announcements, and a video billboard advertises space cruises to the Land of the Ewoks. The audience is already physically immersed in an interactive spectacle even though its role, similar to that of the movie spectator, is simply to move forward in the proper lane and to react without any possibility of altering the enveloping narrative. At amusement parks, in particular, such an organization of space is both a pragmatic way of controlling noisy crowds and an effective means for maintaining efficient traffic circulation. But it also encourages rowdy crowds to behave like idealized mass movie audiences of distracted individuals who respond more to the stimuli of the spectacle than to each other.

Once inside the ride film theater, the patron is greeted by an animatron of c3po, the flight attendant. A screen lowers and shows a safety video much like the ones on today's airplanes except that this one is populated by *Star Wars* droids and aliens. Thus, before he or she encounters the main attraction, an audience member has already been subjected to several movies or videos played on conventional screens in the theater, hall, and lobby.

Shutters part to reveal the cockpit and front glass windshield/screen. The lights dim, and the journey begins with a view out the front windshield of the cinematically animated landscape and the robot-pilot's acknowledgment that this is his maiden voyage. His ineptness prompts a series of wild turns, near misses, and dramatic adventures. So, even in these simulation rides that do maintain a strictly cohesive subjective point of view, narrativization still plays an important role for upholding a cinematic realism. But the narrativization in *Star Tours* avoids the kind of fractured split in spectator positioning characteristic of the earlier installation of *Hale's Tours* or even of *Secrets of the Lost Temple*.

More than wild narratives that reposition spectators, rides like *Star Tours*, *Body Wars*, and *Back to the Future* also completely recover the gap between the index and the referent. This also happens in such rides as *Space Race*, *Secrets of the Lost Temple*, and *Aliens: Ride at the Speed of Fright*. It is not accidental that these ride films appear more realistic to the rides' patrons than do ride films of roller coasters, runaway trains, race cars, and bobsleds. In these films, the referent is not a landscape to which the spectator might in reality have physical access but is instead a movie. In other words, the space landscape of *Star Tours* need not be measured against an ideal referent that it can never equal but only approximate since it *is* its own referent. The *image of* the landscape *is* that which it refers to—

the cinematic space of *Star Wars*; it is after all a movie of a movie. As one computer artist put it: while it may be difficult for computer animation to look like the real world, it is easy for computer-generated imagery to look like computer-generated images (Rubin 1996: 8). These movie- or game-themed rides close the gap between index and referent, achieving a sublime realism that is the subject of postmodern fantasy, of being not so much in outer space but more properly in a well-loved movie or video game. Even the *New York Times* (1998) acknowledges this particular effect: "It's like being inside, not just at, the movies."

Conclusion: From *Hale's Tours* to *Star Tours*

Previously marginalized means of cinematic exhibition like ride films illustrate that cinema has never left behind its function of refashioning the subject for the radical demands made on the viewer as a spectator. At important historical moments of epistemological crisis, travel ride films from *Hale's Tours* to *Star Tours* have covered the disjuncture between the materiality of the body and the body's de-emphasis in distracted cinema viewing. In this regard, they provide an important model for further work on the spectator's experience in general and for understanding, in particular, the spectatorial pleasures of porn, horror, action, melodrama, and other genres that coordinate an address to out-of-the-body and in-the- body experiences. However, travel ride films have accomplished this in different historical circumstances and thus should not be conflated for an ahistorical sense of effect. There are important implications in their differences.

Hale's Tours functioned in relationship to the standardization of photography and cinema; this standardization provided the context in which the radical abstraction and reconstruction of optical experience was being redefined as subjective vision. *Hale's Tours* accomplished that autonomization of sight and its concomitant normalization in voyeurism by grafting visual pleasure onto motion shocks, by retaining the focalization of visual perception in relationship to the body's other perceptions. By accustoming the body to the privileging of sight in relationship to other subjective sensations, *Hale's Tours* helped cinema to accomplish a subject position pleasurably identified with panoptic surveillance.

Almost a century later, the confusion of visual knowledge in the face of too many visual stimuli and even certainty about the image's truthfulness—its referentiality—is compensated for in modern simulation rides. They likewise make visual knowledge coherent by articulating its certitude in relationship to the subject's bodily experience of multiple sensations. Simulation rides rectify and compensate for the loss of a unified subjectivity by literally grounding a subject position in all its material positions and sensory capacities. They are a response to the modernist subject position of visual omnipotence and the authority of panoptic surveillance (that was held out by *Hale's Tours* and then by cinema in general): they nostalgically address their spectators as diegetic movie characters, who become for the moment unified subjects living inside movies.

It is therefore possible to respond emphatically to Amos Vogel's earlier posed rhetorical question, "The jury is stumped: Has film left behind the 'illusion of art' and become reality itself?" Ride films seem to enjoy their greatest popularity at exactly those moments when the jury *is* stumped. In times of epistemological crisis, cinema answers loudly with the reaffirmation that its constructions of subject knowledge are "reality itself."

Notes

1. *Hale's Tours* had many competitors of either rail or auto travel: *Palace Touring Cars, Hurst's Touring New York, Cessna's Sightseeing Auto Tours, Citron's Overland Flyer, A Trip to California Over Land and Sea, Auto Tours of the World and Sightseeing in the Principal Cities. White and Langever's Steamboat Tours of the World* applied the *Hale's Tour* concept to water travel. *Hruby and Plummer's Tours and Scenes of the World* made these concepts more generic for traveling carnivals so that they could set up a train, boat, or automobile. For a detailed description of *Hale's Tours* and its many competitors, see Rabinovitz 2001.

2. One of the first widescreen products after World War II, Cinerama was a peacetime application of this military technology and was designed by Fred Waller, who invented the Waller Gunnery Trainer for the Army and Navy. Cinerama frequently took up the travelogue as its subject matter as well as the point-of-view "movie ride" (e.g., the roller-coaster-ride introduction to *This Is Cinerama* [1952]; the same film's climactic fly-over the Grand Canyon; the bobsled run down St. Moritz in the 1955 *Cinerama Holiday*).

3. For descriptions of Hale and Gifford's patents of an amusement device (patent no. 767,281) and a pleasure-railway (patent no. 800,100), see *The Official Gazette of the United States Patent Office* 1904, 1905. In 1906, they sold the rights east of Pittsburgh to William A. Brady of New York and Edward B. Grossmann of Chicago for $50,000 (*The Billboard* 1906a: 20). They sold the

southern states rights to Wells, Dunne, and Harlan of New York. They sold additional licenses to C. W. Parker Co. of Abilene, Kansas, for traveling carnival companies. They sold the Pacific Northwest states' rights to a group of men who incorporated as "The Northwest Hale's Tourist Amusement Company" in Portland, Oregon.

4. As early as its initial 1906 season, *Hale's Tours* and its competitors became top-grossing, popular concessions across the United States (*The Billboard* 1906d: 28). At Riverview Park in Chicago, the nation's largest and best-attended amusement park, *Hale's Tours* was the fifth biggest moneymaker of the fifty concessions there, earning $18,000 for the season. It was topped only by the Igorotte Village ($40,000), the Kansas Cyclone ($28,000), and the Figure 8 roller-coaster ($35,000), Rollin's animal show and ostrich farm ($26,000), and the dance pavilion ($22,000). It even surpassed the revenues from the park's other moving-picture venue, the electric theater, which took in $16,000 for the year (*The Billboard* 1906e: 28). See also Brown 1916: 373.

5. A history of ride film companies since the late 1980s would entail its own chapter. Initially, the biggest manufacturers of installations and movies were the Ridefilm Division of IMAX Corporation, Showscan (which Trumbull sold when he went to work for IMAX), and Iwerks Entertainment, Inc. The latter was started in 1986 by two former Disney employees, one of whom is Don Iwerks, son of Ub, Disney's very first animator in the 1920s. In 1996, both Iwerks Entertainment and Showscan filed antitrust lawsuits against IMAX. Showscan settled with IMAX in 1997, and Iwerks lost its claim in 1998. In 2000, IMAX sold its Ridefilm division to Iwerks Entertainment and, in 2002, Iwerks Entertainment was acquired by SimEx, Inc. and became SimEx!Iwerks. The same year, Showscan went out of business.

6. Of course, motion simulation rides continue the work of twentieth-century amusement park thrill rides, and it is in amusement park settings that many ride films are found.

7. It is noteworthy that in this report spectators do not jump out of the way (as they did in the reports about Lumière film showings) since they do not understand things coming at them inasmuch as they understand themselves moving forward; they instead yell out at pedestrians in the frame to get out of the way (Thomas 1916: 373).

From Lecturer's Prop to Industrial Product

THE EARLY HISTORY OF TRAVEL FILMS

RICK ALTMAN

IIIIIIIIIIIIIIIIIIIIIIIIIIIIIIIIIIIIIIIIIIIIIIIIIIIIIIIIIIIIIIIIIIIIIIIIIIIIIIIIIIIIIIIIIIIIIIIIIIIIIIIIIIIIIIIIIIIIIIIIIIIIIIIIIIIII

The history of cinema has by and large been configured as a history of films. Understandable in a post-1915 world dominated by feature films, a film-oriented approach to cinema reveals its shortcomings all too rapidly in the field of early cinema. Early moving pictures were in many cases like theatrical props: they gained meaning only to the extent that performers were able to integrate them into their acts. When film entered the American scene, the entertainment arts were heavily dominated by performers. The leading theatrical trade organs of the period — *The Billboard*, the *New York Clipper*, and the *New York Dramatic Mirror* — organized their reporting around acts and the people who performed them, not around products and the people who produced them. Even though the era was hardly without its entertainment products (including sheet music, phonograph records, and moving pictures), a long tradition of covering the stage led the trades to consider these products as little more than props for singers, impersonators, and lecturers. During cinema's formative years, films often existed only to the extent that they could be included in a live performance. Edited or combined to suit the situation, moving pictures long remained subservient to existing forms of entertainment and the performers who provided them.

In order to understand certain aspects of early cinema, we must therefore put aside our firmly entrenched film-oriented approach to cinema in favor of a performer-oriented position. This is especially true for the study of documentary films in general and travel films in particular. For many years, histories of documentary film began with the twenties, lionizing Robert Flaherty and ignoring virtually everything earlier (e.g., Barsam 1973). Even Kristin Thompson and David Bordwell have recently claimed that "before the 1920s, documentary filmmaking had largely been confined to newsreels and scenic shorts" (1994: 202). While this claim might seem to be borne out by production company catalogues, it fails to reckon with the full range of production during cinema's first quarter century. Though it may be possible to base a history of *Hollywood* cinema on studio production, a history of travel films must start elsewhere. Because early cinema was a world not of films but of performers, the history of travel films must begin with those who "performed" them.

In order to discover early travel films, it is useless to search indexes under "films, travel." Instead, we must look under the rubric "lecturer." During cinema's formative years, many different types of lecturers used or accompanied films. Some simply read out loud the film descriptions provided by production companies. Others made up their own commentary on existing films. For the history of travel films, however, the most important lecturers were the performers who traveled the Lyceum and Chautauqua circuits with projector and homemade film in hand (Gaudreault and Lacasse 1996; Lacasse 2000; Musser and Nelson 1991; Altman 2004b). Since the 1830s, when the National American Lyceum grew out of lectures given by Josiah Holbrook in Millbury, Massachusetts, Americans had regularly been regaled by public lectures designed to educate and uplift. Recognizing a widespread hunger for spiritual and intellectual revival, in 1868 James Redpath established a talent bureau to provide lecturers for the many established lyceums spread throughout the country. In 1874 Lewis Miller, a businessman, and John Heyl Vincent, a clergyman, established a summer version of the lyceum on the shores of Lake Chautauqua in western New York. Soon, year-round lyceum lectures (on what was often termed the "platform circuit") would be joined by short-lived chautauqua meetings all over the country. In 1904 these chautauquas were organized into circuits, thus facilitating performer scheduling and travel. The Redpath Lyceum Bureau continued for decades to contract with lecturers for both lyceum and chautauqua performances.[1] Lyceum circuit lecturers typically held forth in the many public buildings that dotted the turn-of-the-century cityscape, especially town halls and public auditoriums, concert halls and opera houses, union halls and churches. At first borrowing the same venues, chautauqua lectures were eventually moved to more easily ventilated tents for the summer season.

For several decades, lecturers remained the featured performers on the lyceum and chautauqua circuits. Moving from town to town, they would typically repeat the same lecture or coordinated course of lectures throughout a season, using the summer slow period to develop a new lecture or course for the following year. Not until around 1915, with the growing popularity of so-called tent chautauquas that filled the summer season, would this familiar pattern be disturbed. During the final quarter of the nineteenth century, this schedule had been followed by many well-known travel lecturers who illustrated their lectures with lantern slides shot in foreign countries, including Edward L. Wilson, the legendary John L. Stoddard, and his successor E. Burton Holmes. Whereas Wilson had begun lecturing before the heyday of the lyceum circuit, Stoddard's career began with lectures on Constantinople as part of the Redpath Lyceum Course at the Boston Music Hall, and on the Rhine and the Alps for the Concord Lyceum in that city's town hall (Barber 1993: 700). Like Wilson, Stoddard illustrated his lectures with lantern slides taken or purchased during his travels. Only the text was included when Wilson's lectures were published, but Stoddard's photographs were reproduced in the immensely popular published versions of his lectures (Wilson 1874–88; Stoddard 1897).

Wilson's and Stoddard's lectures provided Burton Holmes all the education he needed to develop his own illustrated lecture style. Like all other late-nineteenth-century travel lecturers, Holmes practiced the art of what is rightly called the "illustrated lecture." At the heart lies the noun—the lecture itself, the verbal discourse simultaneously assuring temporal and geographical continuity, accompanied by continuous communication with the audience. The illustrations occupy no more than an adjectival role, helping to define and exemplify the words of the lecture. Because Holmes usually took his own photographs (or had them taken to his specifications), he managed to provide greater continuity within his illustrations than many other travel lecturers, who often bought stock slides from catalogues (Figure 1). Even Holmes always subordinated his illustration program to the verbal lecture, however (Holmes 1901; Altman 2004b: chap. 4). Though Wilson, Stoddard, and Holmes each made a career out of showing slides, to their audiences it made no difference whether they shot their own pictures or not.

In 1897 Holmes began to make moving pictures to supplement his lantern slides. Working with his cameraman, Oscar B. Depue, Holmes filmed many of the famous sites that he had previously photographed (Depue 1967: 60–64). In a move that is entirely predictable from his previous practice, and that would presage the next two decades of travel film-making, Holmes managed his moving pictures in exactly the same way

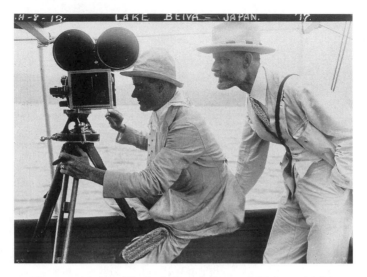

1 Cinematographer Herford T. Cowling and Holmes (right) on
location shooting at Lake Beiva in Japan in 1917. Courtesy of the
Burton Holmes Collection, Seattle, Wash.

that he handled his photographs. At first treating his films as a novelty, he
located them at the end of his lecture, as he might place a series of unusual
photos or trick slides. Then, a few years later, he began to intersperse
them within his program, using them like lantern slides to illustrate particular portions of his lecture (Barber 1993: 81–82). When he was working
with still photographs, Holmes had never been thought of as a photographer but always as a lecturer. Now that he had begun to make films and
to integrate them into his performances, he would continue to be known
as a lecturer, not as a filmmaker. Ads for Holmes's performances thus
always stressed his name and the term "lecture," consigning his illustrations—even when they included moving pictures—to the small print. A
27 February 1898 *New York World* advertisement, for example, announced
Holmes's performances at Daly's in the following manner:

BURTON HOLMES

LECTURES

MAGNIFICENTLY ILLUSTRATED IN COLOR

accompanied by a series of original

MOTION PICTURES

Tomorrow at 11. Tuesday at 3. Wednesday at 11.

"CYCLING THROUGH CORSICA"

Thursday at 11. Friday at 3. Saturday at 11.

"YELLOWSTONE NATIONAL PARK"

Reserved Seats, $1.50 and $1. Admission, 50¢.

Over the next twenty years, many a travel lecturer would complement his stock of travel slides with motion pictures (Figure 2). In most cases, these films were made by (or under the supervision of) the lecturer himself. A particularly representative example is provided by Edward Burton McDowell (who called himself "Dr." and who around 1907 changed the spelling of his name to MacDowell, perhaps to capitalize on the fame of contemporary American composer Edward MacDowell). Prior to 1902, McDowell offered typical fare for a travel lecturer on the platform circuit: lectures recounting his own trips, "illustrated by lantern slides which were developed by his own hands" (McDowell folder). During the summer of 1902—the platform circuit off-season—McDowell traveled "Through Arizona Canyon and Yosemite to the Glaciers of Alaska," where in addition to his photographs he made the first in a series of annual travel films. Ever since they had become national parks in 1872 and 1890, respectively, Yellowstone and Yosemite had constituted prime targets for travel photographers and lecturers. Now McDowell would complement his lantern slides by motion pictures representing, according to his publicity, such animated subjects as

Feeding Time on Pigeon and Ostrich Ranches in California
Surf Lashing a Rocky Coast
Parades during the Carnival of Roses
Waterfalls of the Enchanted Yosemite Valley
Panorama of the Yosemite Mountains
Yosemite Stage Coach passing through the Mariposa Grove "Tunnel Tree"
Bathers Diving and Toboganning
Locomotives Laboring Up Steep Mountain Grades
Ocean Steamer in a Storm, Tossing and Plunging through a Heavy Sea
Railway Panorama of the White Pass, Alaska
Klondike Miners Shooting the Perilous White Horse Rapids, etc.

Projection of these films in alternation with lantern slides was facilitated by the design of contemporary projectors, which always combined

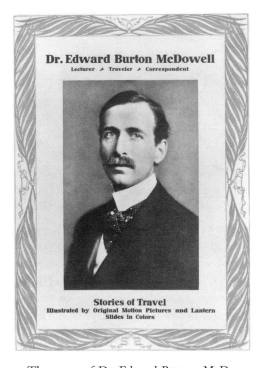

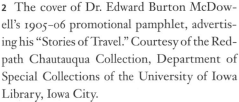

2 The cover of Dr. Edward Burton McDowell's 1905–06 promotional pamphlet, advertising his "Stories of Travel." Courtesy of the Redpath Chautauqua Collection, Department of
Special Collections of the University of Iowa
Library, Iowa City.

a lantern slide light source and transport mechanism with an add-on
"motion head" permitting the unspooling of motion pictures. Of course
McDowell did not himself project his films. Turn-of-the-century platform lecturers always depended on a confederate to handle projection
duties while they lectured. When McDowell added films to his arsenal,
motion picture projection was thus added to the duties of "Mr. D. C.
Denmark, Assistant, Stereoptician and Motion Picture Expert." From
a 1909 document in the Redpath Chautauqua Collection we know that
the railroad fare for McDowell's projectionist was paid by the Redpath
Lyceum Bureau as part of McDowell's lecturing contract (McDowell
folder). During the century's first decade, contracts were typically made

between the lecturer and the booking company, with the projectionist handled just like the motion picture portion of the projector—as an add-on.

In 1903 McDowell photographed and filmed "Samoa: The Tropical Paradise of the South Pacific." His 1906 publicity doesn't spare the italics to claim that "*his motion picture camera was the first to be operated in either the Samoan or Fiji Islands*; and that his moving pictures of savage life and customs in these remote lands are *today the only ones in existence.*" Though McDowell's films of Samoa are not known to still exist, his description helps us to grasp how he understood his filmmaking activity. McDowell never says that he made a film about Samoa, nor does he advertise that he will show a film about Samoa (Figure 3). Instead he promises "The Story of a Summer Cruise, Illustrated by Original Motion Pictures, and Copyrighted Photographic Slides Colored by a Master Hand." Whenever they are mentioned, "motion pictures" are always subservient to the verbal lecture, and always in the plural. In Samoa, we are told, "Dr. McDowell, with an equipment of three cameras, secured 40 motion pictures and more than 1,000 negatives of still subjects." Designed to replace lantern slides when the lecture calls for illustration of an activity rather than a landscape, building, or still life, McDowell's motion pictures put the accent on motion, including:

Samoan Dance by Twenty Men and Women
Canoe Race
War Dance
Waterfall
Food Offering and Processional March
Samoan Youths Bearing the Roasted Pig
Running Dance of Taupou and Manaia
Depositing the Cocoanuts
Moonlight Dance
Diving Scene by Thirty-five Native Boys
Firing Gun on U.S. Man-of-War
Surf Dashing on a Lava Walled Shore
Remarkable Samoan Children's Dance
Ship at Sea

Just as contemporary catalogues designated and sold individual Passion play scenes as separate entities, for McDowell each of these "subjects"

Cocoanut Lunch—
Interior Forest
Copyright 1903
By E. B. McDowell

Original Samoan Moving Pictures
By Edward Burton McDowell
(Copyrighted)

Samoan Dance by Twenty Men and Women; Canoe Race; War Dance; Waterfall; Food Offering and Processional March; Samoan Youths Bearing the Roasted Pig; Running Dance of Taupou and Manaia; Depositing the Cocoanuts; Moonlight Dance; Diving Scene by Thirty-five Native Boys; Firing Gun on U.S. Man-of-War; Surf Dashing on a Lava Walled Shore; Remarkable Samoan Children's Dance; Ship at Sea.

Samoan Dance—
Portion of Motion Picture
Copyright 1903
By E. B. McDowell

The above reproduction is exact width of a segment of motion picture film 150 feet long. This picture, in its entirety, consists of a series of 2,400 miniature negatives, no two exactly alike, which were made in rapid succession at the rate of one seventy-fifth of a second for each little picture.

Devotees of the
"Banana Habit"
Copyright 1903
By E. B. McDowell

MR. D. C. DENMARK, Assistant.
Stereoptician and Motion
Picture Expert

3 A page from one of McDowell's promotional pamphlets, highlighting his "Original Samoan Moving Pictures." Courtesy of the Redpath Chautauqua Collection, Department of Special Collections of the University of Iowa Library, Iowa City.

constituted a separate "motion picture" capable of replacing a lantern slide. In a sense, these films were still defined as "views," according to the era's conception of still photographs. They did not yet constitute the stand-alone object that would later be understood by the term "motion picture" (in the singular). In 1904 McDowell returned to the South Pacific in order to film the Fiji Islands. The following year he would join a bevy of filmmakers to record the building of the Panama Canal. His publicity is careful to point out that the motion pictures were "made by Dr. McDowell with his own motion picture camera; and these motion pictures of the canal work are the first and only ones yet made" (McDowell folder).

In 1907 McDowell (having now changed the spelling of his name) took his Goerz-Anschutz camera to Cuba, where he filmed not only well-known tourist and battle sites but also the back country. Whereas his previous film footage had always consisted of separate short "subjects," each appropriate to replace a lantern slide, McDowell's Cuban motion pictures are in large part organized around the story of his own difficulties:

> After feasting his cameras along these beaten paths of travel, and in accordance with his reputation for seeking out of the way places because of his great love for "roughing it," he then answered a "call of the wild" and began to follow the muddy bends of an alligator stream, the only navigable river in Cuba, far up into the interior forests.
>
> Dr. MacDowell there visited Estrada Palma, the recently deposed president of Cuba, who, with his children and grandchildren, has retired to a lonely cattle ranch that he may more easily bury his crushed ambitions and try to forget an ungrateful world.
>
> From the Palma ranch Dr. MacDowell journeyed farther up the river toward the interior to near the head of navigation where there is a little grass hut village, which does not possess a resident who knows a word of English.
>
> A bed among the salt and sugar barrels in the back room of a country store was his resting place for several days.
>
> His story about how he "got out of the wilderness" is most interesting and thrilling.
>
> How the rainy season came on suddenly and how a long forced horseback ride was made through the forests and flooded swamps back to civilization.
>
> How the floods had swept away the bridges and how his horses swam three rivers during the trip are among the strenuous adventures which Dr. MacDowell's motion picture camera has faithfully reproduced.

McDowell's increasing tendency to organize his short motion picture subjects into self-contained stories was shared by several other itinerant lecturer/filmmakers of the period.

As we know from the route slips kept by the Redpath Bureau, late in the first decade of the century McDowell took his illustrated lectures to an extraordinary range of small to medium-size Midwestern towns. From 8 to 23 January 1909, for example, he lectured in the Michigan towns of Adrian, Traverse City, and Muskegon, before dipping down to Covington, Kentucky, on his way to Chillicothe, Columbus, Hebron, and Glenford, Ohio. After four weeks' break, McDowell then moved on to Medina and Lima, Ohio, plus Peru and Warren, Illinois, and, after an excursion to Mankato, Minnesota, the Iowa towns of Toledo, Osage, Manchester, and Thornton. All of this from 22 February to 4 March. In just a month on the road, during the coldest months of the year, McDowell had thus taken the warm climates of Samoa, Fiji, Panama, and Cuba to seventeen towns in six states.

During this period, several other lyceum circuit lecturers took to making their own travel films. Best known for his Passion play lectures, delivered over two thousand times to over two million people, John J. Lewis also delivered travel lectures illustrated with motion pictures (Lewis folder). Like John Stoddard and Burton Holmes, Lewis had not hesitated to provide a travel frame to make his locally shot Passion play pictures appear to have been made in Oberammergau. By prefacing the play itself with scenes on an express train and an Atlantic liner, and footage from Paris, Switzerland, and Munich, Lewis reinforced the impression that his religious tableaux were shot as the culmination of an actual trip to Oberammergau. In other films, Lewis used motion pictures to illustrate everything from the Canadian Rockies and old New England to Vesuvius and the 1900 World's Fair.

Like Edward McDowell, George Earle Raiguel had taken advantage of universal fascination with the building of the Panama Canal to expand his repertory. In subsequent years, he would make motion pictures of Paris, Switzerland, the shores of the Mediterranean, Japan, and China (Raiguel folder). One of the few female filmmaking lecturers, Bernyce Childs, began in 1906 to film the North American West Coast from San Diego as far north as Nome, Alaska. For years her lectures were accompanied by these films, until she eventually sold her negatives to the Charles Besler Company (*Moving Picture News* 1911). By 1910, virtually every corner of the globe had been included in travel films shot by itinerant lecturers. Robert Dyball Scarlett parlayed his time in the Philippines into a series of films that supported his lecturing career for many years (Scarlett folder). In support of his "Travelogues," Clarence Price offered "the most wonderful moving pictures ever exhibited in the United States. These pictures were taken in foreign countries under the personal direction of Mr. Price, with his own photographers and picture machines." Price's films covered the great cities of Europe and the Mediterranean, including Pompeii, Venice, Algiers, Paris, and Copenhagen, as well as Holland, Sweden, Switzerland, Egypt, and China. In addition, his publicity promised "smugglers at work on the France-Italy border" and "scenes in darkest Africa, India, Ceylon, Japan, Russia, Germany, England, and Norway" (Price folder). Though these films have not to my knowledge been preserved, their role in a program of platform lectures is made clear in the lecturer's publicity pamphlets.

Throughout the first and into the second decade of the century, traveling lecturers continued to fill out their programs with moving pictures. When the summer tent chautauqua movement was organized, ever new opportunities were created for lecturers. As Jane Schulz put it: "Residents of Chautauqua communities were searching for inspiration and enlightenment, but they also were looking for stories that took them outside the limited orbit of their experience. Sensing this interest, Chautauqua management made sure that they booked an occasional travel and adventure program for each summer season" (2002: 104–6). With his wife, A. W. Stephens accompanied his performances with moving pictures wherever he lectured in the upper Midwest. The press clippings dossier included in his publicity pamphlet related his triumphs in such towns as Earlville, Iowa; Camargo, Illinois; Peebles, Ohio; and Pardeeville, Wisconsin (Stephens folder). George Earle Raiguel and Frederick Poole featured their films of Europe and China in Philadelphia's Witherspoon Hall, as part of a University Extension Society lecture series (Raiguel folder). Arthur K. Peck offered not only traditional views of the landmarks of European culture and the beauties of American nature in many high-profile East Coast venues as well as Midwest chautauquas but also a series of moving pictures depicting the activities of the coastal lifesaving service—a topic destined to help free travel films from their dependency on accompanying lectures. According to his publicity, Peck "was among the very first to offer moving pictures to his patrons to supplement Travel Lectures when desired" (Peck folder). J. E. Comerford not only projected films in support of his lecture "A Day and a Night with

Our Life Savers," his troupe also provided "sensational stage effects," including sound effects of every sort (Comerford folder).

In addition to travel films in the tradition of Stoddard and Holmes, many platform lecturers produced nature films to accompany their lectures. John P. Gilbert shot his own nature study and "microphotography" films (Gilbert folder). Richard E. Follett, director of the Detroit Zoological Society, was a leader in producing wildlife films (Follett folder). In this domain he was joined by the curator of the Bronx Zoological Park, Raymond L. Ditmars, with his 1914 film *The Book of Nature* (Hanson 1988: 89). Other nature films were produced by lecturers Howard Cleaves and Lee Keedick and by Kadow Productions (Cleaves, Keedick, and Kadow folders). Before he perfected his famous camera, Carl Akeley used films shot in Africa to complement his lectures (Akeley folder). The lectures delivered by the naturalist Arthur C. Pillsbury were accompanied by motion pictures made with the help of x-rays.

During the second decade of the century, several developments conspired to break travel films and nature documentaries out of the performance orientation that had previously defined them. Until about 1910, moving pictures were considered by travel lecturers as essential props in their program. Like comedy routines, stage dialogue, and specially confected sets, moving pictures provided necessary differentiation among live performers. For this reason, lecturers carefully protected their films from duplication. When they showed films taken by others, they often claimed authorship of those films in order to promote their own individuality. The growing complexities of film production and the difficulty of balancing a lecturing career with production of moving pictures (along with the development of summer tent chautauquas, which offered lucrative engagements during the very period when lecturers had previously shot their films) eventually combined to change this situation. Increasingly, lecturers collaborated with film production companies to shoot and edit their films. As early as 1907, the veteran journalist Alfred Patek had illustrated his lectures with films of the Panama Canal made in conjunction with a cameraman from the Edison Company (*Moving Picture World* 1907: 137). J. E. Comerford's life-saving films were produced in collaboration with the Kinetograph Company (Comerford folder). Edwin L. Barker developed the first of his so-called industrial photoplays, *Back to the Old Farm*, with the Essanay Company (Barker folder). The professional support of an established production company was much appreciated by lecturers who had a hard enough time meeting a busy lecture schedule.

Once their signature films were widely distributed, however, some of the shine was instantly rubbed off their performances. In many cases, lecturers responded by shifting their focus. Once a renowned monologist, impersonator, and lecturer, in subsequent years Edwin L. Barker would turn his entire attention to filmmaking, as director of "Barker's World Picture Stories," including *The Dawn of Plenty*, *The Dawn of Power*, and *The Dawn of Commerce* (Barker folder). Another lyceum-circuit lecturer, F. Tennyson Neely, would eventually style himself as "publisher and lecturer," thanks to his "Wonder Pictures." These films, including *The Nations at War*, *With the German Army*, *Submarine Warfare*, *The Bandits of Mexico*, *Great Italian-Austrian Struggle*, and *Our Country at Peace*, were advertised as having been shot on the battlefields of the Great War (*Exhibitors Herald* 1916; Neely folder). As Neely put it, he began booking his films "with or without lecturer" (Neely folder). This potential separation of the film from its lecturer-author bespeaks a major change in travel and other documentary films. Once tied ineluctably to a lecturer's performance, films might now be understood as separable and even separate commodities, a potential source of income for any exhibitor, even in the absence of the film's author-lecturer.

This process had been facilitated by two important 1912 film events. In February 1912, Kinemacolor opened its most successful film in New York City. *Durbar in Kinemacolor* showed King George V of Great Britain and Queen Mary participating in the durbar held in Delhi, India. At first presented with Lawrence Grant's lecture, the film was so successful that it took on a life of its own, independent of Kinemacolor's house lecturer (Musser and Nelson 1991: 162ff.). Two months later came the unprecedented success of *Paul J. Rainey's African Hunt*. Originally eight reels long, this record of a high-profile African safari — led by the explorer Paul J. Rainey accompanied by John C. Hemment, a photographer, and a taxidermist from the Smithsonian Institution, Professor Edmund Heller — was edited to five thousand feet for its April 1912 release and subsequently expanded to six reels for a November 1913 re-release. Initially, a lecture by Hemment accompanied the film, but by November 1913 subtitles had been added, thus facilitating distribution of the film "with or without lecturer" (Hanson 1988: 703). In June 1914 a sequel, *Rainey's African Hunt*, opened at New York's Casino Theater (Hanson 1988: 755).

Both of these films were extensively covered not only by the trade press but by the popular press as well.

The success of Rainey's films led to a boom in expedition and nature films. Though destined for traditional distribution (usually on a states-rights basis), many of these films were at first presented by a lecturer in a lyceum-like context. When it opened in New York in May 1912, *The Alaska-Siberian Expedition* (Alaskan-Siberian Motion Pictures, 1912) was accompanied by a lecture delivered by the filmmaker, Frank E. Klein-schmidt, himself. In Philadelphia the lecture was presented by another member of the expedition (Hanson 1988: 10). In all likelihood, the com-peting *Atop of the World in Motion* (Beverly B. Dobbs, 1912) received the same treatment. The photographer Martin Johnson documented life in the South Pacific in the 1913 *Jack London's Adventures in the South Seas*. A year later, Kleinschmidt was back with *Captain F. E. Kleinschmidt's Arctic Hunt* (Arctic Film Co., 1914). The same year, Albert Blinkhorn offered *The Capture of a Sea Elephant and Hunting Wild Game in the South Pacific Islands* (Albert Blinkhorn, 1914); the explorer Vilhjalmur Stefansson pro-duced *Rescue of the Stefansson Arctic Expedition* (Sunset Motion Picture Co., 1914); and J. Campbell Besley produced *The Captain Besley Expedition* (Captain Besley Motion Picture Co., 1914). The following year, Besley would offer a sequel, *In the Amazon Jungles with the Captain Besley Expe-dition* (Captain Besley Motion Picture Co., 1915). Lady Grace Macken-zie also recorded her safari in *Lady Mackenzie's Big Game Pictures* (Lady Mackenzie Film Co., 1915). Even America participated in this movement, through films like Frank M. Buckland's and J. F. Cleary's *American Game Trails* (Education Films Corp. of America, 1915).

In many ways, these expedition films served to perpetuate the tradi-tion of films made and accompanied by platform lecturers. Always closely identified with a specific explorer, who often made personal appearances and provided lectures in conjunction with film screenings, these films were usually distributed by the explorer himself or herself rather than by one of the era's well-known production companies. A series of films pro-duced by the explorer Edward A. Salisbury helped to break this bondage to a personal appearance aesthetic. In 1915 Salisbury had lectured in San Francisco, New York, and Chicago to accompany *Wild Life of America in Films* (Edward A. Salisbury, 1915), made in cooperation with government officials (Hanson 1988: 1039), but Salisbury's next film would break free from the filmmaker/explorer-returns-home-as-lecturer approach. Using footage shot on a year-long expedition down the East Coast of the United

States, through the Caribbean and the Panama Canal, and up the western coast of Central America, Salisbury produced three films—*On the Spanish Main*, *Pirate Haunts*, and *The Footsteps of Capt. Kidd*. At first presented by the explorer himself in a traditional lecture-oriented fashion, the films were soon outfitted with titles by the novelist Rex Beach (who had also participated in the exhibition) and shown in March and April 1917, without a lecturer, in New York's prestigious Rialto Theater. Subsequently, these films were distributed by the Grand Feature Film Company.

The rise of newsreels shortly after 1910 further aided in wrenching documentary films out of the live performance lecturing world and establishing them as viable products available for general distribution. Every year would bring additional competition for Pathé's pioneering newsreel, which had begun in August 1911. In February 1912 Gaumont began offering its *Animated Weekly*. On the first day of 1913, the *Mutual Weekly* was introduced. In 1914 Selig teamed up with the Hearst newspapers to produce its own newsreel (Bowser 1990: 185). Before and after the turn of the century, traveling lecturers had regularly built programs around news from the other side of the world. Many lectures on Cuba and the Philippines were spawned by the Spanish-American War; these were often accompanied by moving pictures showing important locations and reconstructing newsworthy events. During the 1904–05 season, both Lyman Howe and E. Burton Holmes showed films presenting aspects of the Russo-Japanese War, with special attention to the siege and capture of Port Arthur (Musser and Nelson 1991: 162ff.). When the building of the Panama Canal was the big news, everyone from Holmes and McDowell to Patek and Raiguel got into the act. Every year, as they struggled to produce or cobble together films to support their routines, lecturers looked to current events as one potential guide. The increasing popularity of newsreels in the new decade put a decided brake on the production of contemporary-event films in support of traveling lecturers. For example, the Mexican Revolution was virtually ignored by lecturing filmmakers but provided material for several feature films, including *Barbarous Mexico* (America's Feature Film Co., 1912), *Mexican War Pictures* (Lubin Mfg. Co., 1913), and *The Life of General Villa* (Mutual Film Corp., 1914). Produced for regular distribution, these films went straight to movie theaters rather than to the lecture circuits.

When war broke out in Europe in 1914, many companies rushed to produce and distribute feature documentaries. While a few of these, like *The Battle and Fall of Przemysl* (American Correspondent Film Co., 1915), were outfitted with lectures meant to be read during screening (Hanson 1988: 48), by far the majority were prepared for commercial theatrical distribution by the inclusion of explanatory intertitles. Within eighteen months of the war's beginning, American exhibitors had been offered such forgotten gems as *On the Belgian Battlefield* (Tribune Company, 1914), *The War of the World* (Lewis Pennant Features, 1914), *The Battles of a Nation* (American Correspondent Film Co., 1915), *The German Side of the War* (Chicago Tribune, 1915), *The History of the World's Greatest War* (Selig Polyscope Co., 1915), *History of the Great European War* (Picture Playhouse Film Co., 1915), *European War Pictures* (Apex Film Co., 1915), *On the Firing Line with the Germans* (Industrial Moving Picture Co., 1915), *Russian Battlefields* (Chicago Tribune, 1915), and *The Warring Millions* (American Correspondent Film Co., 1915).

During the first decade of the century, homemade films about foreign places and events had provided itinerant lecturers with personalized props for their programs. Like other contemporary stage performers, these lecturers used every means at their disposal to individualize and popularize their routines. Moving pictures provided a perfect medium for this process. By the middle of the next decade, however, films about faraway places had earned a new status. Travel and war films had been severed from the live stage, turned instead into commodities expected to stand by themselves. With information previously provided by a lecturer now built into intertitles, these films were able to enter into a new type of commercial configuration, where the films would do the traveling, without the need for a lecturer to accompany them. No longer lecturers' props, these films had now become industrial products.

Note

1. This essay relies heavily on the papers of the Redpath Lyceum Bureau, which are deposited in the Department of Special Collections of the University of Iowa Library. The largest existing collection on this topic, the Redpath Chautauqua Collection includes 7,949 publicity brochures, promotional advertisements, and flyers for 4,545 lecturers, teachers, preachers, politicians, actors, singers, concert companies, magicians, whistlers, and other performers who traveled the lyceum and chautauqua circuits at the beginning of the twentieth century. All subsequent mentions of named folders refer to portions of the Redpath Chautauqua Collection. For further information on this collection, see Altman 2004a.

II

Travelogues and Silent Cinema

"The Nation's First Playground"

TRAVEL FILMS AND THE AMERICAN WEST, 1895-1920

JENNIFER LYNN PETERSON

IIIIIIIIIIIIIIIIIIIIIIIIIIIIIIIIIIIIIIIIIIIIIIIIIIIIIIIIIIIIIIIIIIIIIIIIIIIIIIIIIIIIIIIIIIIIIIIIIIIIIIIIIIIIIIIIIIIIIIIIIIIIIIIIIIII

Reviewing a travel film of Austria in 1910, a disgruntled *Variety* critic wrote, "This is another one of those scenic things with mountains, streams, castles, water fronts and all other things that go with this [*sic*] scenery exhibitions. The scenery is pretty, of course, it doesn't take any great amount of intelligence to pick out a pretty spot, and the makers can go on indefinitely turning them out. It would probably be more interesting, however, to show the American public scenes of our own continent" (*Variety* 1910: 13). Such mocking of an undeniably formulaic genre is certainly understandable—travelogues did indeed depict a familiar itinerary of "pretty spots" with maddening repetition. But the review is more interesting for the way it contradicts itself: the reviewer turns a complaint about scenery in general into a nationalistic plea for specifically American scenery. What the writer does not acknowledge is that, from the beginning, the cinema had already been doing just what he suggests: showing the American public scenes of its own continent.

The western United States was one of the most frequent locations for travel films in the first decades of film history. During the earliest years of the cinema, when the medium was still a novelty, single-shot views of the American West were featured in many moving picture shows, such as *Royal Gorge, Colorado* (Edison, 1898), *Upper Falls of the Yellowstone* (Edison, 1901), *Panoramic View of Moki-Land* (Edison, 1901), and *Gap Entrance to Rocky Mountains* (American Mutoscope and Biograph, 1902).[1] By 1907, when the nickelodeon era was underway, travelogues had become an established genre and were a regular component of many film programs. Travel films from this second, transitional phase of silent cinema continued to highlight the American West, with titles such as *Grand Canyon, Arizona* (Nestor, 1912), *Glacier National Park* (Pathé, 1912), and *The Taos*

Indians at Home—New Mexico (Selig, 1912).[2] Commercial interests encouraged this picturing of the West. The major railroad companies, sponsors of filmmaking since the cinema's inception, increased their participation in the promotion of the West in the years following 1910, subsidizing
more film productions and initiating a major campaign designed to promote tourism, featuring the slogan "See America First."[3]

It should be apparent from this brief inventory of film titles that a
few specific points of interest—mostly national parks and Indian reservations—came to stand for the vast region of the western United States in
silent-era travel films. By extension and following the same logic of synecdoche, the West frequently came to signify the entire United States.
While one might presume that these films would reaffirm the popular
image of the "wild West" as an untamed wilderness, what is striking about
early travel films, besides their often spectacular landscapes, is how frequently they are filled with tourists. Even the earliest Edison release set
in or near a national park, *Tourist Train Leaving Livingston, Mont.* (1897),
features a train heading for Yellowstone "crowded with tourists waving
goodbye" (Musser 1997: 316). This is not a film about the wild West but
a film about modernity, for to see tourists waving from a crowded train
is to witness the modern world. While silent travel films do indeed represent the West as an Edenic garden, then, they also upset the myth of
the West as an uncivilized wilderness by depicting a region traversed by
trains and peopled with tourists.

This essay explores the representation of the West in early travel films,
arguing that travelogues both reaffirmed and modernized the myth of
the American frontier. With the onset of modernity, the popular image
of the West was reconstituted: what had once been seen as a mysterious and rough land had now become a tamed region of natural wonders,
a land ripe for tourism and recreation. As travel films represented the
supposedly primeval nature and cultures of the West, they enacted an
aesthetic of nostalgic preservation. In displaying preserved pockets of
land such as Yosemite, Yellowstone National Park, or the Taos Pueblo,
travelogues worked to create a hermetically sealed series of landscapes
frozen in time, rather like a collection of snow domes. Yet by filling these
"primitive" views with the mediating figure of the tourist, the films also—
perhaps unintentionally—modernized and domesticated those wild landscapes. In tandem with this nostalgia for a vanishing wilderness, travel
films also displayed images of the new, modern West in growing cities
such as Los Angeles and San Francisco. I argue that this dialectic in which

the nostalgic past meets dynamic modernity worked to promote the West as a desirable destination for tourism and, ultimately, immigration. With the commodification of the West as a tourist playground, the region was made to support contradictory myths in which the frontier coexisted with modernity.

National Scenery

At the beginning of the twentieth century, the world had become a field of competing scenic attractions. Illustrated magazines, stereographs, postcards, and other mass media catered to a popular curiosity about foreign lands and colonial territories. Middle-class citizens were now provided with a seemingly endless flow of information and pictures from exotic lands they would probably never visit. With the arrival of motion pictures, the cinema became the preeminent marketplace of exotic images. Early travel cinema entered into this crowded field of exotic visual culture, contributing moving images poached from preexisting notions of what foreign views should look like. In the new motion pictures, nineteenth-century pictorial conventions such as the picturesque were reconfigured in more popular and commercial terms. The scenic was now more than an aesthetic ideal—the scenic had become a commodity.

The United States' entry into this international contest of scenic marvels was its celebrated western landscape. Defensive comparisons between American and European scenery were commonplace at the turn of the century. Clearly, many people perceived the United States to be locked in a contest with Europe that was being waged on the level of scenery. Travelogue films explicitly took up this campaign; as a writer in the motion picture trade magazine *Motography* explained in 1912:

> If people only realized that in our own country we have mountains more picturesque than those in Switzerland, lakes more beautiful than those of the Emerald Isle, rivers far more interesting than the Rhine, forests that make the Black Forest look like a postage stamp, and magnificent prairies and plains that cover areas as big as many European principalities ... There are now on the market moving pictures showing the wonders of our own Yellowstone National Park, the beauties of Colorado, the grandeur of the Canadian Rockies, the splendor of our Northwestern territories, and other gems of our wonderlands, which when disclosed motographically cause the

most phlegmatic "yes-but-in-Europe" bug to acknowledge that his own country offers him the best travel "buy" available. (Rothacker 1912: 169)

As this passage demonstrates, famous places around the world were being brought into accord with a hierarchy of tourist value, and North Americans were game to have their scenery compete. Similarly, in his classic study of tourism in the American West, Earl Pomeroy lists a series of commonplace comparisons: "Colorado was the Switzerland of America, or, in a more daring mood, Switzerland the Colorado of Europe, though along the 'Switzerland Trail of America' one found Eldorado Springs and Boulder, respectively, the 'Coney Island of Colorado' and 'the Athens of Colorado'" (1957: 34). Every place was open to comparison, but only the most valued places could become recreational icons, places ordained appropriate for touristic consumption. Not just the landscape but also indigenous people became part of a nationalistic American agenda. The photographer and writer George Wharton James wrote in 1915, "The Hopis, Havasupais, Apaches and Navajos are more picturesque than the Swiss, Irish, Serbian or Russian peasants" (Hyde 1990: 208). In the economy of this popular picturesque, natives and peasants are valued only as decorations aiding the agenda of national scenery.

In the early twentieth century, the West's landscapes and locales were consumed as *representations* first and foremost. Although many people traveled west on the new railroads, it was not until the era of the automobile in the 1920s that the western United States was really accessible to mass tourism. Supporters of the new motion picture medium were fond of bragging that the cinema made travel accessible to all, as did a commentator writing about a new series of Yellowstone National Park films in 1914: "By these pictures . . . the scenic wonders of the nation's first playground will be brought to the millions of people in the United States who are unable to visit the park" (*Motography* 1914: 458). Significantly, Yellowstone is figured here not as a wilderness but a playground. Natural landscapes had ceased to be threatening and were now safely marketable as national icons. Facilitating the West's role as the land of scenic nationalism, the entire diverse region was represented as a coherent whole — but a whole that was dotted with singular attractions. A veritable Grand Tour of the American West was constructed, the itinerary of which might include Yellowstone, the Grand Canyon, the snake dancers of "Moki Land," Yosemite, and San Francisco, along with occasional "slice of life" topics such as ranching. Travel representations focused on singular examples to invoke a larger whole: the Grand Canyon stands as an icon of the West, which by extension stands as emblematic of the larger United States. While to some extent all knowledge formation works in this way, representation by synecdoche is particularly central to the logic of tourism.

The fact that by 1900 previously unfamiliar regions could be promoted as premiere tourist destinations was the result of a more general fascination with the West in the nineteenth century. As Edward Buscombe points out, the idea of "the West" is "essentially a nineteenth-century invention" (1984: 25). The traditional American frontier myth conceived of the West as a pristine wilderness, a virgin land ready to be conquered by a virile European-derived society (Goetzmann 1966; Smith 1970; Nash 1973; Slotkin 1998). Many scholars have traced the history of nineteenth-century pictorial depictions of the West as an untouched Eden, from the paintings of Albert Bierstadt and Thomas Moran, to the photography of Eadweard Muybridge and Timothy O'Sullivan, to the government-sponsored expeditions led by Major John Wesley Powell and Ferdinand V. Hayden, and beyond (Solnit 2003; Snyder 1994; Krauss 1983). The West was well-documented in the nineteenth century, and these abundant representations fostered an understanding of the landscape that was explicitly tied to U.S. national identity: the West became the land of scenic nationalism.[4] The West and its representation had become an important part of a larger U.S. nationalistic project, its scenic grandeur supposedly reflecting the glory of the people who territorialized it. However, the mythology of the West was not immutable; part of its power was that it adapted to changing times. The historian Anne Farrar Hyde describes how the meaning of "the West" shifted over the decades of the nineteenth century. What began as a threatening wilderness filled with incomprehensible desert landscapes, mountains, and rock formations that challenged European aesthetic standards slowly emerged in the second half of the century as a monumental landscape that bolstered nationalistic pride. Hyde writes, "Instead of claiming that the western United States replicated Europe, many writers [began to use] Europe as a reference point to claim that the far western landscape was bigger, better, and more wondrous" (1990: 208). As we have seen, these kinds of comparisons persist well into the twentieth century, recurring in discussions of travelogue films.

Part of the impulse driving all these representations of the West was a desire to preserve landscapes and lifestyles that were perceived to be disappearing. Such nostalgia for the vanishing West is more immediately apparent in fictional westerns, and the relation between fiction and non-fiction set in the West is illuminating. The fictional western, it should be pointed out, is perhaps the only film genre that is semantically dependent on place: western stories cannot be set outside the West. Westerns were one of the earliest fiction film genres to regularly capitalize on actual western landscapes. Westerns seemed more authentic when shot on location—the mythic space of the western resonates more strongly when the actual place is signified by documentary realism (Leutrat and Liandrat-Guigues 1998). Both fictional and nonfictional westerns depend on a sense of place, but nonfictional imagery is used to anchor this decidedly mythical fiction genre with the claim of realism. Some films even featured scenery more prominently than narrative, demonstrating that landscape also could have a mythologizing function. For example, an advertisement for Selig's melodrama *A Painter's Idyl* (1911) highlights the scenery of Yosemite more than the film's story, which seems a mere pretext for the film's magnificent real-life setting (Figure 1).

Besides being set in the West, another of the fictional western's generic requirements is that the stories must be set in the past. As Robert Warshow put it: "Where the Westerner lives it is always about 1870—not the real 1870, either, or the real West" (1970: 141). The genre is concerned to reenact the conquering of "wildness" and must be set in a particular place and time to have national-historical resonance. Unlike fictional westerns, however, travel films must necessarily show the West in the present, as it looked at the moment of its filming. Thus travelogues always enunciate in the present tense, but they are also very much about the past, or a nostalgia for a mythologized past. Rather than working through national identity by means of storytelling, as the fictional genre does, early travel films of the West instead present spectacular landscapes and indigenous cultures as though they always were—and always will be—the way they look now. Travel films attempt to create worlds that exist outside history, timeless worlds that correspond with the fantasy of the old West. In practice, however, the inclusion of tourists in these timeless worlds complicates the films' antihistorical project.

The western travelogue's display of a pristine natural world relies on the nostalgia of the picturesque, an aesthetic that values landscapes and people precisely when they are perceived as being lost. The art historian Linda Nochlin has observed that one of the functions of the picturesque is to "mask conflict with the appearance of tranquility" (1989: 50), and indeed, in these films we see idealized visions of a world that

1 Promotional flyer for *A Painter's Idyl*, Selig, 1911. Courtesy of the Academy of Motion Picture Arts and Sciences.

seems preserved in formaldehyde. The films present a tourist-friendly landscape that persists only because of the artificial support system of the National Park Service; they depict tribes contained within the boundaries of Indian reservations who stage traditional dances for the benefit of the camera. This fantasy of a primeval, prelapsarian landscape only appears once the land and the lifestyles have ceased to be a threat, once the savage wilderness has been reinvented as benign nature. This picturesque nostalgia represses anxieties about the changes and upheavals that have actually occurred in the places being shown. But, in fact, the West had always been seen as fading away.

By the turn of the century, academic credence had been given to the idea that the "authentic" West had disappeared. Frederick Jackson Turner famously declared the western frontier closed in his lecture "The Significance of the Frontier in American History," delivered to the World's Congress of Historians at the Columbian Exposition in Chicago in 1893 (Turner 1920). With this overdetermined proclamation of closure, Turner observed that western expansion itself had shaped the national character. Thus the old West's bittersweet loss cleared the way for the myth of the West to be ritualistically reenacted in representations for decades. In other words, as Bill Brown writes, "while an authentic West is reported to be absent, its authenticity remains insistently present, to the point of being internalized within the visual and literary culture of the East—indeed, seemingly internal and central to America itself" (1997: 3).

Like fictional westerns, travel films reproduce the myth of the West as a wilderness on the verge of being conquered. Or more often, with the inclusion of tourists, the films show a West that actually *has* been conquered—but only just. Richard Slotkin writes, "According to this myth-historiography, the conquest of the wilderness and the subjugation or displacement of the Native Americans who originally inhabited it have been the means to our achievement of a national identity, a democratic polity, an ever-expanding economy, and a phenomenally dynamic and 'progressive' civilization" (1998: 10). Fictional westerns do more work to propagate the myth of the West than nonfiction, but travel films still participate in this mythologizing in interesting ways. Fictional westerns have been analyzed in terms of the frontier myth for decades. But nonfiction has been much less interrogated for its propagation of myth. In fact, it is surprising how rarely the nonfiction film's mythologizing function is acknowledged. This is in great part, I believe, because landscapes and scenery seem unassailably authentic, while cowboys and Indians, for example, are understood to function as caricatures. The representation of nature is one of the primary means by which travel films are able to mask their mythologizing. Armed with documentary authenticity, travel films are marketed as actuality, and national myth becomes naturalized as truth.

Wonders of Nature in the National Parks

With the new belief in recreation, exercise, and fresh air that characterized the late nineteenth century, nature became constructed as a site of authenticity, a place where people could go to recuperate from the shocks of modernity and urban life. The cinema emerged just as the national parks system was being established in the United States (Runte 1987), so it is hardly surprising that national parks were a favorite topic of early film. It is somewhat ironic, however, that the cinema, a quintessentially modern technology, should become such a significant promotional outlet for the parks, which celebrated wilderness and encouraged fantasies of primeval nature. In fact, it is that very tension between the modern and the primitive that these films can illuminate for us. Early films of the American West show us a wilderness in the process of domestication. Traditional views of the West's sublime natural landmarks such as Yosemite's Bridalveil Falls or the South Rim of the Grand Canyon, familiar from nineteenth-century photographs, remain staples of the films, but such views are now often cluttered by tourists frolicking in the foreground. Something new has entered into the iconography of the western wilderness in these films. Their ultimate quest is still magnificent scenery, but the films are equally invested in representing the *process* of getting to that scenery—the railroads, cars, horse paths, and walking trails the traveler must use to reach the scenery—and the *experience* of viewing the scenery once one has reached it. The films solicit spectator attention by providing mediating tourist figures within the landscape, essentially holding the audience's hand while leading it into the spectacular places on-screen. But as nature is made easier to access, the fantasy of virgin wilderness becomes more difficult to maintain. The myth of the western frontier is still at work here, but it requires a greater effort to reach: in order to engage with the myth of an unspoiled wonderland, the spectator must on some level pretend that the tourists are not there.

The earliest single-shot films of the national parks alternate between views of pristine natural sights such as waterfalls and views of tourists enjoying the parks. The American Mutoscope and Biograph Company released a series of actualities filmed in Yosemite in 1902, for example, featuring six titles: *Artist's Point, Glacier Point, Cascade Near Wawona Cal., Wawona Big Tree, Coaching Party Yosemite Valley*, and *Tourists Arriving at Wawona Hotel.*[5] Each of the six films comprises a single shot, and each prominently features movement. *Artist's Point* and *Glacier Point* are both landscape views; Half Dome is visible in both films along with other bits of the Yosemite Valley's striking landscape, but taken from such an extreme distance the image is somewhat difficult to make out. These two landscape panoramas create a striking effect of movement and depth, but the specific Yosemite context remains unseen as the camera pans across a vast expanse of abstracted air and earth. *Cascade Near Wawona Cal.*, on the other hand, is a stationary shot, but here the movement is that of the waterfall; without outside knowledge of the subject filmed, one would not know that this image was specific to Yosemite. Finally, *Coaching Party Yosemite Valley* and *Wawona Big Tree* feature another kind of movement: vehicles filled with tourists move through the frame, while the camera remains stationary.

A series made by the Edison Company at Yellowstone three years earlier focuses exclusively on tourists, with titles such as *Tourists Going Round Yellowstone Park, Coaches Arriving at Mammoth Hot Springs*, and *Coaches Going to Cinnabar from Yellowstone Park*.[6] In these three films, very little of the park is visible; instead, vacationers and vehicles are the focus. It might seem strange that the filmmakers went to the trouble of shooting this footage at Yellowstone when virtually none of the park is visible; however, the sightseeing coaches shown in these films are quite distinctive, and at this time they were just as much icons of Yellowstone as the park's geysers.

These early actuality films must be distinguished from the multi-shot travel films made in subsequent phases of film history. The films in these early series were all sold separately; they could have been combined to make one mini-program about Yellowstone or Yosemite, or they might have been purchased individually and shown juxtaposed with shots of entirely different subjects or locations. If single films were shown alone without the other films for contextualization, there would in fact have been nothing on-screen to verify that these views were actually taken at the places they claim to depict. The unusual framings and single-shot structure create an almost mystical separation of the images from any actually existing geography. However, in most early moving picture shows a lecturer would have been present to explain the subject matter to the audience. These very early films are formally distinct from the travelogues made later, which are much less abstracted from their context. While actuality films and foreign views dominated cinema in the early years, they became marginalized with the rise of the story film around 1903 (Musser 1990). However, though they were no longer the main attraction, travel films persisted as an important component of film programs through the end of the second decade of the century and beyond (Peterson 2004). By 1906, with the advent of the nickelodeon era, travelogues were a familiar staple of moving picture programs, shown in between comedies, dramas, and song slides as part of early cinema's variety format. Travel films from this period were often released as part of a split reel, sharing the bill with a fiction film and running less than five minutes.

National parks continued to be a favorite subject, and travel films made in the years between 1910 and 1920 focused even more on the resort qualities of the parks. Rarely is an untouched natural wilderness depicted; few places appear free from human recreation or intervention. A film from these years called *Paradise on Earth*, for example, particularly highlights Yosemite National Park as a tourist playground.[7] The film has a distinctly promotional feel, displaying Yosemite's stunning landscapes and also celebrating tourism, showing white, middle-class vacationers relaxing and enjoying nature and fresh air. Groups of tourists on horseback are led by guides down a switchback trail, through a grove of trees, and across a wooden bridge. Cars filled with tourists pass through the landscape. Glacier Point is shown with a female tourist standing precariously atop its rock jutting out over the spectacular valley (Glacier Point has often been photographed with tourists standing brazenly on this jutting rock). In over half the film's shots, pristine nature is penetrated by tourists who disturb that pristine quality. Significantly, most of the tourists shown are women (some children are also visible); this was probably a strategy aimed at demonstrating how easy and enjoyable it was for all sightseers—even ladies—to visit Yosemite's wilderness. In one staged shot, three young women run into the frame from the left and kneel down at the edge of the Merced River to drink. They lie prostrate on their stomachs, drinking the river water, laughing and shaking the water out of their leisure clothes as they stand up. The women are just as idealized as the nature depicted here, but in a larger sense what is being idealized is the *experience* being shown. Travel to Yosemite, the film seems to beckon, and you too can enjoy nature's wonderful regenerative powers. In addition, there are several shots of waterfalls in the film with no mediating tourist figures in the frame. These images, like the single-shot views of waterfalls made a couple of decades earlier, have an abstract quality, inviting the viewer to meditate momentarily on the spectacle of flowing water. The persistence of such shots indicates that dramatic, unmediated scenery still remained a travelogue ideal. Yet the images are contained by the commercial rhetoric of the larger film, creating a spectacle not of boundless wilderness but nature domesticated.

Some films from this period do focus more exclusively on landscape. The film *Yellowstone National Park* (Pathé, ca. 1917), for example, is composed mostly of images of geysers.[8] This film opens with an extreme long shot of a striking, otherworldly landscape filled with small, steaming geysers. The horizon line is about halfway up the frame, and the many tufts of steam blowing toward the left of the frame are mirrored by the cloudy sky in the top half of the image. The rest of the film shows a series of single geysers in action, preceded by intertitles explaining facts about the geysers, much like a tour guide: this one shoots one hundred feet in the air, that one shoots from fifty to seventy-five feet, Old Faithful goes off once an hour. The movement of the water and steam shown in these shots of geysers is the inverse of waterfall movement, one of the travel film's favorite images. More so than the films I have been describing, this film bears some resemblance to pictorial traditions derived from landscape painting. Several shots are carefully framed with picturesque sidescreens, and the human figures, when visible, are so distant that they function more as mediating lead-in figures who help guide the viewer into the scenery, rather than as explicitly touristic characters.[9] Yet the geysers in this film do not fulfill the traditional aesthetic function of landscape: they are not pastoral, contemplative, or even allegorical. Rather, the Yellowstone shown here is a parade of wonders, a series of famous landmarks, a commercialized landscape. Landscape in the travel film is rarely sublime; instead, it provokes the wonderment of a fairground attraction.

Over and over, travel films promote the national parks as "wondrous." Describing a series of films of Yellowstone National Park, a 1907 catalogue from the Selig Polyscope Company explains that "by common consent the term 'Wonderland' has been given to the marvelous region which the United States Government has forever dedicated to public use and enjoyment."[10] Similarly, the 1902 Biograph catalogue describes the film *Artist's Point* as "a turning panorama amid the marvellous scenery of nature's wonderland in the Yosemite Valley of California" (Musser 1985: 143). "Wonder" is a concept well suited to the commercial imperative, with its fairground-style appeal to amazement rather than contemplation. As Tom Gunning (1990) has shown, early cinema specifically catered to the aesthetic of the fairground attraction. It is early cinema's allegiance to such popular entertainments, I would argue, that allows it to challenge and modernize the traditional myth of the West. Travelogues depicted the commercial, recreational aspect of the parks, to the exclusion of the parks' other uses such as conservation and wildlife preservation. In so doing, they did as much to undermine the mythic West as they did to promote it.

Railroad companies played a large role in the establishment and pro

2 Santa Fe Railway advertisement, *Chicago Tribune*,
5 February 1909.

motion of the new parks. Railroad officials quickly understood the power
of modern marketing and promoted the idea of the scenic West in many
advertisements at the beginning of the century. For example, the Santa
Fe Railroad regularly advertised the wonders of the Grand Canyon after
opening its line through the Southwest in 1881 (Runte 1987: 44–46; Hyde
1990: chap. 6), though it was not until tracks were laid leading directly
to the Canyon's south rim in 1901 that the area's full tourist potential
was realized (Figure 2). A "See America First" campaign, initiated by
the Great Northern Railroad in 1910, was quickly adopted as a general
railroad slogan. Intended to lure American tourists away from the European destinations they had so long favored, this promotional campaign
brought visitors and their money instead to the national parks. The campaign was such a success, in fact, that the slogan entered into the general parlance of the time. The slogan of the American Film Manufacturing Company, for example, which specialized in fictional westerns,
was a pun on the railroad campaign: "See Americans First." One re-

viewer in 1912 wrote of a film entitled *Glacier National Park*: "We heartily commend the Pathé company's apparent purpose of making a series of 'See America First' pictures" (*Moving Picture World* 1912d: 142). Here the issue of nationalism gets an international twist, since it is a French company focusing on American wonders. The motion picture industry played a great role in this promotional effort, sometimes working with the railroads, which regularly granted filmmakers free access to trains, and sometimes working independently of the railroads. For example, *Motography* reported that the Great Northern Railroad was working in 1911 to contract a series of scenic films to be made in all the cities along its line (1911a: 45).

Auto travel became another alternative shortly before 1920, though car companies did not yet promote travel as aggressively as the railroads (Belasco 1979). *Moving Picture World* reported on a series of national park films in 1918 commissioned by Pathé; the series was filmed completely by one cameraman, Ralph Earle, and his wife, who traveled around the country in their Buick. "[Earle's] Buick car [is] the only one which has been in all of the National Parks, and he was accompanied on his trip by his wife, formerly Hazel Brown, once queen of the Tacoma Montamara Festo. The American flag, which graced the car during the trip, is likewise the only one that has been to all of the parks and this is to be sent to the Secretary of the Interior as a souvenir" (*Moving Picture World* 1918: 680).[11] All alone in nature with a camera, a beauty queen, and the American flag, the experience of this Pathé cameraman underscores the extent to which travelogues resemble home movies. With travel films, American scenery has truly become domesticated.

Natives, Tourists, and Immigrants

I have been arguing that travel films modernize the myth of the old West by populating the region with tourists. But tourists are not the only people who appear in these films. As one might imagine, Native Americans are frequently featured in films of the West, dressed in traditional clothing and performing tribal dances for the camera. In contrast to the modernizing Western figure of the tourist, American Indians appear in these films as emissaries of a "primitive" human past. Typically, little attention is paid to tribal specificity; instead, Indians are presented as generic "primitive types." They are frequently posed on horseback or posed in close-up, statically frozen in their wilderness context, semantically equated with the landscape. The Indians are thus essentialized, made into ahistorical "primitives" rather than mobile subjects with a history. This is very different from the way tourists are shown playing happily at water's edge or moving through landscapes in sightseeing buses, always in contrast with their surroundings. The films are quite clear in their staging of who is visiting and who is here to stay.

Just as the "wild frontier" is threatened but preserved in these films, so the trope of the "vanishing Indian" helps the films construct themselves as a window into the past. Publicity for the numerous films of Native Americans in the years between 1910 and 1920 often carries a tone of nostalgia and loss. The Selig film *The Taos Indians at Home — New Mexico* (1912), for example, is described thus: "Panorama of North Pueblo Indian village, showing in detail the modes of living and customs practiced by this almost extinct tribe" (*Moving Picture World* 1912a: 510). Likewise, the explicit project of the quasi-ethnographic photographer and filmmaker Edward S. Curtis was to photograph all the North American Indians before their ways of life "vanished" completely. This trope of the "vanishing Indian" (alternately labeled the "vanishing American" [Dippie 1982]), recurrent well into the twentieth century, was a popularization of anthropological concepts. As Fatimah Tobing Rony writes, "a central premise of much of anthropology was that the native was always already vanishing, and the anthropologist could do nothing but record and reconstruct, racing against the evolutionary clock" (1996: 91). Lurking behind this notion of vanishing was a kind of displaced national guilty conscience. The vanishing Indian myth smoothed over the nation's responsibility for its genocidal origins, hiding the destructiveness of nation building behind a screen of nostalgia. Travelogue films both invoke this sense of loss and also repress it by depicting worlds in which native life appears timeless and eternal, using a representational strategy that Rony calls "ethnographic taxidermy" (101-2). The native is thus presented as a static being who exists in another dimension outside history, frozen forever in an idealized form.

The National Park in America epitomizes the travelogue's simultaneous affirmation and denial of the frontier myth by contrasting Native Americans with tourists.[12] This remarkable film is more complex than most from the period, traversing the themes of tourism, landscape, and ethnography, subjects that were often treated separately in individual films, and it even includes several animated segments. The first half of the film

3 A still from *The National Park in America*, manufacturer unknown, ca. 1918. Courtesy of the Nederlands Filmmuseum.

depicts Glacier National Park as a natural paradise for tourists. In one shot, a male and female couple are romantically silhouetted against Two-Medicine Lake (Figure 3). Next follow several shots of gigantic glaciers; vacationers can be seen hiking on them in almost every shot. The land-scape dominates the frame, but the figures are still visible. Several water-falls are also shown, some with tourists hiking around them and some without. But while the first half of the film is dominated by magnificent landscapes filled with tourist figures, in the second half, which focuses on Native Americans, the tourists drop out of the scenery. It is as though the fantasy of primeval "Indianness" would be diluted if tourists were shown in the same space with them. Dressed in full tribal costume, a series of "Indian types" are introduced one by one in medium close-ups, first in profile and then in frontal portraits. This kind of anthropometric posing was an early travel film convention, drawn from the contemporary "sci-entific" practice of photographing ethnographic subjects from the front and in profile to allow for later measurements and racial classification (Griffiths 2002: 93–100). The men are next shown standing in a line, one by one each turning his head to look at the camera, in a kind of parody of a chorus line. The men are clearly performing their "Indianness" for the tourist gaze, as though they were characters in a fictional western. (In fact, Native Americans were one of Glacier National Park's main attractions, which was not the case at other national parks [Buchholtz 1976].) However, this extra level of performativity does not mitigate the racist essentialism of the film—subjugation of the Indians being a key part of the American frontier myth. The "vanishing Indian" is merely a quaint aesthetic spectacle in this film, and once again the picturesque masks a legacy of actual violence.

Travel films set in the American West are explicit about their solicitation of tourists and obvious in their use of Indians as essentialized primitives. But what the films erase is the complexity of actual migration patterns to the West in the early twentieth century. Tourism was still within financial reach only of the upper middle class, after all, while migration was a fact of life for millions; therefore we might speculate that these films had more of an impact on immigration than on tourism. In fact, the motion picture trade press contains several accounts of travel films being used to encourage immigration to the western United States. In one story, films of the West were to be shown by the Hebrew Sheltering and Immigrant Aid Society to European immigrants on ocean liners. "Thus foreigners on their way to America will be shown the advantages of the west over city life before they land, and will have this in mind before they are swallowed up by the tenement districts of New York" (*The Nickelodeon* 1909: 130). In another story, a series of films produced by the Great Northern Railroad is "to be shown in all parts of this country, especially in the East and in Europe, where they are expected to command much attention among prospective immigrants seeking information about Western America" (*Motography* 1911a: 45). Even though the films' tourist figures are clearly not meant to resemble immigrants, the films' idealization of the West may well have worked to encourage migration to the region. There were, in addition, a number of travel films that focused not on national parks and Indian reservations but instead on new western cities.

Alongside the picturesque and "timeless" West of national parks and Native American lands, a new image of the West began to emerge in early cinema: the modern, urban West depicted in travelogues of cities such as *Glimpses of San Francisco* (Pathé, 1911), *Seeing Los Angeles* (Imp, 1912), and *Seeing Spokane* (Selig, 1912).[13] Though contradictory, these two images— the scenic West and the modern West—worked in tandem to create a pleasing image of the West with something for everyone: a place to visit, a place to settle, a place to consume. Although these films of cities are set in the geographical West, they resist visions of the so-called wild West, instead depicting a region dotted with civilized urban modernity. *Seeing Los Angeles*, for example, was clearly intended to serve a promotional function for settlement of that city, which was being vigorously championed at the time the film was made. The film depicts a bustling downtown business district and seems positioned directly against popular notions of the wild West. Likewise, a pamphlet promoting the city of Los Angeles in 1910 cautions: "Don't imagine when you come to Southern California that you will find here a portion of the 'wild and wooly West.' Southern California is fully on a par with any of the Eastern states, and ahead of some of them, in what our Boston friends refer to as 'culture'" (Brook 1910: 75). *Seeing Los Angeles*, along with a host of other early travelogues and promotions in other media, encouraged viewers to see the West as a part of the modernizing world.

These early films of western cities evince a remarkable optimism and faith in the transformative power of modernity, as though any locale touched by the magic wand of urbanization would, of course, bloom into a major metropolis. The promotional pamphlet for Selig's *Seeing Spokane*, for example, advertises: "Another city in that delightful, educational series of sight-seeing trips to principal cities of the world" (Selig Collection 1912). If modernization was such an unstoppable force, it is perhaps no wonder that the natural scenery presented in the national park films feels contained and domesticated.

In travel films of the West, then, we see a disruption of national myths about the American frontier. In these films, the West is no longer a barren wilderness waiting to be conquered. Instead, the West has become a picturesque destination for tourists and immigrants. The explicit empire-building objectives of nineteenth-century imagery have been replaced by twentieth-century commercial objectives: travelogue films market western scenery as a commodity. Rather than a frontier in need of taming, the West appears in early cinema as a space for recreation. What's more, cinema audiences could play in "the nation's first playground" without ever leaving their theater seats. Thus the true national playground constructed by these films would seem to be not the space of the western landscape but the space of cinema itself.

Notes

1. These films are all in the Paper Print Collection at the Library of Congress, Washington, D.C. Descriptions and frame enlargements for the Edison films *Royal Gorge, Colorado*, and *Upper Falls of the Yellowstone* can be found in Musser 1997: 356–57, 319.

2. Reviews and descriptions of these films were published in *Moving Picture World*, 24 February 1912: 716; 12 October 1912: 142; 10 February 1912: 510.

3. For an excellent history of tourism in the West, which thoroughly traces the uses of this slogan, see Shaffer 2001.

4. The term "scenic nationalism" is also used by Alfred Runte in his environmental history *National Parks: The American Experience* (1987).

5. Prints of these six films are held at the Library of Congress. The Library of Congress dates these films at 1903, but they are already listed in Biograph's 1902 catalogue, indicating that they were shot in 1902 or earlier. Three of the films also have different titles in the Biograph catalogue; for example, *Cascade Near Wawona Cal.* is listed in the catalogue as *A Wonderful Waterfall*, but the film's description clearly indicates that it is the same film: "Showing the splendid cascade near Wawona, California, which attracts tourists from far and near." Similarly, *Glacier Point* is entitled *Picturesque Yosemite* in the Biograph catalogue, and *Tourists Arriving at Wawona Hotel* is entitled *In the Yellowstone*. See American Mutoscope and Biograph Company, *Picture Catalogue*, November 1902: 142–43, in Musser 1985.

6. Prints of these three films are held at the Library of Congress. For descriptions and frame enlargements, see Musser 1997: 317–20. These films were shot between 19 and 25 July 1899 by James White (producer) and Frederick Blechynden (camera).

7. The Nederlands Filmmuseum holds a print of this film. No information is known about its manufacturer or release date, though the nitrate print's Kodak edge marks date it at 1919. Curiously, the title on this Dutch print translates as: "The Horse's Paradise: A Trip through Wyoming (N. America)." The film was clearly made at Yosemite, and it remains unclear whether the print was mistitled for Dutch release or whether the title might have been carelessly put on the film at a later date. Thanks to Nico de Klerk for translating the Dutch intertitles (here and for all the other NFM titles I cite).

8. The Nederlands Filmmuseum holds a print of this film.

9. On lead-in figures in landscape painting, see Mitchell 1994: 23–24.

10. Selig Polyscope Company catalogue, 1907: 134, in Musser 1985. On Yellowstone National Park as a "wonderland," see Shaffer 2001: 49–52.

11. Earle had filmed the national parks for Pathé at least once before, in 1913. See *Motography*, 20 September 1913: 195.

12. The Nederlands Filmmuseum holds a print of this film. No information is known about its manufacturing company or date of release, though the NFM dates it at ca. 1917.

13. Descriptions of these films can be found in *Motography* 1911c and *Moving Picture World* 1912c. The film *Seeing Spokane* is described by a promotional flyer in the Selig Collection, Academy of Motion Picture Arts and Sciences.

Between the "Familiar Text" and the "Book of the World"

TOURING THE AMBIVALENT CONTEXTS OF TRAVEL FILMS

I have traveled a lot—I have read a lot and I knew all the famous men of my time, you can believe me, I don't say this out of vanity, and yet I only considered all this knowledge as a partial goal, what I was searching for was life's path and the universe's functioning principles, which is why I brought together a documentation in which all the world's events have been studied. —Albert Kahn, 1938 [1]

[O]ur senses are our prison, their limits the bars of our human cage. One day it may be otherwise: the whole world may be as clearly visible to my eyes as the room in which I am writing. Extension of vision and with it of sympathy, that is what one wants; but to discover the way to it is as difficult as finding the path which leads to truth itself. —B. Ifor Evans [2]

PAULA AMAD

||||||||||||||||||||||||||||||||||||||||||||||||||||||||||||||||||||||||||||||||||||||||||||||||||||||||||||||||||||||||||||||||||||||

Speaking to a journalist in 1938, Albert Kahn, the millionaire French banker who had spent his life's earnings on an array of humanitarian projects, spoke of travel as a means to an end in which "life's path and the universe's functioning principles" would finally be made known to humanity.[3] Mobilizing his globally developed capital in the service of a vague internationalist utopia, Kahn understood travel to reconcile the search for material markets with the quest for a more immaterial sort of meaning. Yet the lingering instrumentalism that drove this banker with big ideas is revealed in the fact that his dream for "the unification of the world" based on the destruction of "racial and religious intolerance"

(Musée Albert-Kahn 1995: 61) manifested itself in the desire to *document* (rather than change) the world. His goal of producing a "documentation" of "all the world's events" was realized (albeit imperfectly) in a network of projects he funded between the late 1890s and late 1920s, ranging from the Autour du Monde travel grants (which allowed Evans to momentarily escape the "limits" of his "human cage") and fourteen ongoing current affairs publications to a school for preventative medicine, and, last but not least, the Archives de la Planète, a unique global archive that contains 72,000 color autochrome photographs, 4,000 stereographic images, and 183,000 meters of 35mm black-and-white silent film. Impossible to easily classify according to genre conventions, given the vastness of the collection and the mostly unedited form of the films, not to mention the lack of documentation relating to their actual reception and function, the cinematographic component of the Kahn Archive contains a significant number of films that share many features with the travelogue genre of early cinema. With titles like *Water-Spa Towns of Central France: 1926*, *Egypt: Cairo's European Town 1925*, and *Jerusalem, the Wailing Wall 1925*, the touristic frame through which many of the Kahn films were shot is undeniable. Although it needs to be stated from the outset that Kahn's films were not travelogues per se (for instance, even their titles do not function in the same way as those of commercial films, as they nearly always anchor the film historically with a precise date), they were deeply embedded in the culture and crisis of travel that is crucial to understanding the popularity of travelogues during the silent cinema period.

In the first part of this essay I investigate beyond an obviously functionalist scope the role of that "partial aim"—travel—within Kahn's wider system of global "documentation." Far from serving his loftier goals in a purely ancillary way, travel and the attendant ambivalences that recent scholarship (Kaplan 1996; Williams 1998; Green 2002) has associated with their development in the modern period (broadly characterized in the oppositions between and within the pre-1850s concept of travel versus the post-1850s concept of tourism) shaped Kahn's multifaceted projects through and through. His diverse enterprises were structured by the increasingly slippery oppositions between travel (understood as the practice of a privileged subject undertaking a demanding voyage in search of active experiences) and tourism (understood as the practice of democratized masses signed up for recreational tours in search of distracting experiences) as well as the overarching set of tensions common to both forms of journeying (home and away, stasis and movement, memory and forgetting, the familiar and the new, self and other). In other words, travel shaped this Archive in more than an instrumental way and its relevance extends to the concept of travel in its pedagogical, epistemological, philosophical, national, and, not least, cinematographic turns. As a technology of reproduction wedded to the representation of a past event from another place (from the time and space of the viewing experience), early cinema's elsewhere- and elsewhen-ness embraced displacement as a standard condition of its reception. Taking into account all of travel's meanings—as a conduit for training, knowing, thinking, belonging, and viewing as a modern French citizen—it can thus be argued that travel was the governing if not always governable metaphor of the Kahn Archive.

In the second part of this essay I focus on how the Kahn project staged an uncertain encounter between the culture of modern travel and its often-noted convergence with the survey-and-control logic of colonialist expansion. Although the Kahn films are fragmented and without an internal narrative, remaining for the most part in the form of rushes, I will endeavor to edit them, as it were, through textual materials (diaries, travelogues, grant reports, etc.) that were produced in conjunction with the wider enterprise to which they belonged. Viewing the films both individually and in their totality will help force some of the contradictions in Kahn's project to come to the surface. The pressure of these inconsistencies is already evident in Evans's own travelogue. As he indicates, the "extension of vision" and with it "sympathy" for the world's diverse cultures may have been the mission statement under which the many participants in Kahn's planetary Archive labored, but in reality this ideal resembled more a utopian impossibility than a realizable goal. Like all traditional and even more recent technological utopias, it posited a place or condition that was elsewhere and outside time, as hinted at in Evans's image of the unshackled human senses. Yet we must be careful not to equate this striving for the impossible with an unequivocal optimism. For the panoramic hubris of Kahn's desire to collect and order the planet in visual form was always already a symptom of the anxieties that his confident encyclopedism masked, displayed nowhere more forcefully than in the fact that the one subject who was off-limits to the Archive's planetary gaze was Kahn himself, who posed voluntarily for only one photo in his entire life.

Wandering Origins and the Cult of Direct Observation

Not surprisingly, in order to broach the broader implications of the culture of travel for the Kahn Archive one must first account for how embedded Kahn himself was in all its oppositions.[4] Given his early forced migration from Marmoutier in Alsace after the loss of that region in the 1871 Franco-Prussian War, and his coming-of-age and adult travels that took him to Paris, and South Africa (where he made his banking fortune in diamond mine speculation), as well as Tonkin, Venezuela, and Egypt before the turn of the century, and that provided direct inspiration for his multinational gardens begun on his Boulogne property in 1896, Kahn's biography is shaped by some of the central narratives surrounding turn-of-the-century travel. These include travel as the burden of forced migration or expulsion resulting in the condition of permanent exile; travel as the mobilization of expansionist and exploitative economic impulses; and travel as the condition of a humanist world-citizen outlook. As an unwilling and willing mobile citizen for whom spatial displacement was a lifelong condition, Kahn embodied both the oppressive and liberating histories behind modern travel.

The banker's journeys obviously had a profound impact, leading him to initiate in 1898 the Autour du Monde travel scholarship for teachers. Administered by the Sorbonne, although also offered to foreigners like the Englishman B. Ifor Evans, these grants were established to enable young teachers chosen from the "intellectual and moral elite of the nation" to "enter into sympathetic communication with the ideas, feelings and lives of other peoples" (Musée Albert-Kahn 1995: 141). In the instructions for the foundation that organized the Autour du Monde travel fund, the importance of "the value of personal experience" (Musée Albert-Kahn 1995: 64) is referred to three times, while in another directive Kahn stated that the travel funds were intended to encourage future teachers to "come into real contact with life" in order to avoid the risk of being "content with a purely abstract knowledge" (Musée Albert-Kahn 1995: 140). The privileging of concrete observation and active experience as opposed to abstract learning and passive knowledge provides one of the key epistemological tenets of Kahn's projects.

In accordance with this privileging of observation, the teachers who were awarded these travel funds were supposed to contribute to a "vast survey of *réalités*" (Musée Albert-Kahn 1995: 65). Many contributions

1   In Beijing, two unidentified Chinese men and a European woman
stand around the 35mm Pathé camera used on Albert Kahn's 1908–
09 world tour. Photo by Jacques-Richard Gachet. Courtesy of the
Musée Albert-Kahn, copyright Département des Hauts-de-Seine.

to this "survey" were published as literary travelogues with titles such as
"Itinerary from the United States to Canada," "Impressions of America,"
and "Lessons from an Around the World Voyage" in the journal of the
society established in honor of the *boursiers* (fund recipients), the *Bulletin
de la Société Autour du Monde*.[5] The iconographic form of the "vast survey"
took shape when the Archives de la Planète officially began in 1912. Yet the
more immediate plans for this encyclopedic visual "dossier on humanity"
(Brunhes 1913: 38) evolved as a result of a part-business part-pleasure
trip that Kahn made between November 1908 and May 1909 to Japan
and China by way of America. Accompanied by his chauffeur-turned-
cameraman Albert Dutertre, who filmed and photographed along the
way, Kahn produced the first documents that would enter the Archive in
tandem with his own personal travel itinerary (Figure 1). In the diary that
Dutertre kept during the trip (Dutertre 1908–9) we learn much about
Kahn's participation in the masculinist and elitist adventurer-explorer
mode of travel undertaken by scores of missionaries, colonists, Oriental-
ists, and geographers before him. Traveling to out of the way places (like
the Great Wall of China), during the off-season (they are the only "*voya-*

geurs" present at the temples of Nikko), experiencing obstacles along the way (in Japan two agents "survey" Dutertre and prevent him from photographing the Emperor), but pushing through with a gritty determination (they are often aided and fêted by various diplomats and colleagues while at one point Kahn offers to pay local officials to enlist an entire train), Kahn had experiences that fit Ali Behdad's description of the pre- or countertouristic "adventurous traveller who undertook the troublesome journey in search of new 'knowledge,' romantic encounters, and exotic experiences" (1994: 35).

Although the latter two motivations do not seem to have played a role in his priorities, Kahn's own travels were formative in motivating him to create the Archives de la Planète as a visual knowledge compendium, or in the words of Henri Bergson a "*Grand livre du monde*" (great book of the world) (1931: iii).[6] Firmly positioned against the rising discourses of tourism, while also reflecting a distrust of scholarly academic tomes and a renewed adherence to the centuries-old traveler's preference for the objectivity of "on the spot" observations (Adler 1998: 14), the Archive was thus also fashioned as a multimedia corrective to the out of date guidebooks and dusty academic studies that had so frustrated Kahn on his journeys to Japan and China in 1909. As described by Jean Brunhes, the geographer who directed the Archive from 1912 to 1930, the Archives de la Planète was intended to be a storehouse of knowledge that might act as "a sort of true picture of life in our age, constituting the monument par excellence of consultation and comparison for those who will come after us" (1913: 38). From the perspective of Kahn's broader mission, travel was clearly a means to an end (practical knowledge) and not intended (as it was for the tourist) as a pleasure or end unto itself. Another of Kahn's grant recipients, the *lycée* teacher Mme E. Antoine, echoed this sentiment when she justified her visit to Yellowstone Park in America as "not for the pleasure of tourism but in order to understand volcanic phenomena" (1915: 113). Kahn and the "Boulogne community" that participated in his network of projects were thus self-consciously aligned with the elite, edifying, knowledge-seeking, and altruistic labor of travel rather than the mass-marketed, commodified, and sensation-seeking pleasures of tourism that began to dominate the culture of travel in the late nineteenth and early twentieth centuries.[7]

This instrumentalist approach to travel as a means for the acquisition of "useful knowledge" (Pinney 1994: 414) was promoted in the Autour du Monde travel fund and filtered into the accounts that many of the bour-

siers wrote in the *Bulletin de la Société Autour du Monde* on returning from
their journeys. In one such account (originally a speech given to students
at the *Lycée* Sens in 1914), which bears a striking resemblance to Kahn's
own legitimation of the travel funds, F. Bernot defined travel as a "precious object lesson" capable of teaching us from the *livre du monde* once
we had found the courage to abandon "*le texte connu*" (the familiar text) of
conventional scholarly knowledge (1914: 232). Another boursier, Félicien
Challaye, more forcefully drew the connection between travel's object
lessons and the specific economic functions to which they should be put
in his plea to "future traders" and "industrialists" not to "forget the immense clientele that the innumerable populations of Asia and Africa offer
you" (1919–20: 52). In Challaye's advice to his own *Lycée* Charlemagne
students—study "the needs" and "tastes" of the "yellow" and "black"
races (54)—the economic destiny of these pedagogically motivated world
voyages is unashamedly on display.

What these accounts in the *Bulletin* reveal consistently is the contra-
diction at the center of Kahn's idea of travel as an edifying tool for cross-
cultural understanding when in fact what this noble documentation was
intended to produce was not a more sympathetic understanding of the
other (particularly when that other was a colonial subject) but a trans-
valuation of the other into a potential consumer with untapped needs and
tastes. The boursiers' voyages did not so much result in a more truthful
understanding of the other as a more "useful" understanding of the self,
and in particular the French nation, in a time of dangerous geopolitical
reconfiguration, when France was beginning to feel increasing economic
competition from Germany and Great Britain, as well as emerging resistance from her own colonies (in the 1925 Rif War in Morocco and the
1930 Yen Bay rebellion in Indochina). Bernot is clear to state that while
travel can allow one to appreciate more fully "the bonds of international
solidarity" it also makes one "clearly aware of national sentiment" (1914:
235). He thus finally describes travel as a "good teacher since it teaches the
most important of all the virtues of the mind: to doubt oneself in order
to be more sure of oneself" (236). Writing about her own voyages in 1915,
Mme Antoine finds the occasion to affirm this self-assurance during her
stops in the French colonies of Cambodia and Tonkin. Domesticating the
elsewhere-ness of Cambodia into the somewhere-ness of French Indochina (as much a geographical fiction as Kahn's planetary gardens), she
describes herself as "happy" to be finally again "on French soil" (1915:
107). Surveying the terrain before her with an eye on the competition,

she ventures the prediction that in spite of the "manifestly gallophobic" (107) Cantonese presence in Saigon, "our Far-East possessions seem to have in front of them a magnificent future" (109) owing to the wonders of progress delivered by France's heroic engineers.[8] This prediction of course implies that the magnificence of that future depends on France's continued benevolent involvement in Cambodia, just as her feeling of ease in this country depends on an experience of it as a suppliant possession of France. Interestingly, given the emergence of "colonial tourism" during this period (Furlough 2002) as a "softer" tool for selling and justifying the colonial idea to the French public, Mme Antoine's final piece of advice for the successful future of the colony is that it needs "more intense economic activity" (1915: 109) in the form, for example, of tourism.

The Trials of the Travel Film

Hovering above the exploration I have been making of the relationship of travel to Kahn's enterprises are three "reformist" contexts: one, travel as the means to knowledge; two, travel as the conduit for a "benevolent" form of French colonial policy (known as "associationist") that replaced the more militant and expansionist era of "assimilationist" policy (Cooper 2001: 44–52); and three, travel as the practice through which a new form of universalism and humanism might flourish. These justifications for travel combined beneath the Archive's ocular-centric goal of an empathetic "extension of vision." I now want to trace the individual impact made on Kahn's films by these three justifications for travel. Following the directive to make "the whole world" "as clearly visible to my eyes as the room in which I write," as Ifor Evans put it, Kahn's collection of films was shot in more than forty countries, making it one of the most expansive extant collections of early nonfiction film.

Within the recent reinvestigation of the travelogue genre in early film history, travel films have been most often studied in association with the related modern practices of tourism and colonialism, seen as emblems or souvenirs of a culture of imperial expansion experienced at the level of visual consumption and "extension." In accordance with this context travel films have thus been held to account for their bourgeois conservatism and support for the ideological status quo (Musser and Nelson 1991: 54, 179) and for their tendency to embalm the other in the conventions of a picturesque bind that Fatimah Tobing Rony has described as a type of cinematic "taxidermy" (1996: 101). Taking a different approach, Tom Gunning has sought in his essay in this volume to reveal the "utopian" detours from the travelogue's "routes of power and appropriation," while Jennifer Peterson's work has analyzed the connections between the exotic and the banal attractions of the travelogue, pointing to a terrain of tensions that Alison Griffiths has also explored in her analysis of the relationship between anthropology and early travelogues (Peterson, forthcoming; Griffiths 2002).[9] While all these writers might differ on the degree to which early travel films functioned ideologically, what remains clear is that the travel film constitutes a diverse and porous genre.

It is perhaps to be expected that although there is no single type of film that dominates the Kahn Archive, it contains many that follow a travel guide view of the world as well as others that seem to knowingly stretch the conventions of the film travelogue. The definition of the commercial travelogue as a film that strings together (although travelogues can of course be single-shot films) a series of often mobile views of either foreign or local noteworthy sites in order to provide a form of vicarious tourism for Western spectators accounts for this most persistent and popular of early cinema genres only in its broadest applications. Films in the Kahn Archive that follow this pattern of carving up a place (or very often the "phantom-ride" passage through a place) for postcard-size consumption focusing on sensational and curious highlights of cultures both near and far would include films of whirling dervishes in Turkey, Alpine train rides in Switzerland, tours of the markets of Tunisia, boat rides along the Ganges, and religious rituals in Brittany, Jerusalem, and Dahomey.

Sitting alongside, or as Peterson argues, in tension with the exotic or sensational-style travel films are those dominated by the more conventional and banal elements of the travelogue genre: films that are structured around, for example, the "landscape panorama, the street scene, the iconic monuments of a given locale, [and] local 'types'" (1997: 77). The banality of such sites appears in their implicit interchangeability, whereby a scene of a street intersection in Paris might just as well be a street scene from Tokyo or Cairo (were it not for additional local color), given their shared urban structure. On the side of these more banal travelogues, though more troubling than comforting in their familiarity, are those Kahn films that thwart the touristic impulse to reproduce the popularly stereotyped image of a culture (either as exotic or conventional).

They do so not by giving us a necessarily more authentic depiction but by a depiction that is more willing to linger on the usually unrecognizable and ignored repetitive details of daily life. They take another look, that is, at the *texte connu* of touristic imagery. For instance, the film taken by Léon Busy of a troop of young dancers practicing the intricate movements of their performance in front of their teacher and other students—*Cambodge, Province de Kandal, Danses au palais royal de Phnom Penh* (1907/1921)—presents us with too much detail and not enough highlights, too much information and not enough convention. Far from focusing exclusively on the final picturesque performance (the tourist's snapshot), the film is decentered and multifocal in its attention, taking in the audience of students watching, the teacher demonstrating particular movements, and so forth. Such dances, like the iconic ruins of Angkor Vat also shot by Busy, were indeed a familiar tourist destination at the time (Mme Antoine visits both on her tour) and were reproduced in the various visual forms of France's popular imperial imaginary (postcards, world and colonial exhibitions and fairs, commercial travel films, illustrated lectures, etc.). To capture them again was to contribute to the intertextual *mise-en-abîme* of travel discourse and desire whose literary lineage and stock of conventions were passed on with various alterations from Lamartine, Chateaubriand, Volney, Nerval, Flaubert, Loti, and Barrès in a tradition that would have been familiar to Busy, who was both a colonial officer in Indochina and a member of the French Society for Photography. In other words, the texte connu of France's Orientalist imaginary, in its intertwined popular, literary, and military permutations, always already accompanies these films.

And yet if we are to capture the Kahn films' unsettling relation with this texte connu we need to recognize that they are of course not still images or literary texts but films. The unprecedented precision and verifiable nature of the film camera's recording capacities (as crucial when it comes to capturing the intricate movements of dance as it is for simulating movement through space) were what differentiated Kahn and Dutertre's travels from those of their literary ancestors. And it was the camera's same observational qualities that Busy maximized in his filming. To be sure, this attention to dance dovetails with the more "enlightened" or culturally sympathetic approach to the other that was a distinguishing feature of French associationist colonial policy (particularly in Indochina where the French "discovered" much culture worthy of their praise and preservation, such as the Angkor Vat ruins [Cooper 2001: 19–25, 50, 70–71]). Furthermore, it also reflected the bias of a salvage ethnography approach to the other, embodied in Kahn's broadest explanation of his work: "To fix once and for all, the look, practices and modes of human activity whose fatal disappearance is just a question of time" (Musée Albert-Kahn 1995: 74). Even in Busy's ten-second film of a young Vietnamese woman tying her long hair, the indisputable sexual allure of the more intimate though still anthropologically viable subject matter is framed through the scientific attraction of the camera's objective visual description.

Yet, unlike the edited highlights of a conventional travel film, what we have in this and many other Kahn films is ultimately (to borrow a term of Behdad's used to describe tourist guide discourse) a form of visual "prattle" (1994: 45), an excessive accumulation of visual facts and figures contributing to an informational logic bordering on the obsessive and exceeding the domain of the "useful." In such films, as can be seen clearly from those that Jean Brunhes was responsible for directing in Brittany (like *Locronan, la grande Troménie, 1929*, which also happens to be an edited film), we enter the realm of the ethnographic with a focus on detailed and necessarily excessive observation of daily rituals, practices, and gestures deemed within a commercial context to be unwatchable because of their length. Given that there is evidence that Kahn and Brunhes instructed their cameramen to produce views that ran counter to commercial conventions of actuality filmmaking (which at least two of the cameramen were trained in), it is fitting that so many Kahn films are dominated by the authenticating attraction of temporal duration and spatial continuity, the specific cinematic techniques, that is, that are so often associated with the "realist" claims of diverse long-shot, long-take schools of filmmaking and theory (Amad 2001: 148). Although in-camera editing structures many Kahn films, on the whole they favor the patient "flow of life" (Kracauer 1960: 71) that Siegfried Kracauer associated with the material continuum of the uninterrupted shot. In this respect also these single-shot films participate in the one-upmanship of literary and visual travelogues. That is, they seemed to promise that here at last, in this instance anchored by the indexical attributes of film, one had access to the most accurate representation of the other (at least since the invention of photography) captured just in time at the moment when forces of modernization, such as tourism and cameras, were seen to threaten their very existence.

Films for the Future

At this point it is crucial to stress that Kahn's films were in fact never understood to be travelogues. Rather, the films (which are as concerned with urban life as they are with rural or native cultures) were intended to be documents about the present, visual fragments of modernity, collected in a not too dissimilar fashion to the "snapshots from the perspective of eternity" found in the sociology of Georg Simmel (Highmore 2002: 297) and in his wake a whole line of cultural and film critics concerned with reclaiming the overlooked ephemera of contemporary modern life, such as Kracauer and Walter Benjamin. Although the travel films were a crucial genre in popular and intellectual domains of French cinema of the years between 1910 and 1920, Kahn's noncommercial films were never supposed to compete with these "armchair voyages," as Louis Delluc (1917), along with many others, called them. For one, the elite audience who viewed the films on Kahn's property in Boulogne (the major forum in which they were screened) would not have related to them as substitutes for travel because these viewers were by definition well-traveled people. Rather than function as virtual voyages, the films were intended for an archival destiny, as documents for future use. If it is true that there was a sizeable if closed audience to whom a selection of these films was regularly screened, such a characterization of the exhibition context needs to be qualified by the suggestion that what the people who watched these films were getting was a sneak peak at some future film with an imprecise release date. To put it more concretely, Kahn's films were intended more for our eyes than theirs. And unlike the majority of films from this period, Kahn's were deliberately made to travel to the future. As archival documents from the moment of their inception, their meaning was not supposed to be grasped in the present except as a sort of tribute to the monumental collecting process that brought them into existence as a history of the present. That they are unwatchable according to the contemporary conventions of commercial actualities and travelogues is, I would argue, precisely the point: they were not meant to be watched in the present.

However, as I have been trying to demonstrate, Kahn's films may not be travelogues, but the logic of tourism—embedded in modern capitalist networks of transportation, reproduction, and colonialism—deeply inflects the project. That these films must be situated within the history of travel films even though they do not officially belong there speaks to the already mentioned porous nature of the travelogue itself, whose longevity depends on its broad cultural appeal (based on the themes of exploration and discovery, migration and exile, self and other, the everyday versus the extraordinary) rather than on narrow generic conventions. For all the appearances of elitism that surround the Boulogne community, it also needs to be added that by extending travel to the largely middle-class teaching population, Kahn's travel fund had a role in the democratic connotations of tourism (Strain 1996: 73; Green 2002: 425).[10] Even more significantly, Kahn's funds empowered in a radical sense the feminized associations of tourism. At a time when women were still barred from most forms of higher education in France, Kahn opened his travel funds to women.

The touristic logic is, however, particularly evident in the privileged motivation Kahn gave to "documentation." As a decentered, unauthored, and dispersed type of discourse, documentation resembles the multivalent structure that Behdad argues underpins the tourist guide (1994: 43), which differed significantly from the authored, experience-based analysis of the world that characterized the literary travelogue. Like the tourist guide, documentation is more about description than narration and is based on a desire for verification (is the information right?) rather than interpretation (what does it mean?). As we have seen, the autobiographical discourse of the literary travelogue did appear in the *Bulletins*, which have more of a unifying, authorial effect. But the films were not framed by any unifying author, character, or even lecturer.[11] To situate them within a contemporaneous cinematic movement, one could argue that in their accumulative, piecemeal logic the Kahn films shared features with Dziga Vertov's 1926 conception of film as a "factory of facts" (1984: 58) minus the didactic unifying thread. Where Vertov's "documentation" of facts was meant to awaken a proletariat to a new understanding of their everyday oppression, no such direct function existed for the planet of facts accumulated in Kahn's films. Just as one could never possibly make use of all the information in a tourist guidebook, so too is one saturated by the volume of documentation in the Kahn Archive. For all its serious aura, the Archive ultimately addresses us as the tourists (of information) it shunned rather than as the travelers (through knowledge) it cultivated.

Unintended Object Lessons

And yet unlike other forms of simulated travel, such as the commercial film travelogues, the Colonial Expositions of 1922 and 1931, or the fiction genre of colonial films, Kahn's films were never directly propagandistic in function. As Ellen Furlough and others have shown, the function of more popular colonial displays was to "enhance the loyalty of French citizens to the colonial idea and to Greater France, foster identification by French citizens with 'their' empire, showcase imperial accomplishments, and demonstrate the colonies' economic benefits for the metropole" (2002: 442). In contrast, the purpose of Kahn's films remains unquestionably more vague. That is not to say that the Kahn project did not indirectly participate in the validation of the colonial idea or a Greater France (as can be seen, for example, from Challaye's advice to future industrialists to see the market potential in the colonies). However, as unauthored, decentered fragments of visual information the films were not bound by a persuasive logic. And neither were the travel experiences that the boursiers underwent.

Thus, the winners of the Autour du Monde travel scholarships consistently reveal in their diaries how their travels were really underpinned not by a desire to know the other but by an underlining need to know the self, and the nation attached to that self. Driven by that need, these journeys also led some recipients to question both Western imperialism and universal humanism. The most striking instances of this occur in the accounts and writings of Félicien Challaye, who would become one of the most outspoken anti-imperialist voices in the interwar years. Although he clearly supports the belief that Europeans "must understand and practice the essential responsibility of the white race towards other races," he also admits that "unfortunately" whites have "too often abused their power in order to exploit yellow and black people" (1919–20: 54). Providing further evidence of the imperial self-consciousness of some of Kahn's boursiers, Ifor Evans, a British citizen, admits that even before traveling he "was a little ashamed of all the countries marked red in the school atlases" (1928: 67). His travel récit is even more uncensored than Challaye's in its skepticism toward the Kahnian ideal of knowing the other through travel: "One meets the fussy people and at times the important people, the financiers, the social reformers, and the politicians . . . But it was the ordinary man that I missed . . . More particularly it was the women whom I did not see" (66). To be sure, Challaye is not negating the superiority of the white race in calling for the end everywhere to "these abuses and crimes" of colonialism (1919–20: 54), and Evans is not arguing for the return of those countries marked red to self-determination, but their conclusions indicate, at the very least, the ways in which travel produced bad object lessons for those belated emissaries of the French and British empires.

Such unintended object lessons were not only to be learned overseas but within the interior—of the nation as well as the body. In the aerial films shot by Lucien Le Saint over the battlefields of northern France, the devastated towns of Arras and Reims, and the monuments of Paris, the "visuality of surveillance" of the travelogue (see Alison Griffiths's essay in this volume) swivels its gaze toward "home" and delivers an unfamiliar landscape of deep scars whose traumas are barely healed by the capital's more cheery tourist sites. Dr. Jean Comandon's micro-cinematographic films that were also made on Kahn's property in the late twenties were screened for the Boulogne audiences even more frequently than the aerial films. They too belong to the broader fascination with travel that the Archive captured. In films such as *Circulation du sang*, a voyage to the interior of the body was made that allowed viewers to see themselves as if "for the first time" (Cocteau 1919: 2) and experience the human body as a foreign landscape.[12] Overseen by a branch of geography whose central category of investigation just happened to be the humble "home," Kahn's films, no matter how far across the globe they roamed, always seem to have their compasses pointed shakily toward the coordinates of home and self.

My point is that the Archive and the culture of travel underpinning it were just as much shaped by the melancholy of exile (and the impossibility of proper mourning) as by the dreams of expansion, the dis-ease of displacement as well as the comforts of conquest. For if Kahn the individual might stand in as an eccentric but nonetheless typical figure of modernist exile, his Archive also captured the underside to this elitist subjectivity, proving Caren Kaplan's point that "all displacements are not the same" (1996: 2). The disquieting mode of being exiled from the earth, nation, and body provided by the aerial and micro-cinematographic films finds its most haunting members in the Archive's pioneering documentation of Europe's and the twentieth century's newest examples of "homes" and populations in movement captured in Stéphane Passet's films of Macedonian refugee camps in 1913. To argue that Kahn simply desired to escape the shock of modernity's temporal momentum and seek solace in the temporal stasis of cultural otherness would be to ignore such documents and their display of how modernity (and its emergent forms of "ethnic cleansing"), the self (Europe), and the present were always in the peripheral vision of the Archive's global gaze.

Conclusion

Travel was thus not simply necessary to collect the documents that fill the Archives de la Planète but understood broadly as a cultural condition of modernity pinned between the experiences of self and other, home and away, past and present, it was the shadow subject of the Archives. As a practice and a discourse, travel enabled and shaped the content of Kahn's films. By reading a variety of travelogue-related films in the collection of the Archives de la Planète in relation to a group of surrounding texts and contexts, this essay has aimed to open up a new perspective from which to think about the travel film and its troubled associations with the conquest and consumption of space. In its global ambitions the Archive reflected the confidence of French encyclopedism and nationalism while also harboring the anxieties it faced as a result of a crisis in authority experienced at an epistemological, national, and bodily level. In the Kahn films the confidence of the authorial travelogue gives way to the anxiety of interpretation enclosed in the more modern, disunified, and indeterminate documentation of the tour guide, while the containing and controlling gesture of the panorama weakens its grip in the potential for self-surveillance offered by new technologies of totalizing inscription as they took to the skies above and the cells within. While the Kahnian ideal of travel was to doubt oneself in order to be more sure of oneself, what Kahn's films reveal is that the return to the "familiar text" of home (or what Ifor Evans calls the "room in which I am writing" [1928: 68]) was not always guaranteed. The ultimate irony is that in trying to elevate travel beyond tourism in the form of a global visual compendium, Kahn may have ended up producing the only trinket large enough for the global homelessness that haunts his cosmopolitan vision: Call it history's first "world souvenir" — the Archives de la Planète.

Notes

1. The interview with Kahn was conducted for an article in the review *France Japan*; see Musée Albert-Kahn 1995: 62. Given that one of Kahn's life-long mentors was in fact the most famous philosopher of the early twentieth century, Henri Bergson, he is indulging in no exaggeration when he claims to have known the world's most influential men.

2. B. Ifor Evans was a recipient of one of Kahn's Autour du Monde travel scholarships; see Evans 1928: 68.

3. For an overview of Kahn's life and work that gives particular emphasis to the relation between the films in the Archive and the emerging conventions of documentary film, see Amad 2001. For a detailed study of the Kahn phenomenon, which focuses on an investigation of the impulse to archive everyday life within film history, philosophy, geography, and other domains, see Amad 2002. The most extensive treatment in French of Kahn's films is contained in the 2002 issue of *Cahiers de la Cinémathèque* 74 (December), which is entirely devoted to the subject.

4. The most comprehensive biographical account of Kahn appears in Musée Albert-Kahn 1995: 17–54 and 107–31, from which the following information has been culled. Born Abraham Kahn on 3 March 1860 to a Jewish family in Marmoutier, he arrived in Paris around 1875–76, where he became an employee of the Goudchaux Bank. He quickly proved himself to be gifted in finance. Proof of his talents arrived in 1888 (or 1884) on a trip to South Africa, where he reputedly successfully speculated on options in the De Beers diamond mines and Rand gold mines. As a result of these financial coups, by 1892, at the age of thirty-two, he had become a joint owner of the Goudchaux Bank. In addition to his personal travels Kahn also took important business-motivated trips to Japan, where he was one of the first Western financiers to enter that previously closed financial market. For the origins of Kahn's fortunes and dealings in Japan, see Musée Albert-Kahn 1995: 106–31.

5. For examples of these literary travelogues, see Nicole 1915, Nicholson 1928, and Challaye 1919–20.

6. The phrase "*Grand livre du monde*" was actually used by Bergson to describe Kahn's goal in founding the travel funds, but it applies equally to the Archive.

7. The term "Boulogne community" was used by Bergson to describe the intellectual circle who frequented the organizations emanating from Kahn's villa in the Parisian suburb of Boulogne (1931: iv).

8. On the "ethical vision" of colonialism that framed France's industrial-

izing intervention in Indochina as an act of "generosity, benevolence, [and] protection," see Cooper 2001: 29–42, 31.

9. On the connections between anthropology and tourism, science and spectacle, also see Strain 1996.

10. Writing about American travel to France around the turn of the century, Nancy L. Green claims that "from the diplomats and mostly male upper-class voyagers heading for a 'grand tour' to a more feminized and middle-class set of school teachers and businessmen, the class and gender of travelers shifted as tourism was ultimately transformed in the twentieth century into a more democratized, mass event" (2002: 425).

11. For a rare exception to this rule that details the discovery of a lecture accompaniment to a Kahn film, see Trebitsch 2002.

12. *Circulation du sang* is the title of a film that appears in the original projection register of the Kahn film archive for 1921. The title of a film with similar subject matter in the current museum computer catalogue is *Experiences biologiques: Le sang* (Jean Comandon and Pierre de Fonbrune, 1926–29).

Lured by the East

ETHNOGRAPHIC AND EXPEDITION FILMS ABOUT

NOMADIC TRIBES—The Case of *Grass* (1925)

HAMID NAFICY

||||||||||||||||||||||||||||||||||||||||||||||||||||||||||||||||||||||||||||||||||||||||||||||||||||||||||||||||||||||||||

Expedition and ethnographic films encode the nations' ideologies and collective longings for form—expressed in socially acceptable, aesthetically pleasing, and commercially successful generic and narrative schemas —and the psychology and desires of individual filmmakers. As a result, it is important to deal not only with overarching ideologies, such as colonialism, Orientalism, nationalism, and imperialism that shape the thinking and imagination of nations but also with filmmakers' personal histories, politics, and imperatives that help to form both them and their films. One topic in which early traveling filmmakers from the West showed great interest was the Eastern nomads. United States explorers and filmmakers were attracted to such nomadic tribes for personal and national reasons, among them wanderlust; manifest destiny, consisting of national expansionism, exceptionalism, and triumphalism that characterized both American pioneers of past centuries and global explorers of the twentieth century; a desire for authentic experiences and modernist primitivism found in the struggle against harsh nature; and a racialist nostalgia for origins.

As a case study of this complex attraction, this essay examines the seminal film *Grass: A Nation's Battle for Life*, about the semiannual migration of the Baba Ahmadi tribe in Iran.[1] It examines both the film's text and its context—the personal, political, ideological, and cultural forces that informed its genealogy, filming, intertitling, publicity, theatrical exhibition, nontheatrical touring, and reception by diverse audiences and critics both in the United States and in Iran. Recognized as a classic of documentary, ethnographic, and expedition films, it was made by three Americans,

Merian C. Cooper, Ernest B. Schoedsack, and Marguerite E. Harrison—
intrepid explorers, anti-Soviet adventurers, members of the U.S. military
or intelligence services, journalists, and filmmakers.

By the early 1920s, interest in the East and the Orient was keen and
Orientalist conceptions were circulating widely in fiction films such as in
Cecil B. DeMille's *The Arab* (1915), Louis Gasnier's *Kismet* (1920), and
Rex Ingram's *The Arab* (1924). Iran, a subject of many documentaries by
Western travelers (Naficy 1984, 1995), is not Arab but a non-Semitic and
overwhelmingly Muslim country, located in the Middle East where most
of the Arabs and a high percentage of the world's Muslims live. As a result,
its cinematic representations have conformed to many of the Orientalist discourses about Arabs and Muslims and posed problems for them. In
many ways, *Grass* played into these discourses and problematized them.

The Filmmakers and Their Triumphalist Wanderlust

Grass is a silent, 35mm, black-and-white, seventy-minute film that deals
with the trio of American explorers traveling through Turkey, Syria, Iraq,
and Iran in search of a "forgotten" Asiatic tribe. Having "found" them in
Iran and identified them, the explorers follow their transhumance migration from hot, dry regions to cool, green pastures. Cooper is the film's
producer, Schoedsack the cameraman, and Harrison the on-camera personality.

Ernest Beaumont Schoedsack (1893–1979) had been a cameraman for
the Mack Sennett Studio and for the United States Signal Corps; and
he was perhaps the first airborne combat photographer. He devised a
way of filming through the machine-gun openings that synchronized the
camera shutter's motion with the airplane's propeller (Wiley 1981). After
World War I, he joined the Red Cross relief mission, driving ambulances,
helping Polish refugees to escape from Soviet occupied lands, and filming "unparalleled" newsreel footage of the Polish fighters' incursion into
Russia (Goldner and Turner 1975: 25). At least two Red Cross films about
these events, *To the Aid of Poland* (1919) and *The Fall of Kiev* (1919), contain Schoedsack's footage. He also made at least two films for the Red
Cross Travel Film series: *'Neath Poland's Harvest Skies* (1920) and *Shep-
herds of Tatra* (1921). These were upbeat in tone, emphasizing the quaint
and exotic life of the peasants in a devastated Europe (Veeder 1990: 61).
As a freelance cameraman, Schoedsack also filmed newsreels for the U.S.

government as well as for commercial newsreel companies. Among these were scenes of the Versailles Treaty deliberations in Paris and the brutal Greek-Turkish war of 1921-22 that resulted in an independent Turkey under Mustapha Kemal Pasha (Ataturk), which sparked Schoedsack's interest in the Near East.[2]

Merian Coldwell Cooper (1895-1973) worked as a journalist in several U.S. cities and served in General Pershing's army in Mexico, chasing Pancho Villa. In 1917 he was flying low over the western front as a tactical aerial observer when he was shot down over the Argonne. Badly burned, he became for a time a prisoner of the Germans. Like Schoedsack, he viewed the Bolsheviks as a potential enemy, and at the outbreak of the Polish-Russian War, he formed with Major Cedric E. Fauntleroy the Kosciusko Aerial Squadron to fight the Bolsheviks. Again, he was shot down and this time he became a prisoner of the Red Army in Wladykino Prison, near Moscow. For months he assumed the identity of Corporal Frank R. Mosher, the name that was stenciled on the secondhand underwear that the Red Cross had given him. He was certain that if the Soviets discovered his true identity, he would be executed. During this time, Marguerite Harrison, who was spying for the U.S. military in the Soviet Union, smuggled food, blankets, tobacco, books, and money to him. Because of this, Cooper acknowledged that he owed his life to her (Brownlow 1979: 516; Goldner and Turner 1975: 24). Subsequently, in a daring and successful attempt, he escaped to freedom.

In 1922 Schoedsack, who had met Cooper earlier in Warsaw, joined him on a filmic expedition with Captain Edward A. Salisbury, an explorer and conservationist, on his ship *Wisdom II*. This collaboration resulted in a short film, *Golden Prince*, about Ras Tafari—then prince regent of the Abyssinian Empire, later crowned Emperor Haile Selassie of Ethiopia—and some newsreel footage of Muslims on their *hajj* pilgrimage in Jedda, Saudi Arabia. However, an accidental fire by a crewman that burned much of their footage caused Cooper and Schoedsack to adopt an idea they had abandoned earlier: making an epic film about a nomadic tribe's struggle against nature.

As a precocious child who began talking at eight months, Marguerite Harrison (born Marguerite Elton Baker, 1879-1967) had traveled to Europe extensively, thanks to her father, a wealthy transatlantic shipping magnate (Harrison 1935: 8; Olds 1985: 158-59). As an adult, she satisfied her insatiable urge for travel and adventure by becoming a reporter for various papers, including the *Baltimore Sun*, and by contacting the U.S.

Army Military Intelligence Division (MID), offering to become a spy. After preliminary interviews, MID signed her on and sent her to Europe to report on the social climate and psychological conditions of the Germans in the wake of their defeat in the Great War. She worked hard and in a disciplined fashion, chasing leads and regularly filing interesting and accurate reports with her military superiors about the Germans' postwar attitudes, including reactions to the cost of the severe terms of the peace treaty and the emergence of anti-Semitism (Olds 1985: 170). Some of these reports were also printed in the *Baltimore Sun*. Although the Versailles peace treaty brought an end to Harrison's spying in Europe, she soon obtained another intelligence assignment, spying in the Soviet Union. After some success there she was caught and spent ten nightmarish months in the notorious Lubianka Prison and, later, in Novinsky Prison—the first American woman to become a prisoner of the Bolsheviks. It was from Novinsky that a grateful Cooper had planned to rescue Harrison. That became unnecessary, however, as she was released through the intervention of the American Relief Administration, which offered food for famine-starved Russians in exchange for freedom for all American prisoners (Olds 1985: 181–83).

Cooper and Harrison had first met years earlier in Warsaw at a Red Cross ball, an acquaintance that grew once Harrison returned to the United States in the early 1920s. However, she was restless and her powerful wanderlust uncontainable. Her autobiography testifies:

> I knew that I should have been content to live with my boy in New York where I had made hosts of friends, but I could not settle down. During the late spring nights I lay awake listening to the sirens of the ocean liners that were leaving for distant ports. They were truly sirens to me, urging, enticing, irresistible. Finally, I could stand it no longer. I made up my mind that I would have to go somewhere before the summer was over. (1935: 565)

That "somewhere" was nowhere else but the Middle East and Iran, where she went to make *Grass*.

The wanderlust of all three was driven not only by their personal desires for elsewhere and for other times but also by the Great War, which had shaken many people out of their routines, leaving them at a loss, dissatisfied with their own societies, and curious about other places. Modernity and improvements in communication and transportation had made literal travel and virtual travel (by means of film and photography) possible and within reach of ordinary people. The trio's sense of exceptionalism, expansionism, and triumphalism was fueled not only by the victory of the Americans and their European allies over their Western and Eastern foes but also by the emergence of the United States from the Great War as a new global power. It was perhaps also driven by the exceptionalism, expansionism, and triumphalism of the U.S. film industry, emblematized by Hollywood's dominance of the world's screens since that war. Political and cinematic supremacy facilitated the emergence of an American travel cinema.

The film's budget was small at ten thousand dollars, at least half of which was supplied by Harrison (Harrison 1935: 566) and the rest by Cooper and Schoedsack (Brownlow 1979: 516, Wiley 1981: 1), with the latter also contributing his lightweight, hand-cranked French Debrie camera, mounted on a tripod and equipped with a 400-foot film magazine. Although Schoedsack was opposed to taking a woman on a dangerous expedition, he agreed to an equal partnership, according to which all three would share the film's profit in equal parts.

Struggle against Nature and Filmic Conditions

Grass contains two overarching plots of struggles: the filmmakers' search for the "Forgotten People" and the tribes' migration with thousands of animals over rough terrain. The first plot opens the film and lasts the first third of its length, while the latter plot takes up the rest of the film. Schoedsack and Cooper had originally planned to film the migration of Kurdish tribes in Turkey because they had the "most interesting costumes and customs" and lived in a "wildly photogenic country" (Schoedsack 1983: 43).

Indeed, the film begins like an early theatrical feature by introducing the intrepid travelers, much like cast members: in close-up portrait shots, filmed behind Paramount's Astoria Studios, looking at each other or at the camera (Figure 1). After this opening, Harrison is the only expedition member on camera. Such self-referentiality enhanced the film's documentary claims at the same time that, through the artifice of the search for the tribe and Harrison's on-camera presence, it provided Western audiences with a pleasurable narrative world and a figure of identification.

The newly independent Turkey, formed out of the rubble of the Ottoman Empire, suspicious of foreigners, made the explorers' forays into Kurdish region unsafe. During the weeks of waiting for travel and film-

1   Ernest Schoedsack (left) and Merian Cooper being introduced to
the audience (Paramount back lot, Astoria, NY) in *Grass* (1925).

ing permits, Schoedsack filmed some newsreel and travelogue footage
to support the team financially. A few of these sequences made it into
Grass, such as the scene of the dancing bear and village children. As
they became convinced that permits were not forthcoming, they evaded
police surveillance and, following ancient caravan routes, trekked southwest from Istanbul to Angora (Ankara) in search of a new Forgotten
People. They spent a memorable night in an old caravansary, sharing a
hot meal cooked over an open fire with Turkoman travelers. Using flares,
Schoedsack filmed this scene dramatically, which was cut into the film.
Weeks later they entered the Anatolian desert during a bitter winter, but
this did not deter them from fulfilling one of the requirements of desert
travelogues—a sandstorm. They re-created it by having porters shovel
bran out of bags just outside Schoedsack's camera frame while Harrison
and her carriage driver drove straight into the wind. The result on film
was highly realistic, as waves of bran came at them, covering them from
head to foot, entering their hair, noses, and teeth—Harrison having to
remove bran from her long hair for days.

Continuing their search, the trio headed into the Taurus Mountains
toward Syria (Figure 2). In the midst of a blinding snowstorm, with snow
coming up to the bellies of their horses, they encountered hospitable

2 Marguerite Harrison and local attendants in a snowstorm in the Taurus Mountains (Turkey) in *Grass*.

natives, among them a local hunter named Halil Effendi, who provided them with another re-created episode. Using a specially built portable canvas screen as camouflage, with three holes in it for eyes and the gun muzzle, Effendi stalked wild mountain goats, shooting and killing one. However, since the shooting occurred off camera, they re-created it by propping the carcass high on a cliff. When Schoedsack was ready, Halil took a shot and someone pulled a cord that caused the carcass to tumble over the mountainside for the filming. Harrison justified the fakery in the way many documentarists have justified re-creations: "It was merely a repetition before the camera of what had actually happened" (1935: 586).

Disappointed in not finding their picturesque and heroic Forgotten People in Turkey, Syria, or Iraq, the filmmakers finally chose the Bakhtiari tribes in Iran. In this choice they were advised by the British politician Sir Arnold Wilson, chairman of the board of the Anglo-Persian Oil Company, and by the chief of British intelligence for Iraq, Gertrude Bell. The Bakhtiaris' semiannual migration in search of pasturage was massive and dramatic, and their route highly picturesque; it was to begin in April 1924, a schedule the filmmakers could readily accommodate; and their area of migration was within the jurisdiction of the giant oil company's operation, where the filmmakers could benefit from its influence and protection. Sir Arnold's introductory letter, urging local and tribal officials' cooperation, opened many doors to them, including their audience with the Il-Khani, the chief of all the Bakhtiari tribes, and with his cousin and second in command, the Il-Begi, Amir Jang.[3] The older Il-Khani was puzzled by the idea of foreigners accompanying tribal migration for filming, but he was won over by the younger Il-Begi, who had been to the movies in Tehran and had liked them. The filmmakers' desire to follow a tribe whose route was through the wild mountains, not on the gravel road that the British had built, resulted in their joining the Baba Ahmadi subtribe, headed by Haidar Khan.

At this juncture, the filmmakers were justifiably delighted about finally locating the site of the Forgotten People—a delight that is enacted in *Grass* in the drama of discovery, a characteristic of the expedition genre—which is marked on a map of Asia Minor and Persia (now Iran) on which a large caption identifies the Forgotten People's location and the trio's route to find them. As part of this drama of discovery, viewers are treated to the only scenes of nonmigratory aspects of the tribes' life in the film: the tribal black tents in the valleys and women who are spinning cotton, dancing with a handkerchief, feeding a baby, and milking a goat while men perform the stick dance.

From this point on, the film's first plot—the filmmakers' struggle to find their subjects—joins its second plot—the struggle of the Baba Ahmadi tribe numbering some five thousand people and fifty thousand animals to migrate from their southwest winter region near the Persian Gulf to the cooler summer pastures near Isfahan. This massive movement began on 17 April 1924, and lasted forty-eight days, during which Schoedsack and Cooper generally slept on the ground, while Harrison slept in a small tent. As Schoedsack explains in a tape letter, "We ate the food they gave us—we had no supplies of our own—and it was very good. They'd bring us their food every night. We'd stretch out on our bedroll, and they'd give us barley, which they stored in goatskin sacks, and every few days they'd have a shish Kebab—and always plenty of yogurt" (Schoedsack 1971). Cooper, too, loved the outdoors life with the Bakhtiari, considering it, according to his wife Dorothy Cooper, as "one of the happiest periods in his life" (D. Cooper 1984).

Schoedsack filmed by hand-cranking his Debrie camera at the silent speed of 16 fps, exposing some 20,000 feet of black-and-white negative. Tribespeople did not have a problem with being filmed, perhaps because they had developed a good rapport with Schoedsack and trusted him and because they were too busy with their migration to pay attention to the camera. Harrison often slept with the precious film cans and the trio's moneybags in her tent to safeguard them. As the only Westerner with sustained on-camera presence, she stands out among the tribespeople with her white horse, her light-colored Western safari suit, her pith helmet held on her head with a scarf, and her fashionably made-up face. She took care to apply make up for each shot and she washed her clothes regularly to make herself "presentable" (Harrison 1935: 626–27). Schoedsack's shot compositions, which centered her, also contributed to her visibility.

The filmmakers turned the two massive and dramatic obstacles of the migration into the film's narrative complications. One involved thousands of tribespeople and animals crossing the torrential and icy rapids of the Karun River, which was a half-mile wide and without a bridge in the vicinity. In this process, human lives and livestock were inevitably lost annually. Schoedsack, who had gone ahead to secure a position to film the tribes' arrival at the river, sent a note to Cooper, saying: "Coop! I hate to say it before we start shooting, but this is what we have been traveling months to see. Better be here before sunrise tomorrow. This is it!" (M. Cooper 1925: 218–19). The lengthy sequence he filmed shows in graphic detail the way tribesmen inflate goatskins and tie them together to form rafts, which carry their wives, children, small animals, and belongings, while the men swim across the turbulent waters simultaneously herding thousands of sheep, donkeys, cows, and horses. Later, when he had confronted the river and witnessed the Baba Ahmadi's efforts to cross it, Cooper wrote: "It was a show, all right. For five days Schoedsack and I, rushing about with the cameras, watched the greatest piece of continuous action I have ever seen" (1925: 233). The documentary historian Erik Barnouw offered a similar assessment of Schoedsack's filming: "One of the most spectacular sequences ever put on film" (1993: 48).

The other obstacle and narrative complication involved the barefoot tribespeople, dressed in light clothing, carving a narrow zigzag trail into the snow-covered side of Zardeh Kuh up to its vertical 15,000-foot summit. Filming such a massive and moving target posed major logistical and aesthetic problems, one of which was the impossibility of rehearsals or retakes. Another was that, to avoid the intense daytime heat, the tribe generally broke camp in complete darkness, depriving the crew of any nighttime scenes or ethnographic footage of tribal socializing. The blinding early morning sun, and the often bright background, also made it impossible to film the lightly dressed tribespeople. However,

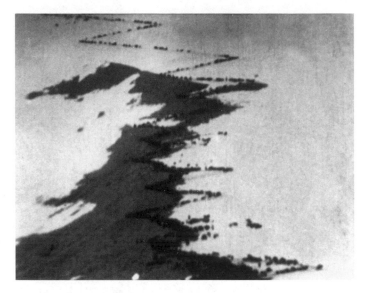

3   5,000 tribespeople and 50,000 animals on the zigzag trail up the Zadeh Kuh (Iran) in *Grass*.

Schoedsack learned to cope with these problems admirably. His cinematography is crisp, dramatic, and breathtaking, particularly where humans are framed against massive mountains, vast valleys, or torrential waters. Kevin Brownlow calls one of these scenes "the most unforgettably epic shot of documentary history" (1979: 526). Apparently based on a painting of Napoleon crossing the Alps, which Cooper had seen in Paris, it pictures the zigzagging multitude of tribespeople flattened against the far valley like thousands of flies (Figure 3). Schoedsack's intimate shots are also dramatic, showing women carrying babies in wooden cradles on their backs, a young girl climbing the rocky path with a lamb on her shoulders, and pack animals creating a traffic jam on the zigzag trail.

The filming of *Grass* itself was also a heroic struggle and achievement, given the weight and bulkiness of the 35mm equipment and film stock and the exigencies of tribal migration, which demanded mobility, spontaneity, and great stamina. In such circumstances, planning was nearly impossible. Schoedsack did well on that account as well, for by the end of the seven-week migration, he had exactly eighty feet of film left with which to record the tribes' triumphal arrival in what the film intertitles call "the land of milk and honey—the land of Grass" (Schoedsack 1971). This is why that scene is so brief and contrived.

The U.S. travelers' search for the Forgotten People and the two key river and mountain crossings are driven not only by wanderlust and desire to escape to elsewhere but also by the theme of the tribes' nomadic life as an elemental struggle for survival against violent nature. Robert Flaherty's *Nanook of the North* (1922) had memorably depicted this theme in the Inuit's efforts to survive in the Canadian tundra. Cooper wanted to achieve a similar effect, for he hypothesized that "when man fights for his life, all the world looks on. And where does man have to fight harder than when he finds his opponent the unrelenting and stern forces of Nature? . . . We decided to attempt to throw on the screen the actual struggle for life of a migratory people" (1925: x).

By the time filming was over, however, Cooper and Schoedsack had grown to regard their film as "half a picture" and a "great missed chance" (Brownlow 1979: 528–29). While their footage was impressive in scale and grandeur, it lacked human intimacy and personality. Their plan to complete the film by raising funds to film the tribes' autumn return migration and Haidar's family life with his two wives and son did not materialize. In their preparation to leave Iran, all three stayed in Tehran for a while, where they had two fateful engagements, with significant impact both on their film's fate in Iran and on the politics of Iran-U.S. relations. Cooper and Schoedsack stayed at the home of U.S. Vice Consul Robert Imbrie, who notarized a testimonial letter for them, written by tribal chiefs, that offered proof of their expedition. Within months, Imbrie would be murdered by a fanatical mob in Tehran. In the meantime, Harrison gained an audience with Reza Khan, minister of war *and* prime minister, who used Imbrie's murder to consolidate his hold on power and become the shah (see below).

Editing and Intertitling the Film

Cooper and Schoedsack took the exposed footage to Paris for development and, later, edited it into a 7-reel film in New York City (about seventy minutes). It was during a private screening of this version that Jesse Lasky (of Famous Players-Lasky Corporation) liked what he saw and decided to complete the film for theatrical distribution—not wanting to repeat his mistake of passing up the opportunity to distribute *Nanook of the North* seven months earlier.

To that end the studio made several major changes and additions to the film, copyrighting it on 21 June 1924. The portraits of the three explorers were added to the start of the film. The tribal chiefs' testimonial letter was inserted at the film's end. Dated 28 June 1924, written in Persian and English by Haidar Khan and Amir Jang, and notarized by Major Robert W. Imbrie, it confirms that Cooper, Schoedsack, and Harrison were "the first foreigners who have crossed the Zardeh Kuh pass and the first to have made the forty-eight day migration with the tribes" (in the Persian version, it is forty-six days).[4] In addition, the film was turned into feature length (ten reels) by padding it with outtakes, which angered Schoedsack in particular (Brownlow 1981: 2). Finally, innumerable intertitles were inserted (some 174 in the version that Milestone is currently distributing). The final ignominy was that the credit for editing the film did not go to Cooper and Schoedsack, but to Terry Ramsey and Richard P. Carver, who also had a major hand in writing the intertitles.

Famous Players-Lasky may have felt they needed dramatic and snappy titles to make what they feared would be a dreary documentary entertaining. In the late silent era, all films employed title writers, whose job was "to make subtitles entertaining," and by 1925 some of them had succeeded too well, eliciting "howls of laughter from delighted audiences" (Brownlow 1981: 1). Of the filmmaking trio, Harrison disliked the intertitles the most. After viewing *Grass* once on the public screens, she could not "bear to see it" again because she "loathed" the artificiality and theatricality of the intertitles (1935: 648).

Taken together, the film's visuals and intertitles create a dichotomous, "split" text. While the visuals by and large document, authenticate, and celebrate the reality, bravery, stamina, and resourcefulness of the tribe, the intertitles are often ethnocentric, Orientalist, narratively manipulative, and overly dramatic. This textual split may be a result of the division of labor, with the filmmakers, experienced about the migration and sympathetic to the tribe, in charge of the visuals, and the studio writers, ignorant of the tribes' way of life, supplying the intertitles.[5] However, this division was not that hard, for Cooper admitted to having written some of the titles himself (Brownlow 1981: 1). That the intertitles in the next Cooper-Schoedsack documentary, *Chang* (1927), and the captions for the numerous stills of the migration in Cooper's book about *Grass* suffer from similar problems underscores Cooper's ethnocentric view of non-Western people.

The film is also a "hybrid" text in the way it borrows from fiction cinema and contributes to an emerging nonfiction cinema. It borrows from the silent fiction films the scenario of search, the filmmakers' "discovery," and the way the intertitles dramatize, narrativize, entertain, characterize, stereotype, and visualize. On the other hand, the documentary footage of the expedition and migration, the film's self-reflexivity, and the way the intertitles and maps provide context, diegetic and extra-diegetic information, and framing give evidence of the codes of the as yet unnamed documentary form.

Racialist Nostalgia for Origins

Another theme that attracted the early Western travelers to the tribes was that focusing on tribes allowed them to establish continuity and hierarchy in the chain of human evolution, with non-Western tribes residing in the earlier stages and Western societies occupying the pinnacle of evolutionary developments. There is a marked difference, however, between the manner in which traveling filmmakers, such as Martin and Osa Johnson, represented African blacks around the same time in such films as *Simba* (1928), *Congorilla* (1932), and *Baboona* (1935) and the way that the makers of *Grass* represented the Iranian nomads. In representing the African blacks, and sometimes Arabs, the traveling filmmakers imbued the social Darwinism paradigm with latent and manifest racism, both of which posited the Africans as inherently different, separate, unequal, and inferior to the whites. They were stereotyped, ridiculed, infantilized, and reduced to the level of subhuman. However, the use of this racialist paradigm was more complicated and more favorable to the Iranian tribes. It was more complicated because the representation of the Baba Ahmadi by Harrison and Cooper in their memoirs differs markedly from that in the film, undermining a unified ideological vision of the tribe. Harrison writes that there was "nothing particularly glamorous about their struggle for existence," as the tribe was terribly poor and existed on a totally inadequate diet (1935: 617). Cooper, too, speaks of the Bakhtiari often in uncomplimentary fashion as "wild nomads" (1925: 9) and "barbarian hordes" (3), and he quotes past observers of Iran who describe the tribes as "a race of robbers" and "bloodthirsty" people (151). Both Harrison and Cooper note that their chief, Haidar Khan, was gorilla-like, brutal, a wife beater, an opium smoker, and a horse thief, who loafed about while his people did the work. Despite these very negative appraisals, both also praise the Baba Ahmadi tribe and its chief for their valor, endurance, and ingenuity.

The film does not visualize the team's negative private observations and prejudices, perhaps because it would have countered the projection of the tribespeople as noble savages, which was its overarching theme. Instead, *Grass* emphasizes the positive public display of tribal bravery and stamina, in support of which it marshals ample documentary evidence. This ideological split between the private and public views of the tribe can be detected in the film's other textual split discussed earlier, between complimentary visuals and condescending intertitles. The racialist depiction of Iranian tribes was more favorable compared to that of Arabs and Africans, because these tribes were construed to be white, non-Semitic, and Aryan, a fact that both the film's intertitles and the filmmakers' writings point up. Like Harrison, Cooper invokes the common racial bond between the tribes and white Americans, musing that "it may well be that the migratory life which we are going to live with them is that of our own Aryan forefathers of many thousands of years ago" (1925: 143). *Grass*'s opening intertitles also reiterate this theme.

Such a racialist differentiation between Iranian "primitives" and African "primitives" is also evident in an unpublished exchange between Brownlow and Schoedsack. At one point, Schoedsack states that he took still portrait shots of the Baba Ahmadi, which they liked very much in general; their only complaint was that they were only head-and-shoulder shots. Brownlow then reminds Schoedsack of Martin and Osa Johnson's expeditions in Africa during which they showed the natives still pictures of themselves and discovered that the natives could not make sense of them. Brownlow asks Schoedsack if he encountered the same problem with the Iranian tribe. This is Schoedsack's response: "These aren't low down stupid thick old coloured, you know. These are very intelligent white folk. They knew what pictures were, and they had a lot of old stone carvings on graves and things like that" (Brownlow 1969–70: 9).

Because of these racial and hierarchical conceptions, the Bakhtiari tribes are included in the line of human progress but are kept safely sealed in their time capsule in the earlier evolutionary stages. They came to represent a bygone era of simplicity and authenticity, and their way of life a prelapsarian world of before—before civilization and modernity separated humans from their Edenic origin. Thus a return to and recovery of such a world, in the form of the search and discovery of the

Forgotten People, became alluring prospects. Of course, the tribespeople were neither forgotten nor unknown to themselves or to the Iranians, a great percentage of whom were then—and are still—tribal or have tribal roots. But it was necessary to create this fiction of loss and amnesia in order to feed the fiction of the documentary: the discovery of the forgotten tribe by Western filmmakers.

The film's play of the gazes replicates a series of binary power relations: between East and West, ethnographer and subject, and male and female. It contains only one instance of diegetic eye contact and eye-line cutting; significantly, that is in the film's opening between the two male filmmakers, who form a small exclusive club among equals. Harrison, on the other hand, is shown in the opening in a single shot by herself, looking at the camera without any exchange of looks between her and them. And in the rest of the film, where she is on camera, her personal point of view is rarely shown. As a result, both Harrison and the tribespeople are excluded from the process of signification; they are objectified and looked at. However, they are objectified differently. As a white mediator, even though a woman, Harrison has a higher status than the tribes, since she is also a diegetic subject from whose narrative perspective the audience sees the migrating tribe and the trio's expedition. The natives, on the other hand, are objectified thrice: first as the subject of Harrison's regard, then as the subject of the camera's gaze, and finally with their muteness, since the intertitles rarely quote any actual native dialogue.

The film's self-congratulatory attitude also bolsters the Western filmmakers' power position.[6] The tribal leader's letter at the film's end must be seen in this light, for it testifies to, and dramatizes, their accomplishment in braving the tribes' primitive world. Barnouw thought the film's final emphasis was not on the endurance of the tribe but on "the brash display of egoism—on the heroic accomplishment of the film makers" (1993: 48).

On the Lecture Circuit: Commercial Exhibition and Reception in the United States

After the film's completion, Cooper and Harrison went on the lecture circuit, extensively screening *Grass* while providing live narration about their experiences of traveling and filming. Cooper acquired an agent who booked his film tours at clubs, scientific societies, and colleges, particularly in the Midwest. The National Geographic Society in Washington, D.C., invited him to lecture with the film, and among the distinguished audience was the president of the United States. His average net profit from each lecture was about two hundred dollars, which he split equally with his two partners. He also wrote a series of illustrated articles about the filming for *Asia Magazine* and published a book about that experience, containing Schoedsack's dramatic photographs (M. Cooper 1925), which was subsequently serialized in newspapers and translated into Persian (M. Cooper [1934] 1955). His publisher also arranged for a one-hour radio appearance sponsored by the Goodyear Tire and Rubber Company, for which Cooper received the high sum of one thousand dollars.

Harrison, too, traveled widely with the film, talked on the radio, and lectured with it, particularly to women's clubs and societies. One example of her public lecturing is her presentation on 13 December 1938, at UCLA's giant Royce Hall Auditorium for the university's "lifelong learning" program. The printed flyer boasts that she was lecturing with "the only complete copy of *Grass* available for public presentation." An organist, Harry Q. Mills, was on hand to provide live musical accompaniment. That the event was scheduled in a hall that could seat over one thousand spectators indicates the size of the expected audience. Although, as she admits, she had "acquired a reputation for unreliability" because of her "incurable habit of going off on trips" and missing her appointments, she secured enough speaking engagements with the film to remain financially afloat (Harrison 1935: 648). Like Cooper, she also wrote a book—narratively more engaging than Cooper's—in which, among her other life stories, she recounts the threesome's experience of the filming of *Grass* (1935).

In those days, women travelers, explorers, and filmmakers were not taken seriously, and the mass media were often more interested in their love affairs with exotic foreigners than in their explorations and accomplishments. Harrison complained that all the reporters wanted to know was "if I had become enamoured of a sheik!" (1935: 650). Cooper and Schoedsack, too, did not sufficiently acknowledge her contribution to the film—although Cooper in his memoir applauded her linguistic facility and her paramedical abilities. Schoedsack was downright hostile, calling her involvement in the film "a sore spot" and "a bad idea." Nonetheless, he acquiesced, since having a "white woman" on camera was a "cute" idea, and he felt "honor bound" to "make a shot" of her every so often. He also asserted that there was nothing romantic between the men and Harrison and that Cooper brought her along to repay her for saving him from starvation in the Soviet prisons (Brownlow 1969–70: 9; Brownlow 1979: 528). His antagonism may have stemmed not only from his sexism but also from his professional jealousy of a woman who considered herself the film's heroine and co-producer. Power was also a factor (see below). Although this hitherto unpublished account of the hostile undercurrent of the relationship among the expedition members was kept private, soon after *Grass*'s first theatrical run, the partnership dissolved. Cooper and Schoedsack, however, joined forces on several subsequent productions, which in some ways replayed, echoed, and signified on *Grass*, notably *Chang* and *King Kong* (1933).

These diverse forms of publishing, publicizing, lecturing, touring, broadcasting, and film screening before general and specialized audiences were part of the cross-fertilizing culture industry infrastructures that were coming together for both fiction films and documentary films. The wide dissemination of such ideologically loaded projections of non-Western people would ensure that these ideologies would become part of the political unconscious of Westerners, helping, in the words of Edward Said, to ideologically "produce" the "East," or the "Orient" (1979).

Famous Players-Lasky produced *Grass*, while Paramount released it commercially. A variety of film archives, independent film libraries, university film libraries, and independent distributors handled its non-theatrical distribution. In 1991 Milestone Films and Video acquired the rights to the film from the Museum of Modern Art in New York City and re-released the most complete version of it on videocassette, laser disk, and DVD, with an added Persian musical score.[7]

Grass performed well at the box office, particularly in major cities. It remained on the screen at the Criterion Theater in New York City for three months (April–June 1926), earning $85,346, and it earned in its first run in Philadelphia, Chicago, and Los Angeles a total of $37,400 (Dannenberg 1927: 253). It did not do as well in smaller cities, perhaps because it was so remote from the lives of ordinary Americans and because there were "no pretty girls in it, no love scenes" (Harrison 1935: 648–49). With this income, the three partners paid their expenses, recouped their investment, and earned several thousand dollars each in royalties.

The film did surprisingly well in terms of critical response, as well (Gerhard 1925; Hall 1925; Lawrence 1925; Johnson 1982). In the United States, nationwide film reviewers voted *Grass* one of the best pictures of 1925. Many reviewers ranked it among the ten best films, and overall they

ranked it number twelve, a high ranking given that it was a documentary in the company of luminary feature films such as F. W. Murnau's
The Last Laugh (ranked number two), John Ford's *The Iron Horse* (number four), Erich von Stroheim's *Greed* (number five), Charles Chaplin's
The Gold Rush (number seventeen), and Raoul Walsh's *Thief of Baghdad*
(number twenty-two). In addition, the National Board of Review ranked
it fifteen in a list of forty best pictures of 1925 (Dannenberg 1927: 417–
26). In 1926 *Grass* was selected among four hundred films "suitable for
children" (Kann 1927: 471–73). Geographers and ethnologists "hailed it
as a substantial contribution to human knowledge" (Harrison 1935: 648),
and historians recognized it as a "classic" of documentary cinema, rating
it second only to *Nanook of the North* (Brownlow 1979: 529).

Sociopolitical Reception in Iran

Apparently, *Grass* was not screened in Iranian public cinemas for about
two decades, for several reasons. For one, it showed armed nomadic
tribesmen freely moving about at the time that the government was
forcibly pacifying all tribes. Showing the film publicly would have countered that national policy, spearheaded by the autocratic prime minister
Reza Khan, with grave consequences. Its depiction of Iran as a "primitive" and pastoral country would also have falsified his modernist projection of Persia (whose name he changed to Iran in 1935). That he was
aware of the film is almost certain, for Harrison met with him in Tehran
after filming in 1924. However, there is no evidence that he had viewed
and banned the film.

The film's screening may also have been hampered by a foreign-policy
crisis that occurred immediately after filming. This was the tragic murder of the signer of the testimonial letter for *Grass*, U.S. Vice Consul
Robert Imbrie, by a Tehran mob angry at his photographing a religious
shrine and procession, which became the first of several major rifts in
Iran-U.S. relations in modern times. The Iranian government apologized
for the incident, paid for the indemnity of Imbrie's widow, underwrote
the cost of the warship *Trenton* to repatriate the body, and hanged three
culprits. Significantly, Reza Khan used Imbrie's brutal murder to consolidate his power by declaring martial law, arresting his political opponents,
muzzling the opposition press, and curbing the clergy. A year later, he dissolved the Qajar dynasty and declared himself the shah of the new Pahlavi

dynasty. The United States government, which had publicly taken a hard-line approach with the Iranian government to save face, implicitly encouraged his assumption of dictatorial power as a "price that had to be paid for satisfactory settlement of the Imbrie dispute." For the Americans, the lesson from this incident reverberated for decades, for as late as the 1950s, the U.S. embassy in Tehran routinely warned Americans against photographing religious events in Iran by invoking Imbrie's unfortunate fate (Zirinsky 1986: 283–88).

When *Grass* was eventually shown after the Allied Powers had occupied Iran and forced Reza Shah into exile in 1941, it was not the feature-length, silent American film. Rather, it was a forty-minute sound version (perhaps produced by the BBC), with Nikolay Rimsky-Korsakov's *Scheherazade* (1888) as the sound track and a Persian-language voice-over narration. The well-known scholar Mojtaba Minovi wrote and read the narration himself, which provided a sympathetic and nationalistic counterdiscourse to the original ethnocentric intertitles. The British Council distributed the film nationally to movie theaters and to cultural and educational institutions as late as the mid-1970s.

According to the filmmaker Mohammad Ali Issari, this version was highly popular with Iranians because seeing themselves on the screen for the first time and in a generally positive light "satisfied their sense of national pride" (1982). The French sociologist Edgar Morin also noted that many grown Bakhtiari men, who on seeing the film recognized themselves as children, were delighted about what they saw. The Persian-language narration must have indigenized the film, increased its attractiveness, and enhanced what Morin calls the "pleasure of auto-identification" of cinema (1977: 109). Issari's auto-identification by means of *Grass* had a lasting effect on him, initiating his lifelong commitment to documentary filmmaking.

At the same time, however, like a Lacanian mirror, the film's wider circulation produced contradictory reactions, causing not only self-identification but also self-alienation. The writer Ali Javaherkalam, who viewed the film in 1931 in a cinema in Abadan operated by the Anglo-Persian Oil Company, relates that during the screening, some oil workers became so agitated by the perceived negative depiction of Iran that they loudly objected to the film and walked out of the theater. The next day, however, a high-ranking Iranian official of the company admonished them for their defensive anger at a film that he thought had honestly documented Iranian reality (Rahimian 1988: 61). Bakhtiari tribal leaders also expressed mixed reactions about it to me. Amir Bahman Samsam confirmed that he had seen both versions, that the migration was depicted "realistically and without errors," and that the Baba Ahmadi's route was their normal route (Samsam 1984). This latter statement, coupled with similar comments below, dispenses once and for all with the notion put forward by some scholars (Sadoul 1965: 105; Barsam 1992: 55) that the tribe had taken an unusually picturesque and difficult route to accommodate the desire of the filmmakers for dramatic footage. Hamid Khan Bakhtiari, the son of the Il-Khani who had facilitated the filmmakers' migration with the tribe, had also viewed the British Council's version as a young governor of the region. He corroborated the accuracy and truthfulness of the film. However, his emotional reaction was mixed: "I was made proud of the defiance of the men and women of the tribe but very saddened by their poverty, ignorance, and illiteracy" (Bakhtiari 1984).

Grass captured the imagination of not only Issari but also other filmmakers, inside and outside Iran, some of whom attempted to reproduce and update that primordial vision of humankind by examining tribal life—with mixed results. *Grass* continues to be screened in documentary film, Middle Eastern history, and visual anthropology courses in the United States and elsewhere. One barometer of its longevity is the statistic from the Museum of Modern Art in New York City, which reported some fifty "circulations" a year as late as the 1980s, about 80 percent of which went to colleges and the remainder to cultural institutions (Sloan 1982). The availability of the film on video in the 1990s bolstered its circulation enormously, as Milestone Films and Video reports sales of over five thousand videocassettes and DVDs in one decade since it began distributing the film (Doros 2003). This sudden surge may owe partly to the presence of over half a million Iranians in the United States, the largest population outside Iran, who are interested in their cultural heritage.

Attempted Color and Sound Remake in 1956

Aware of some of *Grass*'s shortcomings, Cooper attempted another version in Technicolor and sound, but against Schoedsack's advice (Schoedsack 1983: 114). He assembled a large fifteen-person, Hollywood-style crew consisting of technical personnel, guards, and actors along with half a dozen muleteers and some forty-three mules, who carried their gear, tents, cameras, vodka, orange juice (imported from the United States), canned food (corned beef and hash), and sleeping bags. Most would not eat the tribes' food (Sadeqi 1984). Lowell Farrell was to direct the film for C. V. Whitney Productions, with Cooper as executive producer and Winton Hock as director of photography. This was a far cry from the nimble, three-member crew of *Grass*, who slept in the open or in a pup tent and ate what the tribespeople ate.

Their filming approach, guided by first-time director Farrell, was also Hollywood inspired in that it was based on scripted narrative films, unsuitable for spontaneous filming of a massive migratory tribe. Under government supervision, they managed to film scenes of Bakhtiari daily life, migration, river crossing, and city life, but they ran out of time, money, and steam. This footage was edited into a forty-minute "demo" film that was accompanied by a musical track and a verbose voice-over narration designed to raise funds to finance yet another trip to complete the film (which did not happen). This footage, which I have viewed, lacks the scale and drama of the original, a lack that is particularly noticeable in its mundane river- and mountain-crossing sequences. Having been filmed like a scripted documentary, it also lacks curiosity and the sense of wonder and discovery about the profilmic world that distinguished *Grass*, which remains an unsurpassed expedition documentary of one of humanity's vanishing ways of life.

Notes

1. I would like to thank the following people who over the many years of my research on *Grass* agreed to be interviewed; corresponded with me; and put at my disposal documents, photographs, reviews, and other personal items related to the works of the Cooper-Schoedsack-Harrison team. They are Jalal Asghar (Schoedsack's friend), Kevin Brownlow (film historian), Dorothy Cooper (Cooper's wife), Robert Dickson (filmmaker), Dennis Doros (Milestone Films and Video), Dr. John Gilmore (Schoedsack's optometrist), Shusha Guppy (writer and folk singer), Khosrow Zolqadr Sadeghi (Schoedsack's friend), Peter Schoedsack (Schoedsack's son), Maxine Swanson (former Maxine Logan, Maxine Howard, and Maxine Butcher, nurse and caretaker of Schoedsack in his last years), Gerry Veeder (film scholar), and Ken Wiley (Schoedsack's friend). Not all of these sources are cited here. Jeff Fegley helped with scanning the stills. This research was partially funded by a National Endowment for Humanities Travel to Collections grant.

2. By the mid-1960s, Schoedsack had lost his sight due to a detached retina,

glaucoma, and bullous keratitis (Gilmore 1983). He became a bitter, cantankerous, and paranoid man who demanded narcotics for his pain and sometimes hallucinated about fighting the Iranian tribes (Swanson 1984). He communicated with distant friends by audiotapes. I have a copy of his tape letter narrating the complete story of the making of *Grass* (Schoedsack 1971).

3. At the time, the Il-Khani was Gholamhosain Khan Sardar Mohtasham and the Il-Begi was Mohammad Taqi Khan Amir Jang. There were two Baba Ahmadi tribes, Baba Ahmadi-ye Kashki and Baba Ahmadi-ye Sarajeddin. The U.S. filmmakers were attached to the Kashki branch (Samsam 1984).

4. The version of this letter reproduced in Cooper's book (1925: 13) is markedly different, supplying more information about the route taken. Dated 5 June 1924, it states that Cooper, Schoedsack, and Harrison are "the first foreigners who have made the 46-day migration with the Baba Ahmadi tribe of the Bakhtyari, over the Zardeh Kuh trail from the Jungari district in Arabistan to the Chahar Mahal valley in Ehleck."

5. The low regard of the title writer, Terry Ramsey, for the tribes and his instrumentalist view of intertitles come through in his letter in *Atlantic Monthly* in response to a review of *Grass* that the periodical had published. He states: "The fact is that the Bakhtyari are shown merely driving their cows over a mountain to pastures. They do it twice a year. It is a chore, not an epic, even if I did utter considerable typographical excitement on the screen about it." Reacting to the reviewer's admission of enjoying the "wealth of details," he notes that "she may have enjoyed it, but she did not see it. It was not in the pictorial negative. That beautiful detail was Barnumed into words calculated to speed the spectator past the camera's omissions" (1926: 142–43).

6. Even the catalogue of Kodascope Library, which circulated *Grass*, bore such an attitude: "In all the world, only three white people have ever seen this marvelous depiction of elemental life and mighty courage" (*Descriptive Catalogue of Kodascope Library* 1932: 193).

7. Milestone has the rights to *Grass* until 2015, when the copyright runs out (Doros 2000). The musical score is by Gholamhosain Janati-Ataie, Kavous Shirzadian, and Amirali Vahabzadegan.

Trans-Saharan Automotive Cinema

CITROËN-, RENAULT-, AND PEUGEOT-SPONSORED

DOCUMENTARY INTERWAR CROSSING FILMS

PETER J. BLOOM

The major French automobile manufacturers, Peugeot, Renault, and Citroën, sponsored film expeditions across the Sahara during the interwar period in the context of an emerging tourist economy in North Africa. These expeditions served as potent symbols of the French automobile industry and France's geopolitical ambitions. The best known of these films were the feature-length documentaries sponsored by André Citroën, founder of the Citroën automobile firm. The Citroën crossing films featured the movement of caterpillar-tread half-track vehicles, known as *autochenilles*, across the French colonies and into adjacent territories (Figure 1). The movement of these half-track vehicles was featured in *La traversée du Sahara* (Traversing the Sahara, 1923),[1] *La croisière noire* (The Black Cruise, 1926), and *La croisière jaune* (The Yellow Cruise, 1932).[2]

These crossing films featured exotic landscapes from the perspective of an automotive expedition—indexing an archaeological, ethnographic, and geographic repertoire within the context of French colonial ideologies of hygienic, educational, and political reform. More pragmatically, these films served as a moving visual catalogue of French colonial territory presented in an ambiguous relationship to the expanding forces of leisure travel and tourism. The Citroën films featured the automobile as an emerging form of tourist discovery that relied on an extensive network of shipping and railroad lines. By 1923 it took only twenty-four hours to get from Marseilles to most of the North African port cities, thanks to the expansion of the Compagnie Générale Transatlantique passenger ships, which were, in turn, linked to an extensive network of railway itineraries

1 A diagram of the 1926 Citroën caterpillar-tread half-track vehicle, known as the *autochenille*. Copyright Citroën Communication.

and hotel accommodations (Du Tallis 1923: 30–31). Given the history of French conquest, occupation, and integration of Algeria as a *département* of France as of 1881, it was a destination with a well-developed infrastructure for tourism.

However, the appeal of the North African vacation holiday was less indebted to its familiarity than to its proximity to the Saharan desert —popularly perceived as the great decompression chamber of Western civilization. It was in this space, which had been minutely charted on numerous geographic and military expeditions, that a desert fantasy of sexual and temporal dislocation could be imagined. After the First World War, the French fascination with the Sahara was perhaps most evocatively illustrated in Jacques Feyder's 1921 feature film *L'Atlantide*,[3] adapted from Pierre Benoît's popular novel, published in 1919. In *L'Atlantide*, Queen Antinéa (Stacia Napierkowska), with her ancient Egyptian charms, seduces a long history of eminent European men whose bodies are preserved as taxidermic trophies in her castle hidden away in the gorges of the Saharan desert. Significantly, the world of Antinéa was outside time and history and was a site of no return for those men who were seduced, trapped, and finally exhibited in her lair. Furthermore, as Abdelkader Benali relates, Feyder's adaptation of the novel emphasized the lost civilization of Atlantis as the mysterious source of Antinéa's origins (1998: 105). Antinéa's servants and henchmen reinforced her ancient origins, depicting an Egyptian lineage of master and slave as contiguous with Tuareg culture, as opposed to the democratic enlightenment impulse of French civilization. The sexual appeal of Queen Antinéa and the Atlantis referent were so powerful that in the published travel account that accompanied the release of the first Citroën documentary entitled *La traversée du Sahara*, the subtitle for the work was *De Touggourt à Tombouctou par l'Atlantide* (From Touggourt to Timbuktu through Atlantis), which also appeared as a title heading on each page of the text. "*Par L'Atlantide*" appeared on all of the right-hand pages of the volume, directly referencing Benoît's novel and Feyder's film, and "*De Touggourt à Tombouctou*" appeared on the all of the left-hand pages, referencing the politically contentious Transsaharien railroad project.

The Transsaharien was the French trans-Saharan railroad project that sought to create a railroad link between Algeria and sub-Saharan Africa. The Touggourt-Timbuktu railroad itinerary was subject to an ongoing political debate. The Transsaharien was initially proposed by Henri Duveyrier,[4] a French explorer who first traveled to the Sahara in 1859 and made contact with various Tuareg leaders in the region.[5] Duveyrier suggested a trans-Saharan route from Algiers to Timbuktu in order to establish a gateway to an intersecting sub-Saharan east-west junction between Senegal to the west, in French West Africa, and Djibouti to the east, in what was known as French Soudan.

A network of railroad lines was built throughout northern Algeria, Tunisia, and West Africa during the last third of the nineteenth century. Extensive railway service was established in Northern Algeria as early as 1862 with the Algiers-Blida line, and by 1891 nearly 1,800 miles of railway track linked port cities such as Bône, Blida, Algiers, Oran, and Tunis to Algerian regional centers such as Constantine, Biskra, Berrouaghia, and Aïn-Sefra (Philebert and Rolland 1890). By 1918 the Biskra-Touggourt line was built, and the end of this railroad itinerary in Touggourt was the launching point for the first of the Citroën expeditions led by Georges-Marie Haardt and Louis Audouin-Dubreuil.

The automobile journey across the Sahara seized on prevailing public debates about the Transsaharien. The Citroën caterpillar-tread vehicles were a powerful substitute for the railroad, as if the caterpillar tread, in its tractor-like capacity, had cleared the way for a phantom railway system. The caterpillar treads' continuous imprint attempted to unify a geographic surface while demonstrating the accessibility of the colonies to France.

La traversée du Sahara featured the automobile as a survey vehicle illustrating geographic contours of the desert landscape as a metonym for a civilization lost in time and history. The expedition embodied the values of industrial rationality, with seemingly neutral manned half-track vehicles traveling through nomadic Tuareg communities in the Saharan desert. The vastness of the luminous desert landscape was a site of psycho-historical projection for European fantasies of otherness, a "lost" socio-cultural historical past, and an empty space to be mapped, contained, and ultimately used to undertake the first French nuclear testing near Reggane and the Hoggar Massif region in 1960.[6]

Touggourt was chosen as the starting point of the expedition because it was the last stop on the railroad line that ran from Algiers via the northern port city of Biskra, toward the central approach through the Sahara. As a French-produced Dunlop guide for North African automobile tourism published in 1923 explains, the area surrounding Touggourt was an evocative mise-en-scène for Saharan tourism (Du Tallis 1923: 219). The guide continues to describe the attributes of Touggourt:

> Alas, the sand makes normal automobile excursions nearly impossible. Fortunately, caterpillar-tread half-track vehicles have passed through and opened up innumerable paths for Saharan tourism; let us gaze at the sunlight languishing on the dunes, intersecting with towering palms that weave a magical background for the sandscapes of "Antinéa," the site where principal scenes from *L'Atlantide* were filmed. (219)

This passage links the recently completed Citroën expedition with the evocative landscapes that served as an exterior shooting location in Feyder's *L'Atlantide*. The rhetorical interplay between sunlight, sand, and the feminine charms of Antinéa evoked a visual spectacle that appealed to an emerging tourist economy. On the basis of French Touring Club statistics, Patrick Young has claimed that as early as 1910, there were over 35,000 tourists who visited Algiers that year, and Marthe Barbance estimates that there were more than 350,000 who traveled from France to Algeria and Tunisia in 1923 (Furlough 2002: 451). Tourists were attracted to the extended desert geography, where the automobile became an increasingly viable form of adventure.

As André Citroën explains in his introduction to the volume detailing the expedition, it was partially envisioned as a topographic survey for the projected expansion of the railway line through the Sahara, and the half-track vehicles, he asserts, were best suited to this task because they functioned as "moving rails" along this difficult terrain (1923: 5–24). After more than fifty years of wrangling over specific itineraries for the construction of a trans-Saharan railway, the Touggourt-Timbuktu route was a trans-Saharan itinerary that reflected Citroën's political patrons in the partisan debate. In fact, subsequent public discussions about railroad itineraries shifted south of the Sahara. By the time *La traversée du Sahara* was released in 1923, the Transsaharien had been supplanted by the trans-African railroad project known as the *Transafricain*. It was to be a "continental" railroad route serving as the "vertebral column" of the French colonial empire on the African continent, linking raw materials to ports while allowing the swift deployment of large-scale military and labor contingents (Leblond 1944: 129–30). *La croisière noire*, the best known of the Citroën crossing films, served as the illustration of potential continental itineraries for such a project.

It was argued that the Touggourt-Timbuktu itinerary was critical to unifying the various trans-African railway lines, and, ironically, it was never built because airplane and automobile travel as well as expanded port facilities had finally eclipsed its utility. The numerous exploratory missions and detailed surveys of the Sahara turned the desert landscape into a testing ground for the French automobile after the First World War. Automobile excursions in northern Algeria, Morocco, and Tunisia were first introduced by private companies in response to trade and tourism from 1898 to 1908 but were later used by the French Army in the Sahara immediately following the First World War.

The introduction of the automobile into the Sahara by 1916 coincided with a renewed spirit of Tuareg defiance, which might explain why the first Citroën half-track automobiles were, in fact, militarized reconnaissance vehicles. The importance of a road linking Touggourt to the Ahaggar region via Ouargla and In Salah was recognized by French military leaders as early as 1915 (Ferré 1931: 28). One of the first Saharan automobile itineraries was a twenty-day 289-mile journey from Ouargla to In Salah with two vehicles.[7] One of the participants, Commander Bettembourg, recalls that only one of two vehicles arrived at In Salah. One of the vehicles was abandoned along the way, and the vehicle that arrived benefited from "the combined effort of wooden planks, the shovel, camels, and elbow grease" (Gradis 1924: 12). This itinerary later culminated in subsequent automobile and airplane excursions used to establish road itineraries and refueling points. It was in 1920, during one of the early airplane itineraries, that General Laperrine, the architect of French military strategy in the Sahara, died from injuries resulting from a plane crash. The cult of men piloting dangerously fast machines who sought to master

2 The Gaumont
poster used to promote
La traversée du Sahara
(1923) with an image
of Tuareg tribesman
with camel in Saharan
landscape. Copyright
Citroën Communica-
tion.

the desert landscape was established from this early moment and continues into the present with the Paris-Dakar auto rallye.

La traversée du Sahara begins with the following set of intertitles:
"From the dawn of antiquity, communication across the desert could only
be assured by camel-driven caravans . . . which slowly crossed the immense desert landscape . . . The vast French colonial domain in Africa
requires more rapid communication . . . This is being made possible by
courageous men, with the help of the *auto-chenilles*." These opening intertitles are complemented by a series of long shots starting with a group of
camels being led by nomads, followed by a vacant desert landscape, and
an image of the half-track vehicles. The nomadic lifestyle associated with
camels, caravans, the desert landscape, and the fully veiled nomads is opposed to the modernity of the caterpillar-tread vehicle in this opening
segment of the film (Figure 2). The opening intertitles stress the importance of rapid communication, which serves as an oppositional framing
device throughout the film. Facilitating rapid communication meant the

efficient deployment of French troops, the promotion of French hygienic and medical techniques, and French mail service, as well as French educational efforts based on the "universality" of the French language. Short segments throughout the film illustrate these efforts. The opposition between camel-driven salt caravans and the half-track vehicles is a more complicated story.

The salt caravans depicted in this opening scene were a response to an entrenched network of French zones of occupation that altered grazing patterns for livestock and crucial access to water. The French territorial expansion in the region not only shifted how Tuareg groups secured their livelihood but transformed power relationships between tribal leaders in the region. Amenoukal Akhamouk, who appears in a brief segment of the film, exchanging gifts with leaders of the expedition, is introduced as the sovereign leader of the Ahaggar region, which was the largest section of the desert itinerary. The Amenoukal is a leadership role that the French greatly expanded under Akhamouk's predecessor, Moussa ag Amastane (Keenan 1977: 89–92). In the film, the image of Amenoukal Akhamouk, whose face and body were fully covered in the black-veiled garment known as the "litham," reinforces the mystery of the people and landscape of the Sahara.

The even more elaborate greeting and tea ceremony used to introduce Amenoukal Akhamouk in one of the short films[8] derived from the same footage used to make *La traversée du Sahara* illustrates Terence Ranger's observation that "indigenous traditions" were formalized and ritualized in the colonial context as a means of accentuating "traditions of subordination" ([1983] 1992: 223). Public displays of traditional authority figures supported the contention that French colonization efforts were part of a civilizing process, and gave the erroneous impression that the French deferred to local authority figures.

La traversée du Sahara is structured as a travelogue through a set of intertitles interspersed with a brief series of shots. Significantly, the camera movement was almost exclusively positioned in the vehicles themselves in a number of mobile point-of-view shots. The film introduces the significance of the half-track vehicle as a swift and reliable means of communication across the Sahara desert, which is followed by an illustration of the genesis of half-track technology and the organization of the voyage under André Citroën's sponsorship. The film then presents the actual itinerary of the voyage in three parts, subdividing the itinerary into segments, culminating in the arrival at Timbuktu. After reaching Timbuktu the voyagers embark on a brief hunting expedition in Niger[9] and then return to Touggourt following the same route used to get to Timbuktu. Their return to Touggourt is punctuated by the arrival of André Citroën, his wife, and Adolfe Kégresse, the inventor of the caterpillar tread half-track mechanism, who greet the voyagers at the halfway point of their abbreviated return itinerary.

With ten members of the expedition, five vehicles, and their mascot Flossie, frequent reference to maps of the region, the tracing of their itinerary, as well as the ritual departure of the vehicles serve as recurring visual elements. Flossie was, in fact, Haardt's white-coated Sealyham terrier, who later became immortalized as Milou, the canine adventuress in Hergé's celebrated *Tintin* comic strip (Reynolds 1996: 95). As early prototypes of the all-terrain military amphibious vehicle, the half-track vehicles were equipped with machine guns, built-in expandable tents, and flip-down sinks with running water. *La traversée*'s itinerary is a virtual tour of French military pacification efforts in the Sahara, reflecting familiar motifs associated with colonial adventure—the desert sand, the automobile, the all-male military unit, and stereotyped imagery of geographically specific ethnic populations. The film was finally edited into a fifty-minute documentary for the general public.

Georges-Marie Haardt, the co-pilot of the expedition, told Léon Poirier, the filmmaker hired to accompany the *La croisière noire* expedition less than a year later, that *La traversée du Sahara* was made by a film operator who specialized in the travelogue format, such that the film does not convey the full intensity of the desert (Poirier 1953: 63). Haardt wanted Poirier to portray the visual sensation of the desert landscape in *La croisière noire*, transforming the documentary conceit of the film into an evocation of the desert in the first part. Paul Castelnau, the filmmaker who directed *La traversée du Sahara*,[10] was a geographer by training whose involvement with cinematography began through his association with the geographer Jean Brunhes, a primary theorist of *la géographie humaine*. This school of thought linked geography to ethnography in a Bergsonian-inspired colonial encounter. More directly stated, to paraphrase Achille Mbembe, Bergsonian colonialism reduced the colonized to animals in their native habitat, where familiarity and domestication subsequently served as the dominant tropes of servitude (2001: 27). This mode of colonial engagement is even more apparent in Poirier's *La croisière noire*, which has been out of circulation for many years, in part because of its self-assured approach to imagining African subjects as native fauna specific to particular regions of the continent. Castelnau worked as a traveling film operator whose most important benefactor was Albert Kahn. (For more on Kahn, see Paula Amad's essay in this volume.) Kahn commissioned Castelnau to make numerous films in Asia, Africa, and the Middle East.

As was true of many pedagogical and travelogue films of the period, there was more than one version of *La traversée du Sahara* in circulation. In the two versions of the film that I have screened there is a discrepancy between the titles, as well as variations in length and the content of the intertitles. In addition to multiple versions of the same film, a twelve-part series of short films known as *Le continent mystérieux* (The Mysterious Continent, 1924) was released the year after *La traversée du Sahara*. It featured extended thematic reflections with excess footage from the expedition for particular aspects of the itinerary, such as the Saharan oasis, indigenous scenes, extended views of the desert landscape, and views at In Salah, Ouargla, Timbuktu, and along the banks of the Niger River.

A recurrent theme was the depiction of African women in various states of undress. In contrast to the image of Antinéa as vamp in *L'Atlantide*, African women were depicted in the Citroën films as alternatively titillating, submissive, or saddled with arduous forms of domestic labor. Women of the Ouled-Naïl tribe (known as Nailiyat) are shown performing *la danse du ventre* (belly dance) in the fourth episode of *Le continent mystérieux*, entitled *Scènes indigènes à Ouargla* (Indigenous Scenes in Ouargla). The Nailiyat are introduced in opposition to their "warrior" male counterparts as "sirens of love." Marnia Lazreg (1994) has described the precolonial situation of the Nailiyat, who were later considered prostitutes in French colonial Algeria, as a group of women from the Ouled Naïl tribe who enjoyed a degree of sexual freedom that was not uncommon among women in nearby communities. These women would leave their rural milieu and entertain men in nearby towns with song and dance. Nailiyat women did not solicit, nor did they ask for money, but did depend on the generosity of their clients to help their families pay taxes on land used for farming.

The town of Bou Saada, located on the plateau of the Ouled Naïl Mountains, became known as the capitol of Nailiyat hospitality and dance performance. While these women typically performed fully clothed, the regional French Syndicat d'initiative, or tourist bureau, influenced the character of their performances and insisted that they perform nude before their European visitors, transforming them into tourist spectacles by the 1880s. This shift toward tourism initiated a process in which their freedom of movement was restricted, and women associated with Nailiyat dance performance were issued identity cards classifying them as prostitutes subject to periodic medical check-ups (Lazreg 1994: 29–33). By the interwar period, the Nailiyat became synonymous with prostitution in France thanks to the vigorous development of the picture postcard market.

The critics Malek Alloula (1986) and Leïla Sebbar and Jean-Michel Belorgey (2002) have described the way North African women were visually depicted to titillate and promote the availability of these women as part of an emerging colonial tourist fantasy. The population of Algerian prostitutes, though stereotyped as Nailiyat, was, in fact, part of the same population of orphaned girl children, as Sebbar's contribution suggests, who were taken in by the French Catholic missionaries and trained in silk weaving and lace making (2002: 11). Some of the women became practitioners of the highly sought-after Arab lacework technique, which is abundantly visible on serialized postcards depicting Arab women in various poses. Images of their work are presented in *Le continent mystérieux*, and an homage to Cardinal Lavigerie, founder of the Catholic African Missions, appears in *La traversée du Sahara*.

The Nailiyat were a recurrent subject in a number of expedition-related films of the period. In *Scènes indigènes à Ouargla* (episode 4 of *Le Continent Mystérieux*), the Nailiyat dancers appear as the centerpiece of a celebration after other women are shown performing women's work, which included the fashioning of wool spools, rug making, and preparing couscous for a celebration. The segment of three young bare-breasted women demonstrating la danse du ventre is immediately followed by an older woman dressed in white who gestures toward the cameraman, inviting him to witness other dancers. This segment is followed by an image of the Chaamba *fastasia* celebration with warriors on horseback shooting into the air as they gallop by a group of spectators. These images were recycled in *La croisière noire*, as well as in at least two of the more than fifty short films made over the course of the Croisière noire expedition.

In one of these short films, *Lève africaine* (African Awakening), recycled images of the Nailiyat dancers appear. This time, however, one of the dancers is identified as Zina, who is presented as a woman who responds to her clients' desires, but as the intertitles explain, she chooses them carefully and leaves it to her servants to please the crowd. This is followed by an extended dance sequence with images of musicians and Nailiyat dancers. In the film, which primarily incorporates footage shot over the course of the Croisière noire expedition, prostitution, the profession for which the Nailiyat became nearly synonymous, is associated with Congolese women. The Nailiyat practice of prostitution is merely referenced in the intertitle that reads, "Arab penetration did not include the introduction of Nailiyat dancing, nor their practices of prostitution." In one way, this intertitle refers to the art of Nailiyat seduction as opposed to prostitution practiced by Congolese women. The expansion of prostitution under the French occupation of Algeria was formalized by the "Arab bureau" and was zoned to certain quarters of the French colonial cities catering to the appetites of the French military at first and subsequently to the demands of European sex tourism (Lazreg 1994: 55–59).

Further, "Arab penetration" in Lève africaine casts Arab men as the ravishers of Congolese women, imagined here as sexual predators. The denigration of Arab men identifies them with a past historical moment, analogous to the period of the European Crusades. The fastasia segment that follows the Nailiyat dancers in Le continent mystérieux features the Tuareg, presumably examples of Arab soldiers, who were considered reminiscent of warriors from the Bronze Age, trapped in a medieval past. The geographical diffusionist depiction of Africans in La traversée du Sahara and La croisière noire uses geography as a means of charting their historical and civilized state relative to metropolitan France. The fairground-like depictions of African ethnic groups suggested a colonial geographic theme park of cultural and historical attractions. These attractions were codified once they began to appear as popular ethnographic exhibitions and were inscribed into a cinematic travel itinerary.

Automobile travel became explicitly associated with privileged access to exotic landscapes. As André Citroën and Louis Renault vied for a leadership role in the French automobile industry after the First World War, the Sahara became the new theater for automobile performance allied with the cultural trappings of the expedition. The success of La traversée du Sahara was followed by a series of Renault expeditions which culminated in the development of a vehicle outfitted with six large twinned tires for the Mission Gradis.[11] The Mission Gradis introduced a new itinerary that departed from the newly completed Colomb-Béchar (Algeria) railway station. This expedition represented a new beginning for the Transsaharien project, tracing a Western itinerary that was the shortest distance across the desert into French West Africa.

The competition between Renault and Citroën began with the expansion of their factories to serve the military during the First World War, with Citroën applying Taylorist techniques of assembly-line production to produce artillery shells in record time. The intersecting itineraries of Citroën and Renault expeditions continued on the African continent throughout the interwar period. The various Renault expeditions were less sensational than the Citroën expeditions, given André Citroën's flair for publicity and willingness to devote substantial resources toward their organization and presentation to the public. At least two films featured Renault vehicles on the African continent between 1924 and 1926—a Saharan crossing film that documented the first Mission Gradis and a second film known as *Les mystères du continent noir* (1926) that presented the eight-month Mission Gradis Delingette, which followed a trans-African itinerary from Oran to Cape Town. Georges-Michel Coissac, one of the most prolific French film critics of the interwar period, writes that a film featuring Renault automobiles was released in 1924, *La première traversée rapide du desert (329 heures)* (The First Rapid Crossing of the Sahara [329 hours]) (1931: 61). Although there is scant evidence about this film,[12] it would have documented the first expedition led by Gaston Gradis from Colomb-Béchar to Agosango (located in the Niger basin). The title of the film was a direct challenge to Citroën's *La traversée du Sahara*, given the increased speed and agility of the Renault vehicles.

The "rapid crossing of the Sahara" as opposed to "the crossing of the Sahara in half-track vehicles" evokes a theme central to the earliest public displays of the automobile—the overland auto race. The automobile itineraries across the Sahara by Citroën, Renault, and Peugeot capitalized on the enthusiasm in France for open-road auto races that established a proving ground for the first automobiles. A Peugeot film, shot over the course of the Prost-Peugeot expedition, was released as *Images d'Afrique* (1926). It traced part of what came to be known as the Paris-Dakar auto rallye, with a round-trip Algiers-Dakar itinerary that departed from Paris. This film appeared in numerous versions, being re-edited and supplemented until 1942.

As with the advent of cinema, France led in the development of automobile construction. In 1895, the same year that the Lumière Cinématographe was patented, the first nonstop, 730-mile auto rallye was staged between Versailles and Bordeaux and back. The open-road automobile itineraries in France drew spectators from villages and cities alike, successfully transferring the enthusiasm for professional cycling competitions to the speed and agility of the automobile. A community of spectators that validated the Cinématographe as a founding apparatus of cinema was also present to witness the automobile as a physical means of travel, a vehicle of exploration that could penetrate the most remote corners of the country.

The most popular early open-road automobile itineraries in Europe included the Paris-Marseilles-Paris race in 1896, the Paris-Bordeaux race in 1897, and the Paris-Amsterdam-Paris race in 1898, along with many shorter contests (Laux 1992: 9–10). The commercialization of the Citroën half-track vehicles was a bridge to a new type of travel experience that promised an encounter with "primitive civilizations" not previously accessible to the metropolitan traveler. The confluence of the automobile and a new kind of travel experience in the Sahara was recognized by both André Citroën and Louis Renault. The success of *La traversée du Sahara* convinced André Citroën that he should develop an overland Saharan travel package for affluent European tourists, and Renault followed suit with his own Saharan overland itinerary.

While the Renault automobiles eventually dominated the Saharan itinerary, the Citroën films left a lasting impact on popular audiences, initiating a cycle of short documentary films that provided visual tableaux of the French colonial empire on the African continent. The Croisière noire expedition left Colomb-Béchar on 24 October 1924, with eight caterpillar-tread vehicles and entered Tananarive, Madagascar, eight months later on 26 July 1925. Once the expedition was completed, it became the best-known French crossing expedition and documentary film of the interwar period. The will to create an exhaustive itinerary on the African continent was so powerful that once the expedition reached Kampala, it split up into four different units in order to traverse several different destinations, including Cape Town (South Africa), Mombasa (Kenya), Dar-Es-Salaam (Tanzania), and Beira (Mozambique). Approximately 88,582 feet of film was shot over the course of the journey (Haardt 1927: v), which was edited into short-subject documentary films that simultaneously specified and visually stereotyped the continent. These documentary shorts were presented as supplemental travelogues and pedagogical films and were finally used to demonstrate how various objects that were collected over the course of the expedition were used in context.

Those objects were the subject of a popular exhibition held at the Musée des Arts Decoratifs in 1926, which served as one of the models for the large-scale French Colonial International Exhibition of 1931. Significantly, Léon Poirier's feature-length documentary of the expedition was featured at a number of prestigious venues in France and Belgium.[13] The film premiered with a live orchestra at the Opéra Garnier on 2 March 1926, with Gaston Doumergue, the president of the republic, in attendance. The film was dedicated to the youth of France and became a symbol of French colonial humanism on the African continent. It illustrated a trans-African itinerary along the length of the continent, and by special arrangement with the minister of the colonies, the various sub-itineraries were consolidated such that they converged at the port of Majunga, Madagascar, in order to ceremoniously complete the expedition in Tananarive, the capital of Madagascar. This final leg of the itinerary demonstrated the geographic contours of the French colonial empire on the African continent as a unified body that could be revitalized and infused with the spirit of metropolitan France.

As the French historian Gilbert Meynier has written, the French colonial empire represented a body to be activated, strong but incapable of action, in need of centralized mental conditioning emanating from the French mind (1990: 78–79). In France, the crossing films demonstrated these geographic bodily extensions as a conflation of untended geographic landscapes and ethnic populations. Therapeutic reconditioning was promoted in an extended archive of colonial films that prescribed an interrelated set of industrial, medical, military, and physical activities in the spirit of an interwar discourse of colonial humanism.

A compelling feature of the half-track vehicle is the looping of the metallic-rubber caterpillar tread that imprints the geographic landscape, almost like the movement of a mechanical clock, echoing the constancy of modulated propulsion. In other words, the half-track vehicle defined distance and territory in terms of time and the clockwise movement forward. The movement of the clock, which has been so instrumental in the development of the film transport system for the motion picture camera, relies on the interaction of gears and the counteraction of propulsion and stoppage. In the words of the media archaeologist Siegfried Zielinski, "The clock acquires its hold on time by continually and forcibly disciplining it and not allowing it to run freely" (1999: 74).

The motion picture camera, a time-preservation machine, modulated motion, manually at first but soon regulated by a constant current of electricity. Further, the African itineraries of the Citroën crossing films imply the chronological indexing of civilization, with metropolitan France standing in for the most advanced state of industrial and cultural agency. The half-track vehicle disciplines the landscape in the service of its itinerary and charts relative human difference through the hypnotic regularity of the caterpillar tread in motion, overcoming geographic and cultural obstacles.

The relentless caterpillar-tread physically stamps a surface as it grinds forward, and the film emulsion records surfaces through its modulated exposure to light. In the Citroën crossing films, the half-track vehicle and the motion picture camera were both used to create the illusion of a totalizing geographic picture, analogous to a Heideggerian "world picture" that is imagined as a global geographic itinerary and structured as moving pictures (see Tom Gunning's essay in this volume). Creating a totalizing geographic picture of the African continent was precisely the goal of *La croisière noire*. The logistics for the expedition required numerous military supply lines as well as airplane and hydroplane support. The Croisière noire was the equivalent of a large-scale military survey expedition, in spite of the fact that only eighteen men served as members of the expedition.

The culmination of the numerous events planned throughout 1926 was the well-attended Croisière noire exhibiton, which was held in six large halls at the Musée des Arts Décoratifs, located in a wing of the Louvre, for several months. Georges-Marie Haardt's caterpillar-tread half-track vehicle known as La scarabée d'or (The Golden Beetle) stood at the center of the largest room surrounded by a menagerie of taxidermied animals. The other rooms, as reported in the *Bulletin Citroën*, consisted of a "treasure trove" of objects, including jewelry, religious articles, pottery, and musical instruments that were collected over the course of the expedition. Three dioramas were also constructed, which attempted to depict three different scenes from the continent. In addition, one of the rooms was dedicated to an array of drawings produced by Alexandre Iacovleff, the artist sent to accompany the expedition. Finally, adjoining the exhibition halls, a theater projected a steady stream of fifty-two short documentary films that were filmed over the course of the expedition (*Bulletin Citroën* 1926: 397–405).

The films were an attempt to create a context for objects on display at the exhibit. For the numerous galas that were associated with *La croisière noire*, Josephine Baker, the celebrated African American émigré performer, was a reigning presence. André Citroën was an avid fan of her dance and music to the extent that he gave her a Citroën B14 Sports Cabriolet automobile. John Reynolds writes in his biography of Citroën that Baker returned Citroën's adoration by singing that she had only two

154 PETER J. BLOOM

3 A Belgian poster used to promote *La croisière noire* (1926) using the image of a Mangbetu woman with a distinctive headdress. Copyright Citroën Communication.

loves in her life, her country and Citroën (1996: 81). In one celebrated episode, Baker wore a hat and hairstyle that referenced the Mangbetu coiffure, which was the key image on the best-known poster advertising *La croisière noire* (Figure 3). The Mangbetu hairstyle was featured in *Vogue* magazine in 1926, and Mme Agnès, a Parisian hair designer who worked with the fashion houses in the La Madeleine area, developed this fashionable hairstyle for an affluent clientele (*Bulletin Citroën* 1926: 262).

The Mangbetu people of northeastern Congo were represented in numerous texts by German explorers throughout the nineteenth century. The nineteenth-century "Mangbetu myth" depicted them as noble savages who engaged in cannibalism but lived in the splendor of a royal court culture. Christraud Geary asserts that in popular and scholarly thought of the period, the Mangbetu variations in physiognomy and skin color were attributed to a mixture of Bantu with Semitic and Hamidic races, which occupied a higher position in the European racial hierarchy (1998: 147). The image of the Mangbetu that appears on the poster for *La croisière noire* was modeled from a photograph taken during the expedition. The elongated head shape served to sexualize the image of the African woman, with the open end of the headdress, similar to the open end of a funnel, a point of entry into the African geographic body. The poster image of the Mangbetu woman, like the appeal of Queen Antinéa in *L'Atlantide*, pins female sexuality to the mystery of the landscape.

Finally, the Citroën crossing films were indeed part of the modernity culture of the film travelogue. The images of the African continent portrayed in the Citroën crossing films were an invitation to a world of travel accessible through the medium of the automobile. The commodification of tourist adventure became a new way of imagining cultural difference at a distance, transforming the colonial burden from a form of conquest into a humanitarian endeavor. The cinema marked this shift by demonstrating the permeability of frontiers that were visually depicted as thematic stereotypes. The automobile was thus invested with the ability to travel through these projected stereotypes as part of a cinematographic time machine.

Notes

1. The full title of the film varied between *La traversée du Sahara en auto-chenilles* and *La traversée du Sahara en automobiles*. I refer to this film as *La traversée du Sahara* throughout the text. The Gaumont release featured the title ending in "*auto-chenilles*," which was also prominently featured in poster art for the film. A vhs version of the film held by the Citroën archive is entitled *La traversée du Sahara en automobiles*.

2. A fourth Citroën film, entitled *La croisière blanche* (a.k.a. The Bedeaux Sub-Arctic Expedition, Charles E. Bedeaux, 1934), was commissioned but never completed. It depicts a journey across Canada now held in the form of outtakes at the Canadian Film Archive in Ottawa. Charles E. Bedeaux was a scientific industrial engineer who led chronometic studies at the Citroën factories during the 1920s. According to Milestone Films, the Canadian filmmaker George Ungar is currently restoring this film.

3. Because of the enormous popularity of Feyder's *L'Atlantide*, a sound remake was directed by G. W. Pabst in 1932. For further discussion of the two films, see Benali 1998 and Slavin 2001.

4. In a number of accounts, the French linguist Georges Hanoteaux was credited with suggesting the idea of the Transsaharien some time before Duveyrier (Guy 1900).

5. Henri Duveyrier (1840–92) was the son of a well-known Saint-Simonist, Charles Duveyrier. Henri was sent to study in Germany, where he learned Arabic before traveling to Algeria (Pottier 1938). Further, the Saint-Simonists were among the most ardent supporters of railroad construction, holding a utopian socialist view that the railroad embodied the potential for progressive social reform.

6. For more information about the history of French nuclear testing, see Barrillot 1990.

7. Alison Murray writes that General Laperrine was the first to undertake the journey from Ouargla to In Salah in 1916. There is contradictory evidence regarding this voyage because Laperrine was recalled from the Somme only a year later, in 1917. See her informative article for further detail about the Citroën tourism agenda (2000).

8. *Le continent mystérieux: Part VI: Méharistes et Touareg* (Castelnau 1924), 11 minutes.

9. The sequences from Niger to Gao on the return trip were filmed by an officer known as De Ceris, who was part of the support team for the expedition (Haardt and Audouin-Dubreuil 1923).

10. Léon Poirier writes that Georges Sprecht, his film operator during *La croisière noire*, took over the editing of *La traversée du Sahara* upon Castelnau's return to Paris (1953).

11. This was the first of two expeditions led by Gaston Gradis using three specially equipped large six-wheel double-tire Renault vehicles. It departed from Colomb-Béchar on 25 January 1924, achieved its destination in Niger, and returned to Colomb-Béchar on 1 March 1924 (Gradis 1924).

12. Although I have not been able to locate this film or verify its existence, it is likely that it was filmed during the first Mission Gradis if, as Coissac asserts, the film was released in 1924. The second Mission Gradis Delingette was undertaken from 15 November to 11 December 1924 and then continued with Mme Delingette toward Cape Town, South Africa (De Kerillis 1925).

13. Some of these venues included the Belgian Royal Court, the Théâtre de la Monnaie in Brussels, the Grand Amphitheater of the Musée d'Histoire Naturelle. *La croisière noire* was screened at the Sorbonne and was shown regularly at the Théâtre Marivaux for the Parisian public (*Bulletin Citroën* 1926: 292–94).

Homemade Travelogues

Autosonntag—A FILM SAFARI IN THE SWISS ALPS

To travel is to possess the world.
—Burton Holmes, *The World Is Mine*

ALEXANDRA SCHNEIDER

||||||||||||||||||||||||||||||||||||||||||||||||||||||||||||||||||||||||||||||||||||||||||||||||||||||||||

In June 1930, a certain Herr H. traveled together with his wife and another couple from Zurich to the Kloental Valley, where the four spent a weekend at the Richisau health resort.[1] The 16mm film camera brought along by Herr H. recorded flora and fauna, mountain panoramas, and alpine peasants. The surviving five-and-a-half minute black-and-white silent film shows the city dwellers eating, walking, and exploring the mountains.[2] This little film is an example of touristic amateur filmmaking as it has been practiced, as a hobby or recreational pastime, in the private and semi-private sphere by non- or semi-professionals since the invention of cinematographic technology.[3]

In this essay I would like to propose an approach to travelogue and tourist imaginary based on an individual case study of an amateur film. I will argue that the study of tourist amateur films, far from being a marginal concern for film scholars, allows for a more differentiated understanding of the ways in which travelogues contribute to the formation of the tourist gaze. Furthermore, as I will show in my analysis of Herr H.'s travelogue, home movies and amateur films deserve critical attention because they shed new light on the ways in which media texts interact with and inform everyday life.

Amateur films rarely display an autonomous visual aesthetic, but neither are they simply primitive imitations of works produced according to "professional" standards. Amateur films and home movies are based on a desire to participate in established discourses, and they adapt these discourses in more or less skilful and original ways (Puntigam 1994). In *Autosonntag* (A Sunday Drive)—the title Herr H. gave his film by writing it on the film can—the amateur film intersects with the travelogue and we are treated to a safari to the Swiss interior. Oscillating between spontaneous observation, playful staging, and photographic posing, *Autosonntag* proposes an encounter with the rural world drawing on the conventions of home movies, travelogue, and even expedition films. I will concentrate here on the specific structures of representation and mise-en-scène that arise at the intersection of the amateur film and the visual vocabulary of the tourist film and the travelogue. An analysis of these structures will show that, more than just a particular kind of travelogue, amateur travel films constitute a highly significant record of how amateur filmmakers bring their knowledge of films and cinematographic conventions to bear on the filmmaking process, and how they use that knowledge to mediate and structure the tourist experience. I will argue that the tourist's image-making activities actually contribute to the *production* of the tourist experience. The genre term "amateur film" is here meant to include both private family films (or home movies) and the so-called club films made by organized amateurs.[4] Amateur films are first and foremost "utility films" (to use the British term), utilitarian works shown and seen in specific contexts and made in equally specific environments. If we are to more fully understand the ways in which travelogue, touristic gaze, and amateur film intersect, we must take into account a number of particular characteristics of the practice of private filmmaking.

The Private Practice of Amateur Filmmaking:
Home Movies and Club Films

In the early 1920s the 16mm and 9.5mm formats, which had been specifically conceived for the amateur market, began to catch on as standard formats. Shortly after their introduction, the first amateur film clubs were founded, as part of a general "club" culture, first in England, then in Germany and many other countries.[5] The members of these clubs exchanged know-how and techniques, organized competitions, and published newsletters and handbooks. The clubs helped make it possible to produce and screen "real" films, that is, films reflecting current standards of craftsmanship and storytelling, and also played a role in encouraging members' output by—openly or otherwise—promoting competition between them. In practice, however, it was unusual for a film to travel beyond the boundaries of the club. Apart from their filmmaking activities in the club, members also turned their cameras on family and friends. This may very likely have been the case with *Autosonntag*: an organized amateur takes his camera along on a leisure excursion and, as home moviemakers do, records the shared experiences of family and friends as a souvenir, and perhaps for posterity.

In *Le film de famille* (1995) the French film theorist Roger Odin examines the home movie from a semio-pragmatic perspective. Odin addresses the question of the connection between the stylistic characteristics and the corresponding institutional context of individual film genres. His goal is to find out how the family influences the meaning of specific filmic statements, and how the film satisfies the needs of its spectators. As Odin demonstrates, the home movie works for its spectators (family, friends), not *in spite of* being badly made (*mal fait*) from a professional point of view, but rather *because* it is badly made. The less coherent the text, the less the risk of a conflict between the material shown and the spectators' own memories. In this way, the home movie can offer everyone the possibility of remembering lived experiences according to individual emotional evaluations. As a result, the home movie contributes to the production of a sense of family and may serve to strengthen a sense of community.

In their work on pragmatic communication, both Bronislaw Malinowski and Roman Jakobson have pointed out the potential of the phatic function: those moments in communication in which the goal is not so much the transfer of information or the production of creative texts as the reinforcement and maintenance of communicative relationships (Wulff 1993). In the case of home movies, phatic functions may be found in the collective character of their conditions of production and reception. But the use value of the home movie is not limited to its communicative potential through the activity of jointly making or watching films. Its aesthetic potential—the activity of making a "real" film and the viewing pleasure produced by the film—also contributes to the creation of meaning. The fact that the images in question here are *film* images shapes private image-making practice in a specific way. On the one hand, there is the film's ability to reproduce movement, be it the motion of an object or the movement of the camera. On the other hand, there is also the ability of the film medium to intensify representation as such, since the spectator position intensifies the act of seeing.[6] Karl Sierek has pointed out that the goal of the home movie is often not so much to capture an object or an event but "to film the act of filming, or, in fact, to make seeing visible" (1990: 160). Thus, many camera movements and shot changes can only be explained as attempts to mimetically reproduce the act of seeing. Furthermore, seeing is made visible not only through the camera's imitation of eye or head movements but especially when the filming process is revealed. This impression arises because, in the home movie, an ambivalent relationship exists between the social and aesthetic functions. Filmic mise-en-scène and family documentation, familial mise-en-scène and filmic documentation can get in each other's way. It is important therefore to keep in mind that the home movie is always produced and consumed within the context of personal relationships. As a result, the camera is always part of the filmic diegesis—as the following example illustrates: A child runs toward its filming father and tries to climb up his legs. In doing so, the child not only moves beyond the optical range of focus but also crosses the invisible line, which, in a fiction film, separates the camera from the action. Each time contact is made between the camera and the film's subjects, we are reminded that a film is being shot here. Since most home movies are edited only in-camera, and since most people prefer not to cut anything out, these kinds of mishaps—which disturb the filmic illusion and simultaneously reinforce the fact that what is being shown is a home movie—are visible on-screen. At the same time, these mishaps also serve to foreground the medium. Here one could conclude that, in the case of the home movie, it is only when the subject makes contact with the camera that the illusion of being part of a filmic reality may be produced.

Tourism and the Safari—Images of Ambivalence

When I use the term "safari" in the following, I am primarily invoking a concept symptomatic of the subject under discussion: namely, the three-way relationship between "travel," "taking possession," and the process of "cinematic exoticism" (see the chapter "The Wilderness" in Brownlow 1979). "Safari" is to be understood as shorthand for this relationship.

The term refers to a specific form of tourism; it derives from Swahili, where the word means something like "voyage" (from the Arabic word *safar*) (Kluge 1995: 699). In Meyer's German-language *Universallexikon*, the safari is described as a "group trip to Africa with the possibility of *hunting* or *observing* and *photographing* (photo safari) big game" (Ahlheim 1984: 182, italics mine).[7] Over time, the original "trip with trading caravans in East Africa" developed into a tourist amusement closely linked with specific forms of appropriation: hunting and photography. The illustrated lexicon of colloquial German includes a further meaning that reveals the implicit colonial context. In adolescent speech the term "going on safari" can mean both "shopping" and "intimate touching"; in other words, economic or sexual forms of acquisition (Kuepper 1984: 2378). The safari is always linked with curiosity—in spite of the fact that people mostly travel "to see what they already know is there" and "the only thing to record, the only possible source of surprise, is their own reaction" (Boorstin [1961] 1992: 116). It is no accident that historically the practice of hunting animals was followed by the activity of observing them with still cameras and later with film cameras.[8] On the photo or film safari, the image replaces the game as trophy and becomes the symbol of victory. The goal is "to bag a prize, to get a trophy, to capture the experience, and to project it on a screen" (Zimmermann 1996: 91).

Along with modern mass tourism a whole industry of tourist images emerged. In the mid to late nineteenth century, panoramas, postcards, stereoscopic pictures, and travelogues became staples of the tourist discourse (Kirby 1997: 36ff.; Strain 2003: 2).[9] Cinema quickly became part of this industry as well. Ellen Strain specifies the relationship between cinema and the "tourist gaze" when she writes that "the notion of touristic viewing as an historically-specific phenomenon . . . developed in the decades immediately preceding cinema's inception and . . . was imported into cinema as a developing form" (1996: 72). By 1906 the travelogue had developed into a genre, and for about ten years travelogues remained a fixture of film theater programs (Peterson 1997: 79). In this period, travelogues come in two basic types: those concerned with landscape and those concerned with human beings.

According to Jennifer Peterson, the genre as a whole is characterized by an ambivalent tension "between attraction and repulsion: exoticism is presented and then taken away. These tensions appear to have been highly efficient and adaptable; they characterize films of colonial or exotic landscapes and are also present in films of European locales" (1997: 76). This specific form of "ambivalence" constitutes something like the basic mechanism of the genre (84). The dynamics of the travelogue genre, then, are similar to those of the tourist gaze which, as Ellen Strain argues, "is characterized by the constant push and pull of distanced immersion, by the desire to be fully immersed in an environment yet literally or figuratively distanced from the scene in order to occupy a comfortable viewing position" (2003: 27).

One could argue, then, that it is an ambivalent fascination with the unfamiliar that drives the production and consumption of professional travelogues. However, the same fascination also motivates viewers to produce their own images when they become travelers. In fact, the activity of producing images is an essential element of the tourist experience, to the point where it seems "positively unnatural to travel for pleasure without taking a camera along" (Sontag 1977: 9). A breakdown of the enormous collection of amateur films assembled by the filmmaker Peter Forgacs reveals that about one third of the collection's holdings are travel and vacation films (Hertogs and De Klerk 1994: 59). My own research on Swiss home movies provides similar data. The most popular motifs in home movies are indeed children and tourism (Schneider 2004).

Tourist images have an impact on the activity of travel, and, to a certain extent, they even structure the trips themselves. As Tom Gunning argues in this volume, travel has indeed become a means of possessing the world through images. Some critics suggest that the film and photographic media lend themselves particularly well to such an activity because the filmic or photographic frame may acquire a "magic and at the same time imperial power of absorption" that "captures and incorporates" the world (Hediger 1997: 27). Symptomatic of this form of appropriation is the two-shot of hunter and hunted animal in the safari film, in which the hunter taking deadly aim is shown within the same frame as his prey. This type of two-shot not only serves to create an impression of authenticity, as André Bazin describes it ([1945] 1967: 49); it also stages an act of possession that "expresses social power relations" (Hediger 1997: 27). Such shots also, of course, produce a thrill, which arises through the suggestion of risk and danger—such as when the animal tamer is seen in the same cage as the wild animal in the circus.

Perhaps not surprisingly, then, the dominant composition in tourist travelogues is the shared shot. The shot of hunter and trophy is to the safari film what the shot of tourist and tourist attraction is to tourist photography and the amateur travelogue. In the aesthetic repertoire of the tourist home movie or club film, two interesting variations of the shared shot occur. In the first variation, the photographer is seen together with

the object she is photographing. In the second variation, the cameraman
is part of the diegesis of the film. Although he is not himself visible in
the picture, he is far from being a neutral observer. Indeed he partici-
pates in the event being filmed and makes his presence felt by interacting
with those he is filming or by enticing them to interact with the camera. The "absent presence" of the cameraperson creates the impression
that the "hunter" is actually part of the image. It highlights the shooting
situation and stresses the fact that the cameraperson shares the same pre-
filmic space with the object he is filming, thus anchoring the filmmaker-
as-traveler in the space of travel. Variations of the second type become
less frequent with the introduction of the telephoto lens. They do occur
in our example, however, the *Autosonntag*, to which I now turn.

A Sunday in the Country:
"Remember those odd mountain people?"

Autosonntag is part of an incomplete and anonymous collection that I
bought at a photographic flea market.[10] The filmmaker was a dentist from
Zurich, who lived with his wife and son in the Hottingen neighborhood
from the late 1920s onward.[11] The collection, as it stands, consists of
about two and a half hours of 16mm film shot between 1929 and 1959.
Many films are about the filmmaker's son: first haircut, first steps, first
birthday, and so on. In addition, there are reels called *The Year in Review*,[12]
in which various events appear in chronological order. And finally, there
are a few more or less complete films with beginning, middle, and end.
Autosonntag is one of these, although it has neither opening nor closing
titles,[13] and is separated from the other films on the reel simply by black
leader. Still, it is possible to make out a more or less logical temporal and
spatial development—an indication that *Autosonntag* may be the work of
an organized club filmmaker.[14]

    Autosonntag tells the story of an excursion to the mountains, where the
urban "strangers" encounter the "local" dairy farmers and their families.
The film's title might lead us to expect that we would see an automobile,
but in fact not one appears in the entire film. The title simply refers to
the leisure activity, still very common today, of the drive to the country.[15]

    Autosonntag can be roughly divided into three phases or sections: first,
a kind of exposition, where we are introduced to the characters and the
location; second, a middle section where the above-mentioned confron-

1　The clogs. Courtesy of Alexandra Schneider, Private collection, Berlin.

tation between urban and rural occurs; and third, a kind of resolution. The film begins with a glimpse behind the scenes: we see two women in the countryside holding up a pocket mirror for each other so that they can touch up their appearance—for the film. A second introductory scene follows: we see three people, the two women and one man, walking through a meadow. Next we see a building: the Richisau health resort. A woman we recognize from the previous scenes comes to the window and waves at the camera. Behind her, the second woman steps up, as well as the man, who is in the middle of shaving; they approach the window to greet the camera (and the cameraman). Then we see shots of a breakfast table. An in-camera edit: cut to pigs and chickens being fed. Cut again: back to the people eating at the breakfast table. The next scene is a short visit to the goats, where snapshots are taken: city women with animals, or, in other words, the tourists and their game trophies. After that, they go for a walk.

The next cut is one of very few in the entire film that was made by splicing together two sections of the positive film print. From the point of view of the city folk, we see a mountain farmer and his children standing in front of the camera. This is followed by an interesting detail, as the filmmaker points his camera at the farmer's traditional wooden shoes (Figure 1). From then on, shots of wooden shoes are a recurring motif in this section of the film. With these images, the urban filmmaker transposes his feeling of strangeness onto the mountain dwellers, although it is they who are actually at home. Through excessive repetition of shots of their wooden shoes the farmers are both exoticized and dramatized. Their footwear appeals to the city dweller not only as the most noticeable visual evidence of the farmers' authenticity but also for the difference he sees between himself and the people he is filming. It is an ambivalent otherness that Homi K. Bhabha has called the object of both "desire and derision" (1994: 60). The exotic is expressed in the stereotypical tension between what is constructed as "other" and what is construed as "normal." The wooden shoes become the site of the spectacle of cultural difference that the city dwellers experience as they employ "learned touristic strategies to derive pleasure from the spectacle of cultural difference" (Strain 2003: 45).

Cultural critics have come to agree that to an important extent, tourism involves a process of the fabrication and rearrangement of what is culturally specific in view of the tourist experience. As Hermann Bausinger states, part of this process is to eliminate certain characteristics of cultural manifestations in order to make them more manageable for the tourist. Thus, what was once uncanny, threatening, and alien becomes digestibly exotic (1991: 345). Susan Sontag has pointed out that taking pictures contributes to this process since the function of tourist photography is to "help people to take possession of space in which they are insecure" (1977: 9). The city person's insecurity in the country is focused through the camera and reflected back outward. Through the act of filming, the wooden shoes become trophies to be brought home from the safari: "Remember those odd mountain people?"[16] From this point of view, the shots of the wooden shoes are also "authentic" proof of the myth of the mountain dweller as both primitive and natural.

The "story" of this intercultural encounter continues: we see the farmer walking uphill, and then, in an identically composed shot, the city folk hiking upward. The farmer is obviously leading them somewhere: to a mountain hut, as we soon see. In the sequence that follows, the city women appear in the same shot as the mountain folk. But first, we see the latter posing for a group portrait in front of the camera (Figure 2). The above-mentioned difference between city and country is intensified further in this sequence, which resembles a game of tableaux vivants. First the farmers, their children, and typical props like copper milk cans and a large block of cheese are placed before the camera; then the city women join them. The whole arrangement is rather stiff, the people obviously posing for the film, and it all seems a little "unfortunate."[17] This impression does not arise from the "models" themselves but may be explained by

2 Group portrait. Courtesy of Alexandra Schneider, Private collection, Berlin.

their lack of experience with the medium. In contrast to the city folk, the mountain farmers do not seem to have any idea what the camera is doing with them. At the moment the shot is being taken, they cannot imagine how they will look in the film. The farming men and women stand there as if they were posing for an arranged portrait in a photographer's studio: as still as possible. This reaction is most probably also provoked by the "stage directions" of the city people: the mise en scène is that of the group portrait.

The city women, now entering the frame to pose with the farmers, behave very differently. At first they remain reserved, but soon their performance becomes more lively, as they engage in competition with the farmers. One woman, standing in the background, begins to wave at the camera. In contrast to the stiff farmers, she knows what cinema is and tries to bring some movement into the moving image. In doing so, she is also attracting the attention of the camera (operated by her husband) and potential viewers (of which she is one): "Look, here I am, there I was. Don't I have star quality?" The shared shot is further intensified when we notice that the filmmaker himself has joined the group, and someone else is running the camera.[18] Many amateur films reveal that the cameraperson starts to behave exaggeratedly when he (it is usually a he) enters the frame, as if compelled by an urge to stick out from the group and do something that makes him noticeable when the film is shown. The inclusion of

3 Self-description of the urban male filmmaker. Courtesy of Alexandra Schneider, Private collection, Berlin.

the filmmaker in the film is somehow reminiscent of the photographs of anthropologists in the field. Both images document the presence of the person who creates the visual record at the site of the event, and both images root the imagemaker's authority in the implicit statement "I was there" (Strain 2003: 30). The self-inscription of the cameraperson is one of the instances where the amateur film intersects with both the travelogue and the ethnographic film as discussed by Amy J. Staples in this volume, showing "how cinematic representations are embedded in wider cultural discourses about others and . . . about ourselves." Our Herr H. is a case in point. In order to underline his presence on-screen, he takes a little farmer girl onto his lap; she immediately begins to cry, so that he must quickly hand her back to her father (Figure 3). He stands up and walks back to the camera, to resume his place behind it. He shoots close-ups of children's faces and then shows us wooden shoes one last time—the subject we have already identified as the emblem of his sense of difference and mise-en-spectacle of cultural difference.

The film concludes with a short third section, in which we can watch from a greater distance as the city people take snapshots of the children. As if the filmmaker were commenting on his own activities, he shows us the photographer trying to pose a group of children (it is, of course, one of the shared shots discussed above). The film ends with a few shots of meadow flowers and a picturesque Alpine panorama, backlit.

The Alpine Safari: *Autosonntag* as a Voyage in Time and a Home Movie

The three buildings stand together like three different centuries or periods of settlement: the original Alpine hut, the old house and the new health resort. Here we have, simultaneously, two economic stages, mountain and valley lifestyles, meadow and pasture, maple and pine.
—F. Becker describing the Kloental

In conclusion I would like to suggest a few ways in which *Autosonntag* may be situated within the context of contemporary history and media history.

As I have attempted to show, the similarity between an amateur film like *Autosonntag* and the genre of the travel or expedition film lies in its ambivalent staging of the other and the normal. In addition, the travel film may offer urban spectators a glimpse of human beings in their "natural" or "non-alienated" state. But "authentic" images of "primitives" need not be generated by "distant" cultures only. Traveling, Descartes wrote in the early seventeenth century, "is almost like conversing with men of other centuries" (Boorstin 1992: 78).[19] Our amateur filmmaker's staging of the farmers reveals that he too was fascinated by the idea of time travel during his excursion to the Kloental Valley. The life of the Kloental farmers is a life of the past, while his own urban origins remain the secure present to which he can return after a trip into the past. Herr H. seems to be rather ambivalent about the idolization and mystification of nature and natural living that has been a major theme of Western thought since the eighteenth century. The rural Switzerland he depicts is not just a "natural" and authentic refuge for urban dwellers; it also represents an obsolete way of living to which the contemporary city dweller can feel superior by comparison. The farmers in *Autosonntag* do represent more than just folklore and a nostalgic fantasy of a way of life that, alas, has been lost.[20] Rather, they are curiosities. The city dwellers do not wish to exchange their world for this one: at the most, they want to temporarily appropriate it as tourists. "Progress" is contained within the film camera and thus also in the knowledge of how to use it. And it is found in the automobile, which gives the film its name. One could argue that in *Autosonntag* the filmmaker not only draws on established cinematic discourses such as the travelogue or the ethnographic film in order to mediate and structure his tourist experience. He also uses the technology of film and his image-making activity to participate in a rhetoric of progress in which cinema and the automobile prominently figure as emblems of modernity. Among other things, then, *Autosonntag* illustrates that the link between cinema and modernity—variously discussed by scholars such as Tom Gunning (see his essay in this volume) and Miriam Hansen (1991)—extends beyond film as a social and cultural phenomenon situated in the public sphere to include the private uses of cinema as well. More specifically, cinema informs the experience of modernity in that it provides not only models of perception but also models of production—as witnessed in the figure of the amateur filmmaker who uses the technology of film and draws on a variety of cinematic discourses to make sense of the newfound mobility of tourist travel. Furthermore, the models of production provided by cinema not only help to capture and make sense of the experience of mobility. To a certain extent, they help to produce that experience, and they help to make it into a tourist experience to begin with.

As I have already noted, *Autosonntag* constitutes an exceptional case with regard to other home movies in the sense that it is a more or less structured film. Most notably, it features a clearly marked-out beginning and an end. But while the "author" of *Autosonntag* is exceptionally skilled by the standards of the genre, he still behaves like an average home movie maker-cum-tourist in many ways. He acts like a tourist in that he captures his travels on film. As Ellen Strain points out, the tourist experience, regardless of whether it actually takes place "in reality" or is mediated through film, is a confrontation with "the spectacle of difference, the exotic landscape dotted with wondrously 'alien' human and animal faces" (1996: 72). However, the tourist filmmaker not only captures the moment of confrontation, he also creates it. *Autosonntag* establishes the tourist gaze through an exoticizing mise-en-scène that is the result of an ambivalent convergence of desire, bordering on envy, and mockery. The exoticism of the scene is not there a priori. It is related to an experience of distance mediated through the representational technique of film, most notably the shared shot. The shared shot not only certifies the simultaneous presence of the tourist and the object of his gaze in the same space. As much as the shared shot simply records the encounter of tourist and object, it also triggers their confrontation. Thus, filming dramatizes and exoticizes mere occurrences and turns them into tourist events, creating in the process what Hans-Magnus Enzensberger calls "*synthetische Sehenswuerdigkeiten*" (synthetic sights) (1969: 197). In this particular sense, then, more than serving as a simple ingredient of the tourist experience, taking pictures and making films actually contribute to the production of that experience.

As I have tried to show, the tourist experience is not limited to the confrontation with the "wondrously 'alien' human" (Strain 1996: 72). It may include encounters with Alpine dwellers, nature, landscape, and even architecture. Furthermore, sights that are sometimes nothing more than just the sensations of the tourists themselves are crucial to the tourist experience as well. A great many tourist home movies contain shots of landscapes, houses, and other objects that are obviously attempts to record a certain mood or emotional reaction rather than a particular object. The average tourist home movie could thus be characterized as a fragmentary documentation of time spent with the family featuring both sights that are "actually there" in pre-filmic reality and synthetic sights created in the act of filming (although one could of course argue that all sights, even certified tourist attractions, become synthetic sights when photographed and filmed). The filmic devices most frequently used to capture, or create, sights are the shared shot and the panorama shot, which can be a pan or a fixed-frame shot.

The fact that tourist home movies, including the amateur travelogue *Autosonntag*, are usually films made by family travelers or by families traveling is significant and merits further discussion. As Herman Bausinger points out, research on tourism has for a long time, and perhaps for too long, been focused exclusively on the experience of the other, of that which is strange, and on the ways in which the tourist gaze misappropriates the other. What was left out is that tourist travel is also a way of making strange what is familiar, of leaving home in order to be able to experience it in new ways. "Home is perhaps the main point of reference of every tourist trip," as Bausinger writes (1991: 350). Tourism, in other words, is about staying as much as it is about leaving, about that which is familiar as much as about that which is alien and strange. One could actually claim that this seemingly contradictory dynamic is characteristic of all tourism. In specific cases, the tourist activity will tend toward the encounter with the other rather than toward the defamiliarization of the familiar; consider the difference, for instance, between a three-month trekking trip through the mountains of Nepal and a two-week Club Med vacation. But even in cases where the main thrust is to break away from everyday life as much as possible and search out an experience of difference through an encounter with the other, the rift is never complete.

Rather, every trip is, and remains, a kind of improvement upon everyday life, as Bausinger puts it:

> The goal is to "switch off" everyday life, but this is easier said than done, and certainly not done as easily as the technical term implies. Actually, far from being banned altogether, the everyday very much stays on the horizon of the tourist experience, and some tourists even try to make their time away from home into an improved version of their everyday life. (1991: 351)

Tourism, then, is not least about a "correction of everyday life." Better, more beautiful, perhaps a little strange, certainly different or special — and yet somehow familiar: such are the places one wishes to visit on vacation trips. To relax, to go sightseeing, to experience new things and learn something (a little of everything, but of nothing too much): this is the ideal combination that turns a vacation into a better version of everyday life. To make sure that you can tell the difference is the task of photography and film. Taking pictures and making films are ways to celebrate the correction of everyday life, to capture and eternalize this particular experience of difference.

And while most home movies are not nearly as carefully structured as *Autosonntag*, it is no coincidence that tourist home movies as a rule feature a combination of family shots and tourist views. They are family films first and foremost, and their main point of reference is the family circle. Or, to put it in other words: however much the traveler breaks away from his ordinary life, the tourist home movie never quite leaves home.

Notes

1. The Kloental Valley has been a popular Alpine region since the eighteenth century. For their helpful comments I would like to thank Vinzenz Hediger, Christine Noll Brinckmann, Roland Cosandey, and Christina Schumacher. Thanks also to Mariann Lewinsky for kindly reproducing the film stills. This text is a revised and extended version of an essay originally translated from the German by Marcy Goldberg.

2. Only a single copy of *Autosonntag* exists. Like most amateur film of the period, it was not shot on negative but reversal film stock: the film exposed in the camera was processed to produce a positive print rather than a negative. There are only four splices on the film roll; the rest of the editing was done in-camera.

3. With the invention of motion picture technology in 1895, the cinema began to enter the private sphere. In 1923 the 16mm and 9.5mm formats were introduced as specifically amateur systems and eventually established themselves as standard formats. In 1932 Kodak introduced the more economical 8mm format. But amateur filmmaking did not become truly widespread until after World War II, experiencing a further increase in 1965 with the introduction of the Super 8 format. In recent years the Super 8 format has been replaced by the video camcorder, which will soon be supplemented by digital webcams. Today, more people than ever own personal video or film equipment. Never before have so many events in the everyday life of ordinary people been so well documented. For the history and theory of home movies, see Odin 1995, Zimmermann 1995, Moran 2002.

4. Roger Odin (1995) uses the term "amateur film" for club films, but I prefer to see both home movies and club films as subgenres of the amateur film.

5. For the history of the amateur film, see Zimmermann 1995, Schenke 1998, Odin 1999, and Kattelle 2003. Useful bibliographies appear in Odin 1999 and Compton 2003.

6. In this connection it is interesting to observe the aspects shared by the early cinema of attractions, as described by Tom Gunning in this volume, and amateur cinema.

7. In *The Oxford English Dictionary* "safari" is also defined as "a journey . . . often for hunting." The German term was borrowed from the English.

8. On gun and camera topos, see Hediger 2002.

9. On the travel film, see the contributions to this volume as well as the following: Musser 1984, Peterson 1997, Van Dooren 1999, and Filmmuseum Duesseldorf 2002.

10. When I purchased the collection I was informed that it was incomplete. I have since chanced upon a further film by Herr H. that is part of a private collection. Problems of orphaned home movies are discussed in Streible 2003.

11. These facts can be gathered from the films.

12. *Jahresschau* is the German title the filmmaker wrote on the film cans. They include scenes filmed during trips by car, train, and ship, and on mountain hikes; bicycle races; ice skating performances; and a Zeppelin flight over Zurich.

13. In the film itself there is something like a diegetic title: a shot of the health resort's sign, "Kurhaus Richisau." Another example of the filmmaker's penchant for diegetic credits is the postcard addressed by him to his son, which appears as a title in the opening shot of another film, *First Day of School.*

14. Further indications are the men with film cameras who appear in some

of the shots, and some—for a home movie—unusually interesting camera angles.

15. Hellmuth Lange, the business manager of the "Bund der Filmamateure," the association of amateur filmmakers in Berlin, includes a script for the "weekend film" *Mit dem Auto ins Gruene* ("to the country by car") in his handbook (Lange 1930: 40). On amateur film, travelogue, and the automobile see Ruoff 1991, Schneider 2002, and Bloom in this volume.

16. We must assume that even silent amateur films were enhanced during projection by a live "soundtrack." In the case of the home movie, this was often the filmmaker's explanatory commentary or a discussion among the viewers.

17. Compare with the following quotation: "Africans are fundamentally unfortunate models when it comes to 'participating' in film or photo shoots. They think they have to keep still as mice when they are being photographed, and so they stand stiffly, with tense faces, in front of the photographer. But a relaxed pose and a smiling face are essential for taking a portrait" (Schleinitz 1968: 62).

18. The film's immediate public would of course have recognized the filmmaker right away. For outsiders, it is more difficult. Nevertheless, even without knowing the people appearing in the film, at a certain point it is usually possible to identify the filmmaker. I do not know of any home movie maker who does not appear on camera from time to time (filmed by a spouse, children, a guest, or by way of a delayed-action timer). In our example, the filmmaker's identity becomes clear at the moment when he returns to take over the camera.

19. On the temporal dimensions of spatial distance, see also Fabian 1983 and Peterson in this volume.

20. As in the "mountain film" (*Bergfilm*), where the protagonist can undergo purification through contact with nature, or the "petit bourgeois film" (*Kleinbuergerfilm*), where the rural population is presented with its traditional communal social structures socially intact. The same is true for the "homeland film" (*Heimatfilm*), where we are always presented with a morally integral and self-sufficient little community undisturbed by history.

III

Travelogues in the Sound Era

Hollywood and

the Attractions of the Travelogue

DANA BENELLI

||||||||||||||||||||||||||||||||||||||||||||||||||||||||||||||||||||||||||||||||||||||||||||||||||||||||||||||||||||||

Descriptions of the classical American cinema will often note that the standard film program provided by most theaters consisted of a feature-length film (or two, in periods of double features) accompanied by a newsreel and at least one additional short subject, which might take the form of a travelogue, a comedy, a cartoon, or a film about a topical novelty subject matter. But beyond this passing acknowledgment that there were documentary components in the routine viewing of American audiences, little further attention is given to the presence of documentaries in the American commercial cinema. For example, it is infrequently mentioned that in addition to feature film production Hollywood's studios produced or contracted to acquire, and then distributed, most of these newsreel and documentary shorts.

Historiographic overviews of Hollywood and the American cinema as a whole still consistently marginalize, or dismiss altogether, the pertinence of documentary filmmaking as a potential source of insight into the workings of Hollywood and its feature films. I suspect that Gerald Mast articulates a fairly typical generalist's attitude when he observes, in his introduction to *A Short History of the Movies*, that "the aesthetic principles of the nonfiction or documentary film are different enough from those of the storytelling film to require a full-length study of their own" (1996: 7).

Traditional studies of the documentary have helped to reinforce this attitude by concurring in, and often championing, the assertion of documentary's difference from commercial filmmaking and by consequently directing their energies to the production of the separatist studies promoted by Mast, studies that de-emphasize or ignore altogether most occasions of documentary incursions into Hollywood's commercial domain. Within this context films such as *Nanook of the North* (1922) and New Deal documentaries, like *The River*, which did succeed in being exhibited theatrically, are usually acknowledged as exceptions that prove the rule. They become revelatory instances when extraordinary personal initiative, or enthusiastic support from film critics, or unique access to resources and influence outside the film industry, such as those of the United States government, were required just to break momentarily the studios' grip on the marketplace.

More theoretical academic work offers a complementary historical perspective apparently validating the separation of documentary filmmaking from the activity of Hollywood. Tom Gunning, for example, in his important work on pre-classical cinema, calls attention to the early prominence of actuality filmmaking, such as travel films, and describes it as a notable component of a "cinema of attractions" which flourished in the period before 1906–07 (1990: 56–62). The cinema of attractions is characterized by "showing and exhibition" rather than narrative in its presentation of its subject matter to viewers. It emphasizes the visual pleasure of the immediate moment of viewing and frequently takes the form of a series of views edited without clear continuity of space and time. Its use of intertitles and inclusion of individuals looking straight at the camera further fosters qualities of direct address and exhibition, rather than transparency, as a basis for structuring filmic representation and the viewer's experience. According to Gunning, while the cinema of attractions was a dominant film format of the pre-classical period of American filmmaking, it was eclipsed by the narrativization of the cinema between 1907 and 1913.

But does eclipsed mean absented? Gunning states that the cinema of attractions goes "underground" in subsequent Hollywood filmmaking, and he cites several examples of its inconspicuous persistence and, at times, its momentary eruption into filmic prominence, examples such as the musical's suspension of narrative for song and dance performances, slapstick comedy, and the spectacle associated with the display of women. Might there be still other specifiable exceptions to, or disruptions of, the hegemony of narrative in the Hollywood cinema? And, in particular, do any documentary-based attractions remain in the feature films of the commercial American cinema?

In the discussion that follows I propose to take a closer look at a brief period of American film history, specifically the early 1930s, and to highlight a specific film subject matter, namely, the representation of non-Western locales and cultures by travelogue-expedition-ethnographic filmmaking. Such a focus will call attention to the fact that at both industrial and textual levels of film activity documentary representation continued to be a frequent presence, and at times even a disruptive influence, within the established operations of the classical Hollywood cinema.

To begin from a perspective broader than just the travelogue, during the 1930s documentary films in the form of newsreels and short subjects on varied topics (sports, fashion, musical performance, popular culture, non-American localities and cultures, human interest stories, etc.) were either produced by the studios or acquired by studios from independent producers for distribution along with studio features.

Five newsreels competed in the American theatrical marketplace by 1931. And while Erik Barnouw may suggest that in the eyes of the studios "newsreels were only an item in an entertainment package" (1974: 111) and therefore a lesser matter of corporate interest, it should also be kept in mind that these documentaries were an almost exclusive source of moving images of contemporary reality. Thus, their coverage of current events, public figures, and diverse cultural activity was a matter of some ongoing interest for audiences. In fact, in the trade press there is ample evidence that individual theaters promoted the content of their newsreels, even to the extent of giving it marquee status above the feature film listing on those occasions when the newsreels covered events of particularly intense current public interest. Newsreel theaters catering precisely to this public interest appeared in a number of American cities in the early 1930s, following the successful example of the Embassy Theatre, which had been opened in New York, by Fox, in November 1929. They offered continuous exhibition of news programs compiled from multiple newsreels (sometimes filling out their running time with travelogues). In addition, the monthly installments of the topically oriented *The March of Time* played in almost one third of the theaters in the United States by the end of 1935, their first year of production.

Other documentary short subject series distributed by the studios could prove comparably popular as well. Among series of shorts on sports topics, Knute Rockne's demonstrations of football strategy and Bobby Jones's golf tips achieved a degree of popularity that eventually also earned them frequent above-the-feature marquee preeminence in some theaters' promotions of their film programs.

In January 1931 *Variety* noted that travelogue shorts had become especially popular with American audiences. In response, for 1931 almost one hundred expeditions were planned:

> combing every nook and corner of the globe for new material for travelog shorts ... Almost every major studio is financing one or more of the expeditions and around 50 are planned independently. One independent company in the East backed by New York capital is figuring on sending out a dozen different outfits . . . Reason for the activity is the current popularity of two-reel lecture stuff. In the silent days the travelogs were generally looked upon as fillers, but since the addition of sound-effects, plus oral descriptive matter, the scenic material in many stands is getting a better audience play than the short comedies. (*Variety* 1931a: 4)

In addition to short subjects the studios sometimes engaged in the production of feature-length documentaries, and here we are dealing almost exclusively with films in a travelogue-expedition format structured around the adventure of travel and the exotic spectacle of distant cultures, landscapes, and wildlife. Columbia Pictures released *Africa Speaks* in 1930. In 1928 Paramount purchased exclusive film rights to Admiral Byrd's forthcoming expedition and released *With Byrd at the South Pole* in June 1930. But such features were rather rare events in studio filmmaking. For at feature-length scale the process of documentary production was indeed quite unlike the rationalized procedures of the studio system (which emphasized regulated and timely completion of films to meet the needs of release schedules). Furthermore, the results of the out-of-the-ordinary effort to produce these documentaries did not always reward the studios' attempts to venture beyond their conventional practices. Despite coordinating the release of *With Byrd at the South Pole* with the triumphant arrival of Admiral Byrd in New York City, Paramount was disappointed with the film's grosses.[1]

Yet, despite the paucity of studio-sponsored initiatives in the area of feature-length documentary production, such films were still a noticeable factor in the American film marketplace in the 1930s, especially early in the decade. In the four-year period from 1930 through 1933 the *New York Times* carried reviews for sixty documentaries, most of them travelogue-expedition films. There were a number of substantive reasons for this presence of documentary films and for the prominence of the travelogue type in particular.

First, there was the notable precedent of *Nanook of the North* (1922), which had strikingly demonstrated the commercial viability of documentaries about exotic cultures and locales. By the early 1930s, however, the model provided by Robert Flaherty's film had been substantially supplemented, enhanced, and revitalized in its possibilities with the advent of recorded sound (as the above excerpt from *Variety* states). Sound created dynamic textual enrichment in newer travelogues relative to the films of the silent era, which had been hindered by the necessity of alternating written intertitles with passages of recorded images; the intertitles interrupted the visual flow of the film and needed to be kept brief lest they slow the pace of the film as well. Given the availability of a soundtrack simultaneous with the image track, a film's spoken commentary could more effectively complement images by providing more information than intertitles, by allowing for greater expression of commentator personality, and by facilitating dramatic shading of the on-screen subject matter. Also, the inclusion of apparently authentic (though they often weren't) and unfamiliar wildlife and location sounds enabled a film's visual spectacle to be accompanied by equivalent audio pleasures.

Second, travelogues could be relatively inexpensive to produce. Most of the nonstudio productions enjoyed an advantageously symbiotic relationship to scientific or adventure expeditions. While the organizers of these expeditions may well have hoped that subsequent film exhibition would help defray their expedition's costs, the production of the film was still a by-product of, or complement to, other, primary, motivations for the expedition. So the cost of the trip itself was not the pure production expense that it would have been for a studio seeking on its own to produce a comparable film. Moreover, at this point early in the sound period, when the technology and practices of sound filmmaking demanded a level of expertise daunting for amateurs, the standard approach for travelogue production consisted of shooting the film silent and then adding the voice-over commentary and sound effects later. Thus, these films could be, and predominantly were, produced free from the difficulties and expense of trying to get synchronous location sound. They could be made by determined novices.

Third, the travelogue-expedition format, even in the hands of novices, enjoyed some unique competitive textual advantages relative to Hollywood films and most other independent filmmaking ventures. With the exception of low-budget westerns, which addressed a quite specific market need (largely that of rural communities) and that Hollywood seems to have often ceded to Poverty Row studios and marginal independents, most other independent film producers trying to break into commercial filmmaking struggled to simulate passable versions of Hollywood product while suffering from the essentially prohibitive disadvantages caused by their limited access to financial resources, technology, and stars, disadvantages that were only intensified in the early 1930s by the technical, logistical, and aesthetic complications of making movies with synchronous sound. The travelogues, however, could bypass the importance of stars, the need for state-of-the-art photographic and sound technology, and even a great deal of narrative and aesthetic sophistication if filmmakers could successfully convince the public that their films offered, instead, compellingly authentic (and the more exotic the better) reality to paying customers. There is abundant evidence that in the early 1930s filmmakers succeeded in making this pitch to the American public. Reality, as a subject matter that could attract public attention, was one film material that the studios could not appropriate and put a lock on, as they could stars.

It seems unarguable that there was genuine public curiosity about the unknown, and enthusiasm for the opportunity to view moving images of never-before-seen cultures and landscapes. But just as certainly, a prime source of the travelogue's attraction for audiences was its presentation of two quite specific subject matters that could only be suggested or simulated in Hollywood films, namely, bare-breasted women and genuine violence (primarily in the forms of hunting scenes and animal fights). In the studio fiction films such forms of explicit sexuality and violence were absolutely unacceptable to local censors in the 1930s, even in the pre-Code era early in that decade, and therefore were avoided by Hollywood. But the travelogues often managed to fly under the censors' radar, cloaked by the claim that the educational nature of these representations justified their inclusion in the films. In so doing, these films gained a unique and significant competitive advantage in the marketplace.

Admittedly, the expectations generated by the sensationalistic advance promotions that often accompanied the independently produced travelogue feature films were not always fulfilled by the subsequently screened documentaries (and viewer disappointment could have repercussions on the box office fates of the next documentaries to enter a locality). But the point for the moment is that it was the very difference of subject matter, and specifically the alleged authenticity of what appeared on-screen, that provided the documentary with a means of entry into American theaters and gave it a potential basis for successful competition with conventional studio product.

On occasion, the right congruence of factors such as subject matter, public mood, promotion, and market conditions[2] could empower independently produced documentaries to significantly and disruptively compete within the usually studio-dominated American film marketplace. In 1930, for example, the film *Ingagi* successfully and notoriously presented itself as the record of an expedition which had inadvertently stumbled across the solution to the age-old riddle of the missing link, this purported solution being a group of bare-breasted black women living contentedly in the jungle with gorillas. In the wake of this film's box office success a number of other more legitimately authentic documentaries profitably circulated as well, among them *Hunting Tigers in India* (1929), *Up the Congo* (1930), and *Across the World with Mr. and Mrs. Martin Johnson* (1930). In San Francisco, in May 1930, four travelogue features were simultaneously in downtown first-run exhibition locations. In fact, several of the films of this cycle had completed prior and less notable releases before being brought back to theaters and profiting from *Ingagi*'s coattails (*Exhibitors Herald-World* 1930a: 20).

The travelogue's demonstrated potential for profitable exhibition in the sound period provoked a predictable reaction on the part of the studios. Specifically, and in keeping with the industry logic of repeating whatever might have already proven to be successful, the studios actively scrambled to provide comparable material, albeit while continuing to be wary about in-house production of such films. Three broad kinds of competitive and co-optive responses are identifiable on the part of the film industry.

In the short run, some studios sought to immediately participate in cycles of public interest in travelogues, as these occurred, by picking up distribution rights to existing films produced by independent filmmakers. In 1930, RKO temporarily and profitably purchased the American rights to *Ingagi*, until the Hays Office stepped in to ban any involvement with the controversial film on the part of the studio members of the Motion Picture Producers and Distributors Association.

A second approach on the part of some studios was to formulate more traditional future-oriented production and programming plans based on the assumption that audience interests were essentially stable and continuous. As a constant, the interest in travelogues could be addressed by a studio's yearly program of films in the same fashion as other ongoing genre-based audience enthusiasms. The strategy here was to offset non-participation in unpredictable and volatile cycles of sudden, intense, but short-lived audience enthusiasm with the increased quality of production values that studio resources might underwrite. Paramount, for example, sent its own cameramen with three of Admiral Byrd's expeditions rather than simply buy the amateur recordings that would otherwise have been produced by an expedition participant.

Other studios did acknowledge the demonstrated talents and experience of independent filmmakers and made arrangements to fill upcoming program slots with their work. Thus, Fox entered into a distribution relationship with Osa and Martin Johnson and released their films as they were completed. RKO contractually set up a similar relationship with Frank Buck. As amateur production values, increasingly familiar expedition scenarios, and promotional misrepresentation took their toll on public support for many other independently produced travelogue-expedition films, the studio-distributed offerings continued to appear. The Johnsons and Frank Buck maintained the presence of the feature-length travelogue documentary in the American cinema into the late 1930s, bolstered by their associations with the studios' established reputations.

A third Hollywood response to the travelogue-expedition documentaries was to engage in a process that can be described as textual appropriation. In one form this could simply mean intensifying and promoting the documentary qualities already present in existing Hollywood practice. The early 1930s, for example, witnessed the promotional celebration of location shooting by A-picture westerns such as *The Virginian* (1929), *The Arizona Kid* (1930), and *The Painted Desert* (1930).

But in other cases the studios created films that more deliberately and ambitiously set out to combine component aspects of travelogues with traditional Hollywood narrative filmmaking. Hypothetically, the resulting hybrid film form marshaled the appeals of each filmmaking practice to counteract the generally acknowledged weaknesses of the other. In the case of the travelogue features, the diminishing novelty of expedition routines and itineraries, along with the inherent lack of textual suspense and momentum that resulted from the films' tendency to take the form of episodic sequences of mostly random events, had led critics to openly wish for greater narrative dynamism in the films. Hollywood was at liberty to direct the resources of scriptwriters and performers to such a need, as well as to the creation of more reliable enticements for female viewers, who were considered to be indifferent to the normal educational and action-oriented preoccupations of the travelogues. In turn, the authenticity of location shooting, the use of native supporting casts, and the possibility of including recordings of genuine and spontaneous events, could bring revitalizing innovation, if not also heightened plausibility, to the conventional and increasingly too-familiar narrative and character construction of Hollywood's genre adventures.

Hybrid films of this sort were obtained from in-house directors or commissioned from directors with requisite experience outside the studios. Ernest Schoedsack and Merian C. Cooper became specialists in this kind of project, moving from the ethnographic documentary *Grass* (1925) to hybrid films such as *Chang* (1927), *Four Feathers* (1929), and *Rango* (1931). Later, of course, they made *King Kong* (1933), a film that still reveals traces of their documentary experience (in its now completely fictionalized versions of travelogue conventions such as animal fights and exotic native culture).[3]

At MGM, W. S. Van Dyke worked briefly with Robert Flaherty on *White Shadows of the South Seas* (1928) and subsequently directed *Trader Horn* (1931) in Africa and *Eskimo* (1933) in Alaska. He was scheduled for a film tentatively entitled "Jungle Red Man" which would have taken his production company up the Amazon, but the project collapsed, reportedly owing to the logistical challenges of the enterprise.

The *Trader Horn* production is an especially notable undertaking. In June 1928 MGM bought the rights to the three-volume bestseller memoirs of an African trader named Aloysius Horn (written by the novelist Ethelreda Lewis). Within a week *Variety* carried a short article indicating that not only would a full cast and crew be sent to Africa by MGM but also they would bring portable sound equipment and the film's sound would be entirely recorded on location (*Variety* 1928: 12)—in 1928, the first year of feature-length sound filmmaking! The resulting shoot lasted seven months, covered 35,000 miles, and was something of an event in its own right for the trade and popular presses. The *New York Times*, for example, carried twelve "Diary of a Film" articles, by-lined by Van Dyke, detailing the production's progress (Van Dyke 1929a–1929l). When the film was finally released in January 1931, one ad announced that it would "astound you with its beauty, thrill you with its drama and bewilder you with its truth."

Tabu (1931) and *S. O. S. Iceberg* (1933) are among similar projects pro-

1 An MGM publicity still for *Trader Horn* (1931). Courtesy of the Producers Library Service.

duced by studio outsiders. Despite the troubled collaboration of Flaherty and F. W. Murnau, which Mark Langer (1985) has detailed, *Tabu* was ultimately purchased for distribution by Paramount. In 1930 a German movie, *The White Hell of Pitz Palu* (1929), a "mountain film" produced by G. W. Pabst and Dr. Arnold Fanck, attracted considerable critical praise in America for its outdoor photography. This attention enabled the film to break out of the art house and ethnic neighborhood theaters that were the routine restricted-exhibition fate of foreign films. In so doing, the film achieved a degree of box office success that did not go unnoticed in Hollywood. Thus, in the wake of the film's critical and financial success, Universal Pictures, Inc. hired Dr. Fanck and the star of the film, Leni Riefenstahl, to produce a similar film, in English, for the American market. The resulting film was *S. O. S. Iceberg*, eventually directed by Tay Garnett and released in 1933.

The preceding discussion demonstrates that the travelogue feature film was a presence in the American cinema and that at times it attained the power to warrant being incorporated into the Hollywood studios' feature film production and distribution activities. But with respect to the hybrid films that resulted, a closer look deserves to be given to how the industry negotiated the combination of documentary representation and the classical Hollywood text. The travelogue's popular appeal derived from the power of reality as a subject matter of a presumably evident difference of status from Hollywood's fictions. And, as Gunning points out, the presentational distinctiveness of the early (and traditional) documentary formats largely derives from their primary interests in the informational and spectacle values of directly witnessed reality. Such representational priorities are indifferent to, if not sometimes openly at odds with, narrative structure and its dual emphases on causally motivated movement from one event to the next and the primacy of character. Could the Hollywood text, then, appropriate documentary because of its appealing difference and give increased textual prominence to documentary representation, with its inherent cinema-of-attractions qualities, and still maintain its traditional prioritizing of narrative and character?

In fact, films such as *Tabu*, *Rango*, *S. O. S. Iceberg*, and *Trader Horn* suggest that what Hollywood achieved in the early 1930s was less a harmonious synthesis than a set of industrially acceptable conflicted texts. Just as the production and presence of documentaries created occasional disruptions of the fiction-dominated film market, so too does the documentary's presence within Hollywood texts create the potential for, and often the actuality of, disruptions of Hollywood's traditional narrative economy. These hybrid films are recognizably Hollywood product in their overall foregrounding of narrative and character. They are also, however, significantly punctuated by moments and sequences in which reality is no longer subordinated to narrative, as a background context or as a subject matter validated solely on the basis of its relationship to character (for example, as a subject matter for a character to respond to by means of point-of-view editing). Instances of such textual distraction may be as modest as shot duration that holds a landscape-bearing image on-screen a few beats longer than is necessary to convey narrative information required in the moment, or as striking as full scenes in which narrative logic and character motivation are effectively reduced to the thinnest of pretexts for film passages that devote themselves to the observation of landscapes, native life, or animal behavior for their own sakes.

Early in *Trader Horn* three consecutive scenes offer examples of how the accommodation of documentary attractions could retard a film's development of its narrative.[4] As the first of these scenes begins, Trader Horn, his young sidekick Peru, and their company of natives disembark from canoes at a riverside location where the background water of the river is turbulent and the soundtrack carries the roar of rushing water (which forces the characters to shout their lines and occasionally is allowed to obscure the dialogue of the scene). Trader Horn gestures screen-right to call something off-screen to Peru's attention and the film cuts to a landscape shot of Murchison Falls, the source for much of the river's turbulence and the soundtrack's volume. The two shots make up a traditional Hollywood editing structure that neatly binds a documentary image into the fiction text through the motivation of the characters' looks, and thus is an example of that "underground" containment of the cinema of attractions within Hollywood films that Gunning speaks of. But little of the film that immediately follows maintains such traditional narrative control.

The two men next redirect their attention to another point (there is a shift in the vector of their looks) that is also off-screen to the right and begin to walk in that direction. Again, apparently also conventionally, the camera responds, motivated by their movement, and pans right. But it moves faster than they do, effectively leaving them and continuing its panning until the falls come back into view, at which point the camera ceases its movement, in essence taking its motivation from the landscape and the discovery of something attention-grabbing in that landscape. Camera movement that moves away from characters to the off-screen source of their interest is also conventional, albeit infrequent, in Hollywood practice. But Trader Horn and Peru have seemed to be looking at something other than the falls, and, indeed, they reenter the framed field of view and continue across it, with Trader Horn still gesturing ahead toward space that remains beyond the right edge of the frame. At this point the interests of the camera and characters are literally at cross purposes, with the now-stationary camera preoccupied by the falls onscreen and the moving characters interested in something off-screen that is never subsequently revealed. The camera does not move, the characters reach the right edge of the frame, and the shot ends.

In the next moments of the film the two men will discover the body of a missionary they had met earlier and resolve to continue her intended journey to an area above and beyond the falls. While most other films would avail themselves of an economical transitional dissolve to the expedition's arrival at this anticipated destination, *Trader Horn* instead employs five shots of extended duration, with no dialogue, that observe the party making the climb. Narratively, little (if anything) is accomplished. But the shots take the group along the edge of the falls and thereby provide five further glimpses (accompanied by the continuous roar of the waters) of the dramatic upper reaches of that natural attraction. Thus, the film has granted primacy to landscape rather than editorially, and more conventionally, elide space and time during which no significant narrative development occurs.

Following the climb and their movement into new terrain, there is a brief narrative episode involving the natives' anxiety about going any farther into the dangerous region. After Trader Horn restores order the scene fades out with the inexperienced Peru remarking that the area ahead seems peaceful. The next segment of the film is nothing less than a self-contained travelogue short. For a full fifteen minutes the expedition moves through a (somewhat improbably varied) landscape while Trader Horn points out and comments on the diverse animals that live in Africa. The film primarily engages in cross-cutting between shots of Trader Horn lecturing Peru as the two walk along and more extended shots observing the game he continues to describe on the soundtrack as we view them (though the editing also includes punctuating shots recorded from behind the two actors so as to authenticate their presence in the vicinity of at least some of the animals they discuss). This general observation of wildlife eventually leads to a sequence incorporating the travelogue convention of animal fights, with Trader Horn and Peru concealing themselves behind bushes to watch three hyenas fight off the attack of a leopard. But the violence of this scene proves to be only a prelude to the actual climax for this section of the film. Calling up yet another convention of the expedition travelogues, a hunting scene, Trader Horn (and in actuality Harry Carey, the actor portraying Trader Horn) shoots a rhinoceros that the expedition has chanced upon and upset to the point of its charging the group.

It is unquestionable that this extended sequence may be described as contributing to the film's fictional narrative by confirming that Trader Horn is a knowledgeable and expert big game hunter, and by thematically underscoring the dangers of the African locale where the narrative is set. Trader Horn's "Well, lad, that's Africa for you" brings an end to this segment of the film and trumps Peru's earlier comment about the area's peaceful appearance. And it may even be noted that the interlude provides the kind of conventional prefacing calm that serves through contrast to intensify the drama of an imminent narrative crisis, in this case, the group's capture by local tribal warriors. But none of these functions adequately accounts for the excessive duration of this section. It is, instead, the documentary "lecture" (the industry label used to describe travelogue voice-over commentary) and the spectacle of the travelogue subject matter that drive this passage of the film.

It seems naive to describe filmmaking such as this as careless or flawed. Rather, these examples demonstrate that in some circumstances even the most basic tenets of the classical Hollywood cinema could become of negotiable importance to studios whose primary concern was the creation of films with appeal to mass audiences.

In fact, the contradictory impulses of the hybrid films made the resulting movies uniquely well suited for mass audiences and the national marketplace as these were understood by the film industry and the trade press. Specifically, the audience for studio films was still conceived by the industry as all-inclusive, ideally requiring movies that offered pleasures for both urban and rural viewers and all members of the family. The travelogue-based hybrid films were uniquely suited to meet such varied demands (which were stereotypically imagined by the studios) through their inclusion of educational animal subject matter for children; hunting, animal fights, and adventurous narrative for the men; and, in all likelihood, a romance subplot for the women in the audience. Among the listing of twenty-three "Catchlines" provided to exhibitors by the MGM press book for *Trader Horn* was, "See wild animals in the jungles – the savage war dance of the Isorgi – thousands of crocodiles – the savage elephants of Africa – as a gigantic background for a great romance of love" (Metro-Goldwyn-Mayer 1930: 2).

In addition to potentially attracting multiple segments of the mass audience, the hybrid film also allowed considerable promotional flexibility to local exhibitors by providing them with a range of textual components, and related extratextual topics, that could be selectively emphasized in order to tailor local advertising to the particular interests of their communities. The press book for a movie like *Trader Horn* included copy about the educational, biographical, genre, star, and production process appeals of the film that could be forwarded to local newspapers. Exhibitors were free to make use of whatever portions of this information might prove advantageous in their area.

Paradoxically, then, the travelogue-incorporating hybrid films described above demonstrate that documentary representation could simultaneously be a seemingly threatening source of disruption of the normal harmony of the Hollywood text as well as a uniquely beneficial added resource for the industry's marketing efforts.

The feature-length travelogues and hybrid films described above subsequently died out of the American cinema. There were several clear and immediate reasons for this development. Owing to filmmakers' interest in only the most simplistic and obviously distinctive aspects of exotic reality, it became increasingly difficult for them to continue locating new examples of such material with appeals extensive enough to warrant feature-length hybrid productions. And for the studios the effort of creating the hybrid texts, especially when they involved distant-location shooting, may have seemed like more trouble than it was worth. *Trader Horn* was a tremendous commercial and critical triumph for MGM, and it became a kind of signature film ("From the studio that brought you *Trader Horn*") for the next several years. But it was also a cautionary success in the eyes of the rest of the industry, for its completion required a year of additional work in Hollywood (and, according to some trade reports, in Mexico), and its production costs grew to an extravagant two million dollars. In the early 1930s few studios wanted to become entangled in this degree of production effort and financial risk.

Yet travelogue representation did not disappear altogether from the American cinema. First of all, the short feature became a preferred, virtually standardized industry format for continuing to provide documentary representation of the world at large. Newsreels mined this territory as well, quite possibly with adverse impact on the production of the travelogue shorts because of their ability to "scoop" more time-consuming film productions in delivering spectacular exotic material to the screen, that is, recorded subject matters that might have otherwise functioned as the climactic payoff of travelogue short features primarily consisting of more mundane travel footage. Second, the 1930s became a period of greater facility in the use of rear-screen projection. By the mid-1930s *Variety* carried increasing numbers of references to camera crews being dispatched by studios to distant locales to "gather atmosphere" for upcoming films, that is, footage that would be used as punctuating montage passages between narrative segments of films, or as rear-screen contexts to foregrounded narrative action staged and recorded within the studios. Van Dyke (though he had not yet given up hybrid films) followed *Trader Horn* with *Tarzan, the Ape Man* (1932), which contented itself with invoking Africa by means of the excess footage from the *Trader Horn* production. Clearly, Hollywood maintained an interest in more realistic representations of the world in which its narratives were set but stopped short of a commitment to representational authenticity requiring location shooting of narrative. Ultimately, the studios wanted picturesque backgrounds more than reality.

Given the trajectory of the preceding discussion, which has described a striking emergence of documentary filmmaking in American feature film production in the early 1930s followed by its eventual relegation, within a few years, to theatrical program subordination as short features and textual containment as visual backdrops for narrative, it would be tempting to conclude that this period of the American cinema is merely a curious momentary exception that proves the rule—an aberrant occasion of potential challenge that was soon co-opted and normalized by Hollywood's reassertion of its traditional narrative priorities.

Tempting, but not quite accurate. Two broader contexts (each of which deserves more extended exploration than is possible here) provide an alternative, and corrective, perspective on the matter of travelogue and documentary filmmaking and their relationship to Hollywood filmmaking.

First, specifically within the 1930s the travelogue was not the only form of documentary staking out ground within Hollywood films. For example, the unquestionable attraction that made a commercial hit of 20th Century-Fox's 1936 release *The Country Doctor* was the embedded documentary recordings of the Dionne Quintuplets (teasingly withheld to serve as the film's climax), who were objects of extraordinarily intense public enthusiasm since their births in 1934. Warner Brothers' *Boulder Dam* (1936) made use of generous amounts of newsreel footage of the construction of the dam for its film capitalizing on public awareness of that momentous event. The fan dancer Sally Rand, who achieved public prominence at the Chicago World's Fair in 1933, was cast in Paramount's *Bolero* (1934) to do her act. And *Vogues of 1938* (1937) is one of a number of recurrent Hollywood productions incorporating fashion-show segments (here staged with a dozen famous models) catering overtly to public interest in current fashion. In this film the documentary spectacle of fashion was the prime justification for the unusual added production expense of shooting the film in color.

The broader point here is that although the spectacles of the travelogue documentary may have been exhausted, at the same time the field of real-world subject matters that we might describe as the "domestic exotic" realm of 1930s America remained plentiful and engaging and retained their power to disruptively stop narrative in its tracks for passages of documentary recording. Recordings such as those mentioned above, of celebrities, novelty acts, current events, and popular culture fads, were a staple resource of 1930s films and their continuous quest for innovative film material. And they were especially useful for enhancing film projects that would not be carried by big-name stars and/or A-picture production values.

Second, the increased frequency of location shooting in post–World War II filmmaking virtually assures a textual tension between the spectacle value of reality and the character-based focus of narrative, along with the potential for the real world to escape its narrative bounds. The travelogue tradition constitutes a latent presence within any landscape imagery, even while it is a background to narrative action. As stated earlier, it takes only such routine cinematic situations as camera placement at a great enough distance to allow the landscape to compete with narrative action for viewer attention, or screen duration of a shot that extends sufficiently to allow a viewer to read its narrative content and then shift his or her attention to the background, for the compelling power of documented reality to become an attraction in its own right.[5]

It is impossible to close without at least briefly acknowledging the recent appearance in widespread commercial exhibition of feature-length documentaries such as *The Real Cancun* (2003) and *Winged Migration* (2002). For they serve to call into question the degree to which it is appropriate to describe as unique the early 1930s period discussed above. In fact, once again innovative developments in recording technologies, activities on the margins of Hollywood filmmaking (IMAX among them, but more important in this particular moment the explosion of reality and other more traditional documentary programming on television), and increased public interest in the spectacle of reality have created circumstances conducive to the mainstream viability of the pleasures of the travelogue.

Notes

1. Ironically, some trade press commentary speculated that audiences may have misinterpreted the marquee listings of the film as promotions for newsreel coverage. Other assessments noted that the film's exhibition coincided

with the annual downturn in attendance that accompanied hot summer temperatures (at a time when theaters lacked air-conditioning), and that in light of this context the film's box office performance was good even though it may have fallen short of studio expectations.

2. Starting in August 1930 *Variety* carried articles commenting on industry film shortages. This discussion went hand-in-hand with the topic of film quality. Lack of quality in summer and fall 1930 studio releases was judged responsible for the frequent failure of films to cover their scheduled first-run exhibition periods. As a result studios scrambled to fill screen time. In December, in New York City, RKO did a return engagement of *Africa Speaks*, which had not even played strongly in its first run.

3. See Naficy (in this volume) for a detailed study of Schoedsack and Cooper's work on *Grass*.

4. While I am concentrating on this portion of the film because of its succession of scenes and their cumulative digressive duration, it should also be noted that another comparable and striking sequence, devoted to apparent ethnographic observation of Kikuyu village life, occurs earlier in the film.

5. Related to this discussion is the emphasis on spectacle in contemporary high-concept action films, which has resulted in the abandonment of narrative unity in favor of extended (documenting) passages that dwell on the representation of events in excess of their narrative significance.

"The Last of the Great (Foot-Slogging) Explorers"

LEWIS COTLOW AND THE ETHNOGRAPHIC IMAGINARY

IN POPULAR TRAVEL FILM

AMY J. STAPLES

IIIIIIIIIIIIIIIIIIIIIIIIIIIIIIIIIIIIIIIIIIIIIIIIIIIIIIIIIIIIIIIIIIIIIIIIIIIIIIIIIIIIIIIIIIIIIIIIIIIIIIIIIIIIIIIIIIIIIIIIIII

"Travel and travellers are two things I loathe—and yet here I am, all set to tell the story of my expeditions." Thus begins *Tristes tropiques*, the renowned book by the anthropologist Claude Lévi-Strauss, a statement that frames his reflections on travel and fieldwork in Brazil after a fifteen-year absence (1961: 17). In the first chapter, Lévi-Strauss delivers a harsh critique of lantern lectures and other eye-witness accounts by fellow travelers returning from voyages to exotic places. And while he endeavors to distinguish himself from this group, Lévi-Strauss acquiesces to the common "funereal" fate of lecturers (young anthropologists included) at less than prestigious venues in France. Perhaps there are more similarities between anthropologists and travel lecturers in historical hindsight, as the book labors under the social and political concerns of its time—postwar anxieties about the atomic age and lamentations about the destruction of tribal societies—and offers a self-reflexive gaze on the adventurous, traveling anthropologist.

Since the publication of *Tristes tropiques*, anthropologists, cultural critics, and other scholars have initiated a highly debated critique of the scientific practices of anthropology and ethnography. In large part, these discussions have focused on the intrinsic relationships between travel and fieldwork practices and the affinities between travel accounts and ethnographic texts (Clifford and Marcus 1986; Clifford 1988, 1997). Some anthropologists have situated their own fieldwork within travel discourses and popular tourist sites, drawing insightful parallels between explorers, ethnographers, travelers, and tourists (Bruner 1996; Bruner and

Kirshenblatt-Gimblett 1994). Visual anthropologists and ethnographic filmmakers have taken up the reflexive challenge in recent decades, unraveling the complexities of "filming culture" that involve a different set of methodological tools and representational techniques than "writing culture" (Banks and Morphy 1997; Ruby 2000). However, up to this point, few have examined the historical and discursive relationships between travel and ethnographic films. The analysis pursued in this essay is part of a broader research project that aims to uncover the shared practices and discourses of travelers, anthropologists, and tourists.

This essay explores the historical conjunctures among travel, anthropology, and tourism through the popular adventure books and films of Lewis Cotlow (1898–1987), an insurance broker, world traveler, and independent filmmaker. Like Lévi-Strauss, Cotlow traveled in the Amazon region of South America during the 1940s and experienced a series of parallel adventures and encounters with Amazonian Indians. I use Cotlow's commercially released expeditionary film *Jungle Headhunters* (1950) as a vehicle for pursuing critical overlaps among travel, ethnography, and filmmaking, focusing on the construction of an ethnographic imaginary within the film. While I concentrate on specific cultural sequences, this is only a preliminary sketch of the many cinematic, ethnographic, and touristic issues the film raises. However, I hope to illustrate how a serious consideration of expeditionary films like *Jungle Headhunters* has wider implications for a more in-depth study of the relationships between popular and scientific practices of filmmaking.

The decades between Robert Flaherty's *Nanook of the North* (1922) and John Marshall's *The Hunters* (1956) marked the emergence and coalescence of the scientific disciplines of ethnographic film and visual anthropology. There are notable instances of cinema's great potential in the field of anthropology (e.g., Margaret Mead's and Gregory Bateson's work in Bali in the 1930s); however, prior to the institutionalization of ethnographic film at Harvard University and other sites in the late 1950s, expeditionary and travel films with anthropological or natural history content were primarily geared toward popular audiences. The 1920s to 1950s represented a period of great experimentation in the production of motion picture films about exotic cultures, especially during the postwar years as travelers and tourists enjoyed access to remote areas of the globe through modern transportation technologies. Traveling filmmakers also benefited from lighter, more mobile and sophisticated equipment, including 16mm film cameras and sound-recording technologies. Historical archives in libraries and museums around the world contain rich evidence of these early cinematic practices, the majority of which were filmed by amateurs and self-taught filmmakers, not anthropologists or professionally trained filmmakers. In large part, these collections were donated by or purchased from a disparate group of travelers, missionaries, colonial officials, scientists, businessmen, safari hunters, and tourists, to name a few. These collections represent a wide range of cinematic genres including home movies, travelogues, expeditionary films, natural history films, anthropological films, and Hollywood "jungle" documentaries.[1]

As popular discourses on Western and non-Western cultures, travelogues and expeditionary films reached mass audiences through the film lecture circuit and special screenings at museums, scientific organizations, social clubs, church groups, schools, and small movie theaters. Many of the more entrepreneurial filmmakers produced popular travel programs and lectured across the country with their two-reelers or edited films, providing club-like audiences with "expert" testimonials of far-off places and peoples around the globe (Caldwell 1977; P. Imperato and E. Imperato 1992; Musser and Nelson 1991; Zimmermann 1995). The capability of recording location sound (and later synchronous sound and color film) enabled travelogue and expeditionary films to achieve renewed vigor and new audiences during the period of the 1930s to the 1950s (Doherty 1999; see also Dana Benelli's essay in this volume). The Hollywood film industry reacted opportunistically to these developments, especially with the breakup of the studio monopoly and increased competition from television in the postwar years (De Grazia and Newman 1982: 40–76). Major studios like RKO Radio Pictures, Inc., attempted to create a new market niche for travel and exploration documentaries by producing and distributing independent films with commercially exploitable content (e.g., exotic rituals, partial nudity) that would both pass the censors (as educational or documentary footage) and shore up box office receipts. *Jungle Headhunters*, for example, was produced as a B-movie by RKO and distributed in first-run movie theaters in 1950.

Historically, travelogues and expeditionary films provided an important educational venue for popular audiences interested in the everyday lives, cultural practices, and spiritual beliefs of little-known cultures. Often, the filmmaker's connections with museums and scientific institutions served as an endorsement for the authenticity and educational value of their films. Given their popular status and international circulation, these independent filmmakers reached wider audiences than most anthropologists and ethnographic filmmakers and helped shape popular discourses about global cultures. Even today, ethnographic films speak to a relatively narrow sector of the public in classrooms, universities, professional meetings, and film festivals. In view of a spate of popular anthropological television programs in recent decades—the *Disappearing World* series (Granada Television), the *Millennium* series (Public Broadcasting Service), the *World's Wildest Tribes* (Discovery Channel), and the *NGS Explorer* series (National Geographic Television), to mention a few—an analysis of travel films is critical in reexamining the historical roots of documentary and ethnographic cinema.

"Last of the great (foot-slogging) explorers":[2]
A Vanishing Breed of Men

During a meeting at the Explorer's Club in New York City in the late 1940s, a member reminisced: "In the old days, all you had to have to be an explorer was guts and a good gun. Now you have to have brains, too" (Scullin 1948). This anonymous remark resembles Susan Sontag's comment in "The Anthropologist as Hero" on the paradoxical position of the anthropologist. Citing Lévi-Strauss's *Tristes tropiques*, she notes that anthropology "is one of the rare intellectual vocations that do not demand a sacrifice of one's manhood. Courage, love of adventure, and physical hardiness—as well as brains—are called upon" (1970: 189). As an explorer and amateur ethnographer, Cotlow participated in feats of scientific heroism, masculinity, and adventure in the twentieth century. The anthropological principle of salvage ethnography (i.e., to study, record, and collect "primitive cultures" before they disappear) provided a lofty rationale for his expeditions by preserving images of "vanishing" cultures on film for the benefit of humanity. When characterizing his visits with "Stone Age" peoples, Cotlow made his mission more compelling with such public statements as "The twentieth century was breathing down my neck" (Clemence 1977) or "I just got in under the line" (Hubbard 1977). It was, in fact, the myth of "disappearing" cultures that allowed him to construct his own image as "the last of the great (foot-slogging) explorers"—a vanishing breed of men who returned from their adventures with precious cinematic trophies.

Cotlow's global peregrinations spanned seven decades and straddled major historical shifts in exploration, travel, and mass tourism during

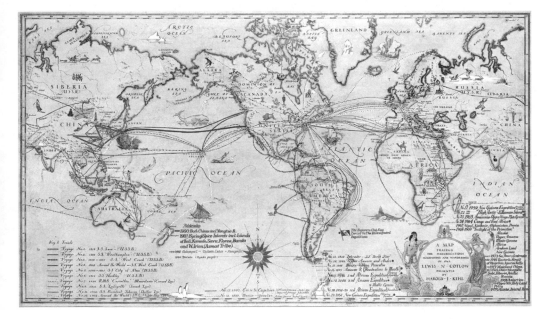

1   A centerpiece in Cotlow's collection, this world map outlines over thirty voyages and expeditions undertaken during his lifetime. Depicted in the iconographic style of eighteenth- and nineteenth-century maps, this artifact evokes an earlier age of heroic exploration and discovery. The title reads: "A Map Tracing the Peregrinations, Migrations and Wanderings of One Lewis N. Cotlow, presented by Harold J. Kihl." A duplicate copy of Cotlow's map hangs in the halls of the Explorer's Club in New York. Courtesy of Museum of Natural History and Science, Cincinnati Museum Center.

the twentieth century (Figure 1). Following in the footsteps of Burton Holmes, Martin and Osa Johnson, Frank Buck, Armand Denis, and others, Cotlow successfully weathered the transition from lantern slide lecturer to independent filmmaker to radio and television personality. Although he took advantage of modern modes of transportation (airplanes, trucks, and all-terrain vehicles), his films tend to focus on more adventurous "foot-slogging" treks through rugged environments to reach isolated peoples. Furthermore, Cotlow's status as a belated explorer situated him at the vanguard of global processes of culture contact, change, and commodification, helping lay the groundwork for what is now marketed as "adventure tourism."

While Cotlow earned his living as an insurance broker, he made an international reputation as an explorer, author, and filmmaker.[3] By 1937 he had made unusual strides in the insurance business and within travel and scientific circles. These contacts and influences prompted his first African expedition to the Belgian Congo (Congo) and Tanganyika (Tanzania), where he shot motion pictures for the lecture circuit and collected ethnological specimens for the American Museum of Natural History (AMNH) in New York.[4] Early color footage produced on this trip was incorporated into a film program entitled *Through Africa Unarmed* (ca. 1937) and Cotlow became a popular personality on the lecture tour. In 1940 Cotlow made his first photographic expedition to South America, visiting groups of Yagua and Jivaro (Shuara) peoples in the Upper Amazon and laying claim to the first color film of these groups. Despite mechanical difficulties with his camera, he managed to salvage enough footage for another presentation, entitled *Upper Amazon and High Andes Adventure* (ca. 1941), launching a second successful lecture tour. With the support of the U.S. State Department and the Office of Inter-American Affairs, Cotlow returned to the Amazon in 1945 and 1949 and continued to collect artifacts for the AMNH. The footage he collected during these various trips was combined to produce his most commercially successful film, *Jungle Headhunters* (RKO, 1950). In 1963 and 1968, with the support of the Indian protectionist Orlando Villa Boas, Cotlow undertook two additional trips to South America, revisiting indigenous groups in the Upper Amazon, Xingu, and Matto Grosso regions of Brazil.

The Ethnographic Imaginary

Historical and discursive affinities between travel and ethnographic films teach us how cinematic representations are embedded in wider historical, social, and political discourses about others and ultimately about ourselves. As a non-anthropologist, Cotlow had few pretensions about maintaining scientific objectivity and openly expressed subjective feelings and psychological states in his books and films. In fact, he developed a reflexive stance that disclosed aspects of travel and filmmaking not normally included in ethnographic monographs. I suggest that Cotlow's work, as unauthorized (or, some might say, profane) forms of ethnography and ethnographic cinema, can be held up as a "cracked mirror" (Ruby 1982; Crick 1985: 78) to reveal an ethnographic imaginary that pervades both popular and scientific representations of other cultures.

   In this essay I develop the notion of the ethnographic imaginary as a historical and ideological construct for examining popular appropriations of anthropological discourses and constructions of realism and spectacle in expeditionary films. The emphasis on previously unseen (and unheard) cultural performances and rituals in films like *Jungle Head-hunters* not only contributed to their commercial success; it bolstered the authenticity of the images and the ethnographic authority of the filmmakers. In other words, filmmakers like Cotlow were playing with a resonant component in anthropological and popular discourses—the idea that cultural rituals are deeply emblematic of the lives of native peoples. For example, classic ethnographic films like *Trance and Dance in Bali* (Mead and Bateson, 1952); *N/um Tchai: The Ceremonial Dance of the !Kung Bushmen* (Marshall, 1966); and *Les maîtres fous* (Rouch, 1955) have contributed in innumerable ways to essentialized portraits of indigenous peoples (even though anthropologists and ethnographic filmmakers have attempted to decode these enigmatic images in ways nonacademic film-makers have not). However, I am not concerned with debunking Cotlow's images by privileging anthropological knowledge. Instead, my analysis focuses on the realm of myth and cultural representation and examines cinematic and narrative devices at work in *Jungle Headhunters*.

My attention to the ethnographic imaginary is inspired by James Clif-ford's discussion of ethnographic allegory, in which he approaches eth-nography "as a performance emplotted by powerful stories" (1986: 98). In *Jungle Headhunters*, Cotlow creates compelling ethnographic alle-gories of salvage, first contact, rites of passage, initiation, participant-observation, and reflexivity in his encounters with South American Indi-ans. Perhaps it should also be noted that Cotlow was no fly-by-night explorer and spent considerable time and energy prior to his expeditions consulting fellow explorers, travelers, filmmakers, and anthropologists. He read extensively from travel and scientific accounts and compiled de-tailed shot lists prior to the film productions. Before filming among the Jivaro Indians of Ecuador and Peru, Cotlow read ethnographic and his-torical accounts by the Smithsonian ethnologist Matthew Stirling (1938) and the anthropologist Rafael Karsten (1923) (Cotlow 1954: 22). These conversations, texts, and illustrations certainly influenced his preconcep-tions of indigenous peoples and form a critical backdrop for any read-ing of his books and films. Therefore, my critique of *Jungle Headhunters* attempts to situate the film within the context of Cotlow's travel writ-ings, and, where possible in this brief essay, to illustrate the cinematic recycling and reinvention of travel and ethnographic tropes produced in the Amazon.

The Explorer as Ethnographer,
or a "Broker in the Bush"

For contemporary audiences, Cotlow's films probably appear staged, campy, and even outright racist. However, in their time they were billed and consumed as scientific documents with educational value. Press reviews of the time unwittingly acclaimed Cotlow as an anthropologist or ethnologist, while his authorizations by museums and scientific organizations added to his reputation as an authority on "primitive" peoples (Bardsley 1972; Scullin 1948). In fact, he often claimed he *was* "part primitive" (Price 1968: 159). At any rate, Cotlow truly believed he had a special flair for getting along with all types of people (the "high brow and the low brow," he was fond of saying), a characteristic he saw beneficial in the business of both insurance and exploration. Contemporary news articles made frequent comparisons between these two vocations and Cotlow assumed a savvy image of the "broker in the bush" (*San Francisco Chronicle* 1955).

Ironically, Cotlow displayed contempt for the scholarly pretensions of many scientists, projecting himself as a kind of folk anthropologist. Speaking of his rapport with primitive peoples, he remarked, "I never treated them like an anthropologist. I never measured their ears or their calf joints. I cared about those people . . . That's why they let me film rituals no outsider had ever before witnessed" (Farber 1983). Through these sorts of quips about the insensitivity and aloofness of anthropologists, Cotlow claimed a kind of quotidian entrée into indigenous societies and offered a point of accessibility for popular audiences. Appealing to his readers and viewers through a brand of palatable anthropology, this self-described "sugar-coated anthropologist" (*The Herald* 1958) provided the metaphorical spoon full of sugar to help the scientific medicine go down.

However, Cotlow's anthropological guise was not simply a ruse to create an aura of scientific authority around his work. Traveling to remote locales in the 1930s to the 1960s, he found himself in the border zones of the ethnographer, surveying and collecting knowledge about little-known cultures. With his tenacious curiosity and lifelong fascination with adventure, Cotlow embodied the salvage impulse in his global search and cinematic preservation of "vanishing" cultures. And as both filmmaker and actor in his productions, he parodied the role of participant-observer in the field, slipping between subjective and objective modalities. In this sense, the "experiential voice" (Pratt 1985: 131) of the traveling filmmaker on the soundtrack contributed significantly to constructions of ethnographic realism in Cotlow's films. Furthermore, Cotlow's use of Kodachrome bolstered the reality effect of his films, perceived as "natural" color in popular and scientific discourses (Staples 2002). Travelogue and expeditionary documentaries of the 1930s-50s, with their focus on chromatic landscapes and visages, played a critical role in "naturalizing" color for their audiences and enhancing public perceptions of realism in color film (Buscombe 1985: 87; Zimmermann 1995: 62).

Headhunters: "Savage Secrets of Nature in the Raw!"

"Why does a man cut off another man's head, shrink it to the size of his fist, and then dance around it?" (Cotlow 1954: 13). With this anthropological query, Cotlow launched his popular travel book *Amazon Head-Hunters* (1954). It is a question that encapsulates his relentless curiosity and preoccupation with "primitive" cultures. In 1949 Cotlow's ultimate goal was to locate and film the Jivaro Indians in color for the first time. While it is difficult to prove whether *Jungle Headhunters* represents the first color footage of the Jivaro, it was certainly among the earliest color feature films to showcase Amazonian Indians. Certainly, the novelty of seeing (and hearing) South American tribes in color for the first time presented RKO with a readily exploitable commodity for marketing the film to American audiences.

The credit sequence opens with a (dorsal) view of a Jivaro *tsantsa* (shrunken head trophy) that rotates on a somewhat shaky pedestal to face its audience—a staged encounter with a (literally) disembodied artifact that simultaneously inscribes the film within the realm of the horrific, cannibalistic, taxidermic, and ethnographic. The shock value of this "encounter" is further enhanced by the use of roughly construed titles and a musical score that resembles those of Hollywood horror films. This particular shrunken head, named "Oscar" by Cotlow,[5] is weighted with symbolic value, for it is both a token of the explorer's success as collector of ethnographic curios and a marker of the film's status as celluloid trophy. The opening sequence also points to the allegorical relationships among head hunting, salvage ethnography, and anthropological filmmaking; to some degree, these practices are involved in the collection, "shrinkage," and preservation of bodies, albeit in different media and cultural contexts.

These taxidermic and archaeological attributes of photography and film have been noted by scholars who suggest that historical reconstructions and practices of salvage ethnography by Carl Akeley, Franz Boas, Edward Curtis, and Robert Flaherty are forms of celluloid taxidermy (Haraway 1989; Morris 1994; Rony 1996; Shohat 1991; Griffiths 1996).

The promotional materials for *Jungle Headhunters* played up the more macabre and sensationalistic aspects of head hunting and head shrinking. Campaign posters featured illustrations of shrunken heads held from their hair by large, hairy hands. Throughout the press campaign, head-hunting practices are compared to America's national pastime: on theater posters, the shrunken heads are held in the palms, with the tagline "For the first time on the screen—SEE human heads shrunk to the size of baseballs!" Cotlow himself made frequent comparisons between Utitiaja (one of the Jivaro chiefs featured in the film) and baseball legend Babe Ruth, whose record of fifty-eight home runs (at the time) proved stiff competition for Utitiaja's fifty-eight heads. In addition to posters, lobby cards, film stills, radio spots, and educational literature on head hunting, the press book offered audiences the chance to buy "simulated Jivaro shrunken heads" at ten dollars apiece. According to the advertisement, the heads were "tinted, with real hair, 6 1/2" high, [and] slightly larger than the real native product for better display." These model heads were used by film exhibitors at theatrical venues and as educational displays at schools and libraries.

A survey of Cotlow's books, films, and promotional campaigns reveals ambivalent, contradictory discourses on practices of head hunting. In *Jungle Headhunters*, the Jivaro are represented as savage, blood-thirsty killers bent on revenge and too "hot-tempered and independent" to live in villages. Their knowledge of the head-shrinking process is described as a "racial instinct," similar to the survival instincts of animals. The film conflates Jivaro culture with nature and attributes their violence to the severity of their environment and geographic isolation. On the other hand, on other occasions, Cotlow presents the Jivaro as noble savages, their head-hunting practices the result of deep religious conviction and spiritual beliefs. In a radio interview with Edward R. Murrow, Cotlow characterized the Jivaro as "warm and friendly" and "kind and patient." Goodness, he proclaimed, was a universal human trait, while evil was like "an ugly dress that can be cast aside" (Cotlow 1953). The idea that "deep down we are all the same" typified the humanistic beliefs and popular cultural relativism Cotlow espoused.

Imaginary Geographies and First Contact

The creation of imaginary geographies in *Jungle Headhunters* is best illustrated by scenes of arrival and Cotlow's "first contact" scenarios with South American Indians. The filmic narrative reinvents a "heart of darkness" topos in the Amazon through ominous shots of the jungle, menacing animals, hostile Indians, relentless rains, and failed outboard motors—all of which add to the narrative suspense and lead up to climactic scenes with Jivaro headhunters. Cotlow's presence among Amazonian Indians—scenes of arrival, first contact, negotiation, rites of passage, and cultural immersion—are theatrical performances that play up the pre-contact mythos of his subjects and the precariousness of his own position. Working in the compilation mode, Cotlow incorporated footage from three Amazonian expeditions during the 1940s, augmenting scenes of animal life with well-worn stock footage from film libraries, a fact that did not escape contemporary reviewers (Brog 1951).

Jungle Headhunters begins in a leisurely fashion with scenes of Cotlow aboard a propeller plane and his touristic encounters with the Kuna Indians of the San Blas Islands, Panama. Upon his arrival at an unidentified Amazonian port (probably Belem), Cotlow boards a commercial river boat and begins his journey upriver. When he transfers to a dug-out canoe navigated by locals, Cotlow switches to the mode of the intrepid explorer. The party proceeds up several (imaginary) tributaries where they encounter Bororo, Xingu (misidentified as Bororo), and Yagua Indians (who live thousands of miles away on the upper reaches of the Amazon). During a brief respite, the film lapses into the touristic as we are taken on a quick detour to the ancient Incan city of Machu Picchu and the Guano Islands off the coast of Ecuador (see Ruoff 1991, and his essay in this volume, for more on the "detour" feature of travelogues). After visiting the Colorado Indians of Ecuador, Cotlow begins a rugged trek by mule and foot through hazardous mountain terrain to reach his ultimate destination—headhunter territory and "first contact" with Jivaro Indians.

In his search for the most colorful, dramatic South American Indians for commercial exploitation, Cotlow sought out the Bororo peoples of the Matto Grosso region of Brazil (Figure 2). His inspiration to film these "curious giants" came from the photographs of Candido Mariano Da Silva Rondon, leader of the Theodore Roosevelt expedition to northern Brazil in 1916 (Cotlow 1954: 140). "First contact" scenes among the

2 Cotlow discusses the filming of a funerary dance with an unidentified Bororo elder in the Matto Grosso region of Brazil, 1949. Courtesy of Museum of Natural History and Science, Cincinnati Museum Center.

Bororo consist of a staged captivity scenario and tribunal where negotiations are presented as initially dubious, but ultimately friendly. As he paddles up the river with two (Bororo) assistants, Cotlow is surrounded by Bororo men who approach their dug-out canoe with poised bows and arrows. This arrival scene recycles familiar codes of frontier narratives in what has been described as "images of encirclement" (Engelhardt 1971, cited in Stam and Spence 1983: 12), especially in the Hollywood western film. The sudden appearance and bellicose posture of the warrior-like Indians, the circling of the party's canoe (not unlike the wagon trains of the western frontier), and the pleading voice and exasperating gestures of the explorer suture the spectator into the position of victim. The party is then taken to a local village where Cotlow undergoes lengthy negotiations with a group of elders bedecked in feather headdresses (a traditional funerary costume). The first person voice-over of *Jungle Headhunters* emphasizes the intransigence of the Bororo and Cotlow's diplomatic skills (although the gifts never make their appearance):

> As they take us into the jungle, I try to fathom what is going on in their minds. Although they aren't actively hostile, I can sense their resentment. We are on trial. As I look across their faces and they look at me, I feel that a judgment will soon be forthcoming. I try to act in a way that I hope will bring us no trouble . . . I do my best to communicate a feeling of friendliness to them, but it's obvious that past experiences are at odds with any present inclination to accept me. It's impossible for me to know what kind of decision they will make and time drags appallingly as they argue. Do I see a trace of understanding? I say again that I'm unarmed and all I want is permission to visit with them. I bring a few tokens of good will. Then the decision—accepted. Not because of gifts, but because they are convinced I can do no harm. Now we're all friends.

The camera pans slowly across the faces of the Bororo men dressed in elaborate costumes of feathers, paint, resin, and palm fibers, providing a colorful spectacle for the audience. In the next scene, one of the elders speaks directly to the filmmaker with gestures Cotlow later mimics when pleading his own case. This particular scene is allegorical of an imaginary ethnographic encounter where diplomacy, trust, and good will are established. Proof of Cotlow's acceptance comes with the performance of the Bororo funerary dance, characterized as a "ceremonial send-off" for the filmmaker. Simulated African drumming is dubbed over the dance which is compared to a "modern Conga line." This sequence and others like them (e.g., Yagua Indians dance to the beat of country square dance music!) are comedic attempts to familiarize the exotic through the playful editing of images and sound and a surrealistic juxtaposition of the "primitive" and the "modern."

Cotlow's literary account of the Bororo presented an altogether different story of his encounter. In *Amazon Head-Hunters*, he reveals that his visit was made possible by the assistance of the Brazilian Society for the Protection of the Indians (SPI; later the FUNAI, of which Colonel Rondon was president). Furthermore, the party approached the Bororo village in a Ford truck, not a dug-out canoe as represented in the film. And rather than threatening the crew with bows and arrows, the Bororo were rather unimpressed with the white strangers in their midst. However, they were genuinely intrigued with the crew's camera equipment. Cotlow writes: "There was no danger of initial contact with the Bororos, nor was there any reticence to overcome. One of them walked up to me and took my still camera, hanging in a leather case from my neck, and looked it over carefully. Another wanted Neves [the cameraman] to show him how the tripod worked . . . And later the chief difficulty in taking pictures lay in the curiosity of the Indians. They wanted to stop everything and look at the camera in my hand, listen to the little whirring noise it made, and then watch me wind it up again. The only solution was to take half an hour and let them satisfy their curiosity about the cameras completely" (1954: 163–64). This version of Cotlow's encounter clearly disrupts the image of the Bororo as cultural isolates in *Jungle Headhunters* and illustrates their fascination (if not familiarity) with cameras and photographic technologies. It also provides insight into the networks of government sponsorship, cinematic representation, and transnational exchange with which the Bororo were becoming actively engaged (Jordan 1992: 52, 200–201; Rondon 1946).

Rites of Passage, Initiation, and Reflexivity

Cotlow's investment in Kodachrome film also prompted his visit to the Colorado Indians on the western slopes of the Andes in Ecuador. In print, he refers to the Colorado as the "red men of the green jungle," alluding to the red achiote plant they smear on their bodies. With the explorer André Roosevelt (cousin of Theodore Roosevelt), Cotlow visited and photographed (in color) several groups of Colorado Indians in 1940. In 1949 he brought along a copy of his published photographs in *Life* magazine as a "velvet carpet of welcome" to revisit and film groups of Amazonian Indians (Cotlow 1954: 151). When one of the men recognized himself in a photograph, Cotlow was considered an old friend and was invited to the village (242–43). In contrast to the Bororo sequence in *Jungle Headhunters*, Cotlow's arrival scene among the Colorado is preceded by a momentary rupture in the discovery narrative through a critical self-reflexive gaze: "As I first meet these various Indian tribes, I feel like a typical white man passing judgment on a human of another color. But as I enter the Colorados' country, it suddenly hits me. Now the situation is completely reversed. As I face the scrutiny of the people, I see myself for what I am—a mildly interesting white oddity." While this reflexive passage registers Cotlow's prejudice and his anachronistic status as explorer, it also hints at emerging popular discourses on race and cul-

3 Cotlow (center left) becomes a "blood brother" of the Colorado
Indians of Ecuador, 1949. Courtesy of Museum of Natural History
and Science, Cincinnati Museum Center.

tural relativism. Cotlow presents himself as an innocent traveler whose
whiteness is only skin deep, detached from the exploitative histories of
European and American exploration, colonialism, and industry in the
Amazon.

This arrival scene sets the stage for an "initiation" sequence where the
explorer's white skin stands out in stark contrast to the reddened skin of
the Colorado. For Cotlow, the threat of "going native" did not carry the
same kind of taboos that emerged in anthropology, and he readily agrees
to have his body painted and hair trimmed in Colorado fashion. "The
jungle allows no individuality," the soundtrack intones, as Cotlow expresses relief when he sheds his identity and becomes like the Colorado in
appearance. His "initiation" as a "blood brother" performs an allegory of
cultural immersion, "becoming" the other that he has sought (Figure 3).
The comedic effect of this sequence is underscored by frequent cross-
cutting between Cotlow's "initiation" and shots of Colorado children
smoking the explorer's cigarettes and donning some of his clothing. His
status is momentarily transformed to that of an adolescent undergoing

a rite of passage, a parody of the ethnographer in the field. In the end, Cotlow's "initiation" is so complete, he exclaims in *Jungle Headhunters*, "they've done such a fine job of turning me into a blood brother that I can't recognize myself!" Scenes of the "self as other" and the "(young) other as self" play with established boundaries between us and them and speak to broader fascinations with primitivism in postwar America. Cotlow's concluding remark, "even today, a little color lingers on here and there," illustrates the fulfillment of an authentic encounter with Amazonian Indians and the appropriation of ethnographic discourses in expeditionary films and contemporary tourism.

Act Naturally: Ethnographic Realism and "Performative Primitives"

Head-hunting scenes in *Jungle Headhunters* highlight seemingly contradictory issues of documentary realism and theatrical performance in expeditionary film. Cotlow's style of filmmaking helped revitalize an earlier tradition of ethnographic melodrama filmed in authentic locales with indigenous actors by filmmakers like Curtis and Flaherty in the early twentieth century. In other words, the Jivaro are in the curious position of playing themselves in the ethnographic present/past, acting in the reconstruction of traditional culture untouched by outside influences. The head-hunting raid and ritualistic scenes that follow promulgate the mythology that the Jivaro were just going about their daily lives unaffected by the presence of the film crew, camera equipment, guides, and interpreters. Cotlow's statements on the natural acting talents of primitive peoples (e.g., that "primitives are great hams who act out glorious deeds at the drop of a hat" [1966: 313]) only added to the construction of ethnographic realism in his films. In fact, these cultural performances, observational modes of filmmaking, and didactic voice-overs construct ethnography *as* theater — staged performances of native life from the perspective of the invisible filmmaker as ethnographer.

Although Cotlow repeatedly claimed he used no script and relied on reality to guide his filmmaking, his books describe in brazen detail the selection of actors, staging of events, and reenactment of daily routines and cultural rituals. Discussing the production of *Jungle Headhunters*, he reveals that the Jivaro were fully aware of the filming process, participated enthusiastically in its production, and displayed talent for their dramatic roles. The translations and interpretations of Cotlow's directions were critical, of course, as was the Jivaros' ability to "act naturally" for the camera. In other words, the filmic production represented a complex process of interaction, translation, collaboration, and exchange. These collaborations can be seen as instances of "autoethnography," a term used by Mary Louise Pratt to describe "instances in which the colonized subjects undertake to represent themselves in ways that *engage with* the colonizer's terms" (1992: 7).

While Cotlow based his selection of actors on physical attributes and warrior stereotypes, the filming of head-hunting sequences embodied aspects of autoethnography and presaged the construction of "performative primitives" in the Amazon. For example, when the initial tsantsa dance did not meet his expectations, Cotlow intervened and demonstrated how he wanted the men to perform for the camera:

> "Everyone of you has come home with a tsantsa!" I cried. "Remember how you danced *then*, how you felt *then*. Dance that way now. Thrust your lance hard, as if you were facing an enemy." Shuara [the interpreter/guide] translated as fast as I spoke. Then I demonstrated what I meant, leaping forward energetically and pushing the lance with what I hoped was a dramatic and vital movement of the whole body. They all burst out laughing! It caught me off balance, for just a moment, and then I realized how ludicrous it was for me to be telling these men how to thrust a *chonta* lance, how to do a victory dance around a shrunken head. I laughed, too, and retired somewhat abashed, but pleased to see this mixed group of enemies laughing together. And my instructions helped. The men got the idea of what I wanted, in any event, and when the dance started again it had zest and earnestness and life to it. (1966: 274–75)

Pleased with the Jivaros' acting talents and his skills as director and cultural broker, Cotlow reflected on this episode in one of his books: "*Acting came closer and closer to reality* as each man remembered other times when he had danced the victory dance after a successful raid" (1954: 112, emphasis added). The mythology that "primitives" cannot distinguish between acting and reality is another common exploration trope that added to the illusion of realism in Cotlow's films. Interestingly, Cotlow eventually comes to the idea that acting can generate the same feelings and emotions as those of a headhunter. In *Amazon Head-Hunters*, Cotlow relates how he was encouraged to join in the dance, completing the processes of cultural initiation and immersion suggested in the film:

> I found myself emitting a hoarse grunt along with the others, and being a part of that movement, a contributor to that weird sound, made me share their feelings, somehow. A steady rhythm can do strange things to people and for a few minutes it almost made a Jivaro out of me. Across the circle I watched the shrunken head as it bobbed against Juantinga's chest. I looked at Juantinga's face and saw a rapt, dedicated expression that welled up from the depths of his soul. And I felt something of that emotion myself. For a little while I was very close to experiencing the feelings of a man who has cut off another man's head, has shrunk it, and now dances around it. (1954: 275–76)

The head-hunting sequence in *Jungle Headhunters* is a dramatic performance in which Jivaro warriors embark on a raid into enemy territory. After crossing a treacherous river, they encounter a trap made of sharp bamboo daggers fixed with curare tips. One of the scouts is "killed," but the men eventually appear from behind the bushes with the decapitated "head" of an enemy warrior wrapped in cloth. The "attack" is not shown (or performed for that matter) but only hinted at through camera pans of the foliage and a musical crescendo. The raiding party returns to the *jivaria* (village) with their dead warrior and enemy trophy, where they are met by grieving relatives. Juantinga, the "victor," begins the head-shrinking process as the voice-over describes in detail the various stages of skull removal, sealing, boiling, whirling hot sand, and drying the tsantsa. These scenes promote an ethnographic sensibility and privileged point of view which allows the audience to vicariously spy on the realm of the sacred, the forbidden, and the taboo. The camera, however, remains at a distance, as close-ups of the head would reveal its pre-shrunkenness. Finally the tsantsa is placed around the victor's neck and a dance is performed by a group of Jivaro men dressed in ritual costume. Portrayed as enacting a "victory celebration," the group shuffles in a semi-circle around the tsantsa, which has now been mounted on a spear.

In *Jungle Headhunters*, the natural world is portrayed as maternal and protective, yet violent, wild, and resistant—an ambivalent nature that "cradles" Amazonian peoples but poses a threat to their very survival. In the final scene, the tsantsa visually dissolves into the mountainous landscape, a transition symbolic of a disembodied male culture threatened by a feminized natural order. Cotlow played within these natural and cultural boundaries, temporally losing himself but emerging triumphantly with his trophies—a Jivaro shrunken head and prized color motion picture film of Amazonian Indians, as his voice-over concludes:

> I've found what I came looking for. And as I look at the shrunken head and try to fathom the cruelties of man, the head seems to dissolve into nature herself, the nature that cradles these people inside barriers whose very appearance cries "Do not enter!" The millions of acres of virgin rain forests, the menacing sentinels of piranha, slithering anaconda, the torrential rivers, the treacherous mountain ranges, behind these barriers only men crueler than nature can survive!

In the final analysis, *Jungle Headhunters* illustrates the capture and "shrinkage" of celluloid bodies on film and the appropriation of ethnographic discourses and idioms in popular expeditionary films. The film foreshadowed reflexive critiques in anthropology and transcultural processes that later emerged with the spread of new media technologies to remote areas like the Amazon. As evident in episodes of cultural performance in *Jungle Headhunters* and the display of Cotlow's photographs in *Life* magazine (Figure 4), photographic and cinematic practices in the Amazon were part of a longer history of colonial contact, exchange, and the global circulation of images. Expeditionary filmmakers like Cotlow also draw our attention to a more complex prehistory of indigenous media in the Amazon, for example, among the Kayapó in the 1970s (Turner 1992) and more recently among indigenous Amazonian political activists and environmentalist groups during the 1980s and 1990s.

As Beth Conklin (1997) has illustrated, signs of visual exoticism and Western notions of primitivism and authenticity now carry symbolic capital in the realm of Amazonian identity politics and global media circuits. Through bodily appearance (adornment, feathers, and nudity) and the use of video technology, Amazonian peoples have learned how to negotiate and manipulate these symbols for empowerment within their own local, national, and international political struggles. While Conklin warns that these representational strategies may have negative consequences as reified images of exoticism (1997: 727), they also point to alternate visions of cultural authenticity and innovative uses of visual media in social and political contexts outside the West. In this sense, indepen-

4 Cotlow shows a copy of his published photographs of "head-hunters" in *Life* magazine (1946) to a group of Jivaro Indians on a return trip to the upper Amazon, 1949. Courtesy of Museum of Natural History and Science, Cincinnati Museum Center. Reprinted with the permission of Scribner, an imprint of Simon & Schuster Adult Publishing Group, from *The Twilight of the Primitive* by Lewis N. Cotlow. Copyright 1971 by Lewis Cotlow.

dent expeditionary filmmakers like Cotlow were at the forefront of postcolonial processes of globalization, transnational exchange, indigenous agency, and change among remote Amazonian communities. As a hybrid form of commercial expeditionary film, *Jungle Headhunters* incorporated aspects of popular adventure, anthropology, and ethnographic realism, preceding by almost two decades the production of academically based ethnographic films in the Amazon.

The Persistent Primitive, or the "Last"
Is Always Yet to Come . . .

Images of the noble savage abound in contemporary forms of mass media
— television documentaries, advertising campaigns, photography books,
and tourist brochures provide ample proof that primitivist stereotypes
hold supreme capital in the arena of global images. Despite the well-worn
trope of the "vanishing primitive," this idea still captures the popular
imagination and continues to be recycled, transformed, and commodified. Amazingly, in 1985, at the age of eighty-seven, Cotlow still toured
around the country with his popular lecture film *Vanishing Africa*, paral-
leling the ongoing travel film lectures described by Jeffrey Ruoff in this
volume. With the introduction of sound technologies and color film,
Cotlow breathed new life into the "primitive" bodies displayed on the
screen. These cinematic technologies and the filmmakers who experi-
mented in the field created new standards of realism and authenticity in
popular forms of documentary and ethnographic cinema. Traveling filmmakers like Cotlow were early pioneers in the representation and commodification of "performative primitives," forging the tourist circuits,
networks, and exchange relations in which global cultures are now thoroughly mediated.

Historical travel and expeditionary films offer a unique porthole into
the production and reception of early forms of ethnographic cinema.
They provide clues to both producer and audience perceptions of realism and scientific truth, especially with the development of new cinematic
technologies. Cotlow's films also help situate ethnographic productions
within a milieu of popular, sometimes competing, cinematic representations of indigenous peoples. As allegories of exploration, travel, and
ethnography, his books and films provide a glimpse into the cultural
mindsets of anthropologists, travelers, and tourists, relating stories about
ourselves and our own desires. The haunting vision of Lévi-Strauss in
Tristes tropiques reflected Western preoccupations with authenticity, nostalgia, disappearance, and the destruction of "natural Man," especially in
the wake of the nuclear age (1961: 389). Perhaps our own anxieties about
truth and artificiality are reassured by knowing that somewhere, in remote pockets of the world, there are still vestiges of humanity uncor-
rupted by the West — the universal essence of man in Rousseau's writings,
which so intrigued Lévi-Strauss. However, we clearly live in a differ-

ent world when Western codes of authenticity and exoticism are re-appropriated by contemporary Amazonian activists and used as political and ethnic symbols in campaigns for self-determination. The tropics, it seems, are not so sad after all.

Notes

1. For example, the Human Studies Film Archives (HSFA) at the National Museum of Natural History, Smithsonian Institution; the Special Collections Library, American Museum of Natural History (AMNH); the University of California Film Archives, Los Angeles (UCLA); and the Nederlands Filmmuseum contain many examples of these collections. See Wintle and Homiak 1995; Root 1987; Hertogs and de Klerk 1997.

2. Throughout his life, Cotlow promoted an image of himself as "the last of the great explorers." A documentary film entitled *Last of the Great Explorers: The Lewis Cotlow Story* (1985) was made about his life. I borrow the phrase "last of the great (foot-slogging) explorers" from the film. A reference videotape is available at the HSFA.

3. Cotlow died in 1987 and is buried in Jupiter, Florida. For more on his extensive publications, films, and television programs, see Staples 2002. Cotlow donated the majority of his collection of artifacts, documents, films, and photographs to the Museum of Natural History and Science, Cincinnati Museum Center (MNHS/CMC) in Ohio. His motion picture films were later transferred to the HSFA for preservation and research.

4. During the 1930s-60s, Cotlow donated over seventy ethnological artifacts from his trips to South America and Africa to the American Museum of Natural History (New York). I am grateful to Dr. Enid Schildkrout, Rene Gravois, and Kristen Mable in the Department of Anthropology there for this information.

5. Perhaps a fitting tag considering the award trophies of the Academy of Motion Picture Arts and Sciences. This shrunken head is now in the collection of the MNHS/CMC, with the rest of Cotlow's donated artifacts, photographic negatives, and manuscripts, catalogue #A12357.

Show and Tell

THE 16MM TRAVEL LECTURE FILM

We are the last of the vaudevillians.
We go from town to town, set up our projectors,
our sound systems, do our shows, and then drive on.
—John Holod

JEFFREY RUOFF

IIIIIIIIIIIIIIIIIIIIIIIIIIIIIIIIIIIIIIIIIIIIIIIIIIIIIIIIIIIIIIIIIIIIIIIIIIIIIIIIIIIIIIIIIIIIIIIIIIIIIIIIIIIIIIIIIIIIIIIIIIIIIIIIII

As this anthology suggests, film history should be about all aspects of the medium, not simply those of the dominant entertainment cinema. Promoting only documentary or avant-garde alternatives, however, further marginalizes other forms, such as newsreels, educational films, industrials, home movies, and, of course, travelogues. In this essay I argue that the travel lecture film—a silent travelogue presented with live narration by an itinerant filmmaker—is the archetypal form of the travelogue in cinema.[1] Still today, travel lectures take place at hundreds of venues across North America, including museums (the Portland Art Museum in Oregon), concert halls (the San Diego Symphony Hall), universities (the University of Colorado-Boulder), and community clubs (the Kodak Camera Club of Rochester, New York) (Figure 1).[2]

The travel lecture formed an important part of early cinema, flourished in later years, and continues today, notwithstanding predictions of its demise in the age of television, virtual reality, and the Internet. Despite continuities with pre-cinematic forms and early cinema, the travel lecture film remains a little-studied genre. Because it involves a live performance, it cannot be analyzed apart from its idiosyncratic screenings. As Thayer Soule eloquently puts it in his autobiography *On the Road with Travelogues, 1935-1995*, a travelogue "lives only when the producer and his audience are together" (1997: 136-37). As such, they leave few historical traces. In

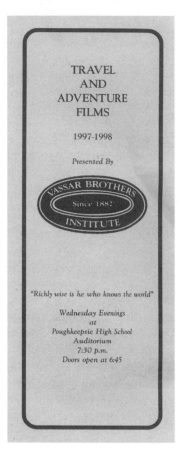

TRAVEL
AND
ADVENTURE
FILMS

1997-1998

Presented By

VASSAR BROTHERS
Since 1882
INSTITUTE

"Richly wise is he who knows the world"

*Wednesday Evenings
at
Poughkeepsie High School
Auditorium
7:30 p.m.
Doors open at 6:45*

1 A live travelogue series brochure from the Vassar Brothers Institute, Poughkeepsie, NY, 1998. Courtesy of the Vassar Brothers Institute, copyright Vassar Brothers Institute.

addition, from the late 1930s to the 1970s most lecturers projected their 16mm camera original—Kodachrome positive film—until the prints disintegrated (Wiancko 1996: 21). As the colors of the camera original are extraordinarily vivid, and the cost of prints considerable, some producers still follow this practice today. Kodachrome positive prints are one-of-a-kind works, like daguerreotypes, that cannot adequately be replicated. Nowadays, even those producers who shoot negative film rarely make more than one or two release prints. As a result, few such travelogues survive, and fewer still have been archived. But the historical invisibility of the travel lecture film is most evident in its total exclusion from film history books. Kristin Thompson and David Bordwell make no mention of the genre in their otherwise comprehensive eight-hundred-page *Film History* (1994).

2 Poster from the French-language live travelogue *Splendors of the United States*. Courtesy of Eric Courtade, copyright Eric Courtade.

Most research on alternative film production and exhibition practices has been limited to the early decades of cinema. While a ground-breaking issue of the journal *Iris*, edited by André Gaudreault and Germain Lacasse, focuses on the film lecturer, all three hundred pages are devoted to the early cinema period. In their introduction, the editors erroneously claim that the lecturer has "definitively disappeared" (1996: 15). And yet the city of Montreal, where Gaudreault and Lacasse work, boasts a remarkable travelogue industry, which celebrated its thirtieth anniversary in 2002. Les Grands Explorateurs presents travel lecture films with live French-language narration in forty-four different venues throughout Quebec. The 2004 season included such titles as *Le Transsiberien* and *Safari-Kenya*. Connaissance du Monde, the Parisian organization that supplies many of the French-language lecturers to the Quebec series, currently distributes fifty-five travelogues to its six hundred venues in France (Figure 2).

In *The Shows of London*, Richard Altick argues that travel lectures with live narrators originated in London in 1850 (1978: 474). The live travelogue's "show and tell" characteristics have remained remarkably consistent over the past century and a half. Most important is the presence of the filmmaker who addresses the audience directly from the stage. A travel lecture offers a "non-fiction drama of people and places, true but dramatized," as one viewer told me, extending the opportunity to "visit vicariously someplace you can't afford to visit yourself." An audience member in Oregon volunteered another definition: "A travelogue is a story about a far away place—it doesn't have to be far away, yet that seems appropriate—that presents a variety of information about a culture, in an interesting, perhaps unique way."

Many current performers trace their origins to Burton Holmes (Figure 3), who gave over eight thousand illustrated travel lectures, using slides and, later, motion pictures, from the 1890s to the 1950s (Caldwell 1977).[3] Different approaches within the live travelogue include comedy, wildlife, history, and tourist emphases. The filmmaker John Holod, who uses slapstick routines and vaudeville humor, exemplifies the comic approach and continues the tradition of his idols Don Cooper and Stan Midgley. John Wilson prefers to explore the natural world in such movies as *Iceland: Europe's Wild Gem*, while Robin Williams uses historical figures for works such as *Amadeus, a Traveler in Italy*. Others, including Grant Foster and Buddy Hatton, stick to the well-trodden path and highlight enduring tourist sites. Harder to classify is the "travel theater" of Howdee Meyers and Lucia Perrigo in *The Magnificent World of the Mountain King: Ludwig II's Bavarian Castles* or the absurd humor of William Stockdale in travelogues such as *Cemeteries Are Fun*.

Travelogue lecturers are cultural brokers, translators, and interpreters for American audiences. As a measure of their widespread availability, 16mm live travelogues play to greater numbers of people than many foreign features and undoubtedly most avant-garde and ethnographic films. More Americans probably saw Frank Klicar's travel lecture film *The Yugoslav Republics* than Emir Kusturica's masterpiece *Underground* (1995). At the moment, there are at least thirty full-time travelogue filmmakers in North America, while, to my knowledge, no such full-time ethnographic filmmakers exist here at all. There is an established travel lecture circuit;[4] John Holod has dates booked several years in advance (Figure 4).

The 16mm travelogue industry, in its current configuration, has remarkable affinities with the production, distribution, and exhibition of motion pictures at the beginning of the twentieth century (Gunning 1998: 258–62). Individual filmmakers are involved in all facets of the business. Exhibition venues are not uniform and often serve multiple func-

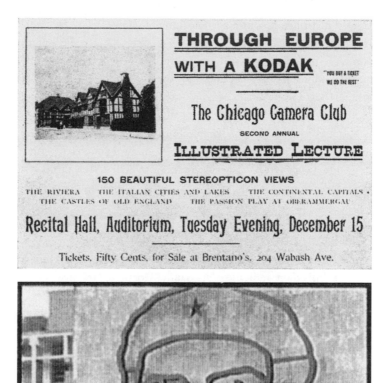

THROUGH EUROPE

WITH A KODAK "YOU BUY A TICKET WE DO THE REST"

The Chicago Camera Club

SECOND ANNUAL

ILLUSTRATED LECTURE

150 BEAUTIFUL STEREOPTICON VIEWS

THE RIVIERA   THE ITALIAN CITIES AND LAKES   THE CONTINENTAL CAPITALS ·
THE CASTLES OF OLD ENGLAND   THE PASSION PLAY AT OBERRAMMERGAU

Recital Hall, Auditorium, Tuesday Evening, December 15

Tickets, Fifty Cents, for Sale at Brentano's, 204 Wabash Ave.

3 A flyer circulated for Burton Holmes's first public performance in Chicago in 1891. Courtesy of the Burton Holmes Collection, Seattle, Wash.

4 A still from John Holod's live travelogue *Cuba at the Crossroads* (1998).

tions. The principal sound accompaniment comes from a live performer in the theater and, correspondingly, varies from show to show. Travel lecturers are not celebrities and, unlike the 1930s the travelogues of Martin and Osa Johnson (Doherty 1994: 38) the films are not usually structured around their personalities. Not only are there no stars in live travelogues, there are frequently no characters at all. As in early cinema, the emphasis is on actuality footage and scenics. Similarly, it is difficult to date travel lecture films. When projected in theaters, many do not have printed titles or credits. Producers have a vested interest in deliberately not dating their films. When I saw Charlie Hartman present *The Sunny South of France* in 1996, I was led to believe the film was new. However, a 1988 advertisement in *Travelogue: The International Travel Film Magazine* indicates that the film had been in distribution for at least eight years.

In venues across North America, travel lecturers enjoy face-to-face contact with their audiences. As Sandy Mortimer, the president of the International Motion Picture and Lecturers Association (IMPALA), said, "If you make a program for television, no one knows your name. When you stand in front of an audience, you are the name above the title." While life on the travelogue circuit may be rewarding, it is not easy. A successful producer typically stays in hotels two hundred and fifty nights a year. One lecturer, recently retired, flew his own plane to his performances. Most travel by car, driving hundreds of miles between shows. Thayer Soule, who apprenticed with Burton Holmes before pursuing his own career, averaged thirty-three thousand miles a year from 1958 to 1995 (Soule 1997: 178). In the end, they spend more time touring cities and towns in America than they do visiting the countries shown in their films.

After a few years lecturing on the road, tired of motels and roadside restaurants, the producer John Holod bought a mobile home. He now lives and tours in this $80,000 vehicle—with satellite TV, VCR, global positioning system, personal computer, films, videos, promotional materials, projectors, and tuxedos—giving over one hundred presentations a year. I accompanied him for two weeks in March 1998 as he presented *Cuba at the Crossroads* on tour from New York to Florida, producing my own documentary about his work, *The Last Vaudevillian* (Figure 5).[5] Holod's motor home is a movie theater and motion picture studio on wheels. When the 1997–98 lecture season ended, he headed north to Alaska to shoot the footage for his next feature, *The Last Great Road Trip: Alaska RV Adventure!* Holod's latest travelogues all prominently feature his motor home as a quasi-character.

The Last Vaudevillian

ON THE ROAD WITH TRAVELOGUE FILMMAKER JOHN HOLOD

A Documentary in Thirty Minutes
By Jeffrey Ruoff

5 A poster for *The Last Vaudevillian: On the Road with Travelogue Filmmaker John Holod* (1998). Courtesy of Jeffrey Ruoff, copyright Vaudeville Vérité.

Mode of Production: The Total Filmmaker

Travelogue producers on the North American circuit are independent entrepreneurs who produce, shoot, record sound, edit, distribute, exhibit, and narrate 16mm movies. Most are Americans of European origin, with university degrees from schools such as the University of Southern California, Stanford University, and Harvard University. Many have had experience in the print, radio, television, and film industries. Like their audience members, many lecturers are over sixty years old. The overwhelming majority of lecturers are men. While there are few women travel lecturers, many wives are involved in the production process and manage the careers of their filmmaker husbands, handling bookings, publicity, and occasionally mixing sound on the lecture tours (*Travelogue* 1992: 49). Producers do not regard learning other languages as a prerequisite to making travelogues. A Canadian filmmaker admitted in his essay "Why the Ukraine?" that the only word he knew of the local language was "*Kanada*" (Willis 1997: 16). Another described filming in

China in the early 1980s "with sign language and a good phrase book" (Green 1996: 23). Even with exceptional ability and the best of intentions, who could learn the languages of the thirty or more countries in which Thayer Soule made travel movies (Soule 1997: 246)?

Travelogues are shot by small crews, often only a few people or a husband-and-wife team, occasionally a lone filmmaker. Location shooting typically takes place during June, July, and August. (There are no screenings during the summer, when it is presumed that travelogue audiences themselves are on the road.) Until the late 1990s, most travelogues were shot with lightweight 16mm spring-wound or battery-powered cameras; few producers record sound in the field. The average shooting ratio for an eighty-minute 16mm feature is five to one. Many older travel lecturers scorn video; one longtime producer referred to the VCR as "an abomination" (Cooper 1996: 36).[6] Despite their disdain, however, many lecturers now sell videotape copies of their works, mostly at the screenings, but also by mail order. (These tapes include recorded voice-over narration, music, and effects that approximate the sound of the live presentations.) For many producers, video sales make the difference between profit and loss.

The initial run of a 16mm travel lecture film is about three to four years, though it may remain in distribution considerably longer. When marketing their works to potential exhibitors, travel filmmakers are anxious to point out the newness of their footage. As the director of *China: The Middle Kingdom* asserted at the 1997 IMPALA film festival, "There are no whiskers on this film; it was shot only six months ago." Given the initial investment, however, producers are inevitably drawn back to film in the same regions, a process that encourages updating films. For example, a director with *Hong Kong* in his catalogue may shoot additional footage during the transition to mainland Chinese rule and then market a new film under a similar title. As a result, the sounds *and* the images of individual films evolve over time.

Exhibition and Audiences: Variety Is the Rule

Travel lecture films are exhibited in the widest possible array of venues, including libraries, museums, service clubs, universities, high schools, institutes, and concert halls. John Holod said that he might play a nine-hundred-seat auditorium with a full house, spotlight, projectionist, and

changing room one evening, then lecture to fifty people in the basement
of a school the following night, where he has to put on his tuxedo in a
bathroom stall and contend with projector noise throughout the presentation. Fees and ticket prices, too, vary. In 1998 the Vassar Brothers Institute paid lecturers $1,050 per presentation; a more common figure was
$500. A season ticket for five screenings at Presbyterian College in Clin-
ton, South Carolina, sold for $25 in 1998, while seven shows cost $52.50
in Portland, Oregon.

At a time when most Hollywood films are explicitly directed at teen-
agers, travel lecture films reach viewers whose average age is approximately sixty. Travelogue screenings, attended by well-to-do audiences,
many in formal dress, have more in common with ballet performances
than with multiplex cinema experiences. Reflecting this difference, lecturers often sport tuxedos for their presentations. The audience for
educational travelogues, now as in the past (Musser and Nelson 1991:
189), is conspicuously middle class. A description of a 1950s audience in
Santa Barbara—"elderly, wealthy, well dressed, attentive, and appreciative" (Soule 1997: 119)—still holds true. An informal industry survey concluded that "most are professional people, i.e., doctors, lawyers, teachers,
etc." (Ferrante 1979: 40). In addition, the travelogue audience is loyal.
A series at the Denver Museum of Natural History awarded plaques to
women, dubbed "Golden Girls" (Perrigo 1994: 12), who frequented lectures for fifty consecutive years.

As during the early cinema period, the film itself is only a portion of
the evening's entertainment. A woman from the Rose Villa Retirement
Home in Portland, Oregon, pointed out, "It's an opportunity for us to get
off the grounds here. It offers camaraderie and a chance to be together."
Door prizes may be awarded and presentations are frequently coupled
with musical performances. Screenings at the El Camino College series
in Torrance, California, have been routinely preceded by live music (Perrigo 1995: 21). At East Carolina University in Greenville, North Carolina,
film lectures are followed by dinner parties with the cuisine of the featured country (Perrigo 1996: 44). In the end, after the door prizes have
been handed out, it may matter little whether the subject of the movie
was Cuba or Canada.

Individual films are always shown as part of a series of travel lectures.
The Geographic Society of Chicago provides season ticket holders with
a "trip around the world" that touches upon all seven continents (Fisher
1991: 28). An article in *Travelogue* magazine, "How to Start Travel Film

Series," offers suggestions for exhibitors: "Vary your presentations geographically. Austria and Switzerland look similar on film. So do Denmark and Sweden. Avoid such conflicts in the same season" (McClure 1988: 34). Responding to a magazine survey, a promoter in Sarasota stated, "We also like to give a bit of education for our season ticket holders. We think they should see a Malaysia or a Tunisia along with Germany and Switzerland" (*The Performer* 1981: 6).

The first travelogue screening I attended, in 1996, took place at an old picture palace in Portland, Oregon, built by the Chicago firm of Rapp and Rapp in 1928. Now renovated, this center for the performing arts seats 2,800. Entering this vintage theater for a live travelogue lecture was like traveling back to another era of movie exhibition. Attendance on the evening of 28 March 1996 was probably one thousand. Unlike screenings at regular movie theaters, tickets were sold for numbered seats; an individual ticket cost $9.75. Though the enormous theater had many empty chairs, spectators nonetheless dutifully filed toward their assigned seats. They were season ticket holders, partial to their regular places.

At the World Cavalcade series in Portland,[7] audience members arrive in couples or small groups of five or six. Senior citizens from retirement communities pull up in buses, well before the 7:30 p.m. screening. Gentlemen dress in suits and ties while some women wear hats they may keep on during the screening. Considerable banter animates the auditorium as ticket holders return to familiar seats. Most travelogue presentations include intermissions when audience members stretch, chat, smoke, use the restrooms, and purchase videotapes and other souvenirs. At the same time, the break gives the lecturer an opportunity to rest and the projectionist time to change the 16mm reels (which, normally, cannot run longer than forty-five minutes).

Since the filmmaker narrates the movie live, each showing resembles a Hollywood preview screening at which the producer directly gauges the audience response. As a result, there is a particularly good match between travel lectures and their public; audiences are rarely disappointed. Travelogue viewers are not in thrall to the images and sounds, an implication often made about spectators of commercial fiction film. The presence of the narrator, as Miriam Hansen has suggested of early cinema exhibition (1991: 142), breaks off this engagement. Viewers are continually reminded of being together with the lecturer in the screening room rather than being transported on some imaginary voyage. Further, live travelogues do not encourage the kind of identification and emotional involvement found in much Hollywood film.[8] It is not uncommon for exhibitors to leave the lights on in the auditorium for spectators to be able to read their programs (which are frequently itineraries of the sites visited). Viewers of travel lecture films prefer information over identification, discourse instead of spectacle.

The World of the Travel Lecture Film

What kind of world is constructed night after night on the travelogue circuit? Of the 284 features in circulation in the United States in 1998, the continental emphasis of works was as follows: Europe (39 percent), North America (26 percent), Asia (15 percent), Central and South America (9 percent), Australasia (5 percent), and Africa (4 percent). There are no films about Antarctica.[9]

Among individual countries, much to my surprise, the United States (21 percent) receives the greatest coverage. The United Kingdom is a distant second (6 percent), Canada (5 percent) third, Italy (3 percent) fourth. If counted individually, Alaska (3 percent) and Hawaii (3 percent) tie with the Russian Federation (3 percent) and appear more than most countries, including France (2 percent), Greece (2 percent), and Spain (2 percent). The most popular subjects on the Asian continent are China, Indonesia, and Israel. In South America, Peru and Brazil lead the way. In Central America, only Costa Rica is represented more than once. In Australasia, Australia and New Zealand appear most frequently. Egypt and South Africa dominate the few films about Africa. Absent were such countries as Rumania, Bulgaria, Algeria, Saudi Arabia, Afghanistan, El Salvador, Nicaragua, Cambodia, Papua New Guinea, Nigeria, and Somalia.

It is intriguing that, unlike most ethnographic films, travel lecture films do not principally deal with so-called exotic cultures at all. Over two-thirds of those in distribution explore Europe and North America. The films about the United States favor the wilderness and the west, particularly the mythology of the frontier, a trait that shows significant continuities with travelogues from the first decades of the cinema discussed by Jennifer Peterson in this volume. Except for two movies, the entire eastern seaboard is ignored. The Midwest, with no single state films, appears merely as a place to leave at the outset of *Along the Santa Fe Trail*, *The Oregon Trail*, and *The Trail: Lewis and Clark Expedition, 1803–1806*.

The topic of a country suggests no automatic approach. Among the most favored, and now clichéd, is the "land of contrasts"—modern versus traditional, rural versus urban—which allows considerable flexibility. Most travelogues offer a smorgasbord of local culture. A viewer in New Smyrna Beach, Florida, praised John Holod's *Cuba* for its breadth: "The variety was good, a little bit of history, climate, geography, nature, the economy." Most travel lecture films endlessly catalogue facts about the locale and quantify the world in every possible way.[10] Exemplifying this tendency, *Across the Bering Sea* takes inventory in a tiny Alaska town: "two trees, one hotel, no traffic lights, and thirteen radio stations." One may learn many specific things from viewing travelogues, including that there are fifty-four kinds of snakes in Belize, that most of the great Gothic churches are in the north of France, and that Guatemala is about the same size as Oregon.

Despite the apparent narrative frame of the journey (departure-exploration-return), most travelogues do not represent temporally coherent voyages. Chronology exists more often as a construct of post-production; *Hong Kong in Transition* includes footage from four different trips to the city taken between 1989 and 1996. The lecture film tends to be an essay on geography or history, not a journey per se, resembling a guidebook such as Fodor's *Exploring Vietnam* (1998) rather than a travel adventure book by Paul Theroux.

As others have noted in this anthology, the travelogue lies at the intersection of the industries of travel and entertainment. "The entertainment industry delivers an experience to its customers," an analyst for *The Economist* writes, "whereas the travel industry delivers its customers to an experience" (Roberts 1998). Like organized tours, travelogues promise safe and comfortable trips, the opportunity to see the world without the inconveniences of traveling on one's own. Lecture films often include publicity for specific modes of transport, accommodations, and restaurants. At a screening in Portland, Oregon, the filmmaker Buddy Hatton thanked then-president Alberto Fujimori for making Peru safe for tourism. Hatton admitted that in the past it had been dangerous to visit the country, but now, "Don't hesitate to go." Some producers also lead tours, a profession that parallels their film lecturing, while sponsors often promote series through offers of free trips (Perrigo 1995: 33). In 1996-97 a Portland agency coordinated its tours with films offered by the World Cavalcade travelogue series. World Travelcade offered group tours of Mexico, Alaska, Peru, France, Scotland, Costa Rica, and Vietnam/Burma, the very countries shown in the travelogues of the previous season. A publicity brochure noted: "The mysterious land of the Inca is well explored by Buddy Hatton in *Peru: The Mysterious Journey*, and by you if you sign up for the tour following in Mr. Hatton's steps." So, the director's comment to his audience—"You might be tired after the long boat trip and prefer to take a short nap upon arrival"—was not simply rhetorical.

Some travelogues are shot on tours. Reviewing the climate of Indonesia, its population, and linguistic diversity, the lecturer Grant Foster concluded: "The ideal way to see both Java and Bali is to take an overland tour by air-conditioned coach" (1991: 12). This tour was the basis for his film *Java to Bali: Overland*. Any reputable travelogue will feature as many modes of transportation as possible, not only on-screen but also, of course, as ways of representing movement. *Adventure along the U.S./Canadian Border* includes POV shots taken from a train, hot air balloon, river boat, dog sled, wagon train, canoe, freighter, plane, and automobile. During a seminar at the School of American Research, the anthropological filmmaker David MacDougall jokingly suggested a definition of ethnographic film as "a film in which a goat is killed." Similarly, one could say that a travel lecture film is not quite itself without an antique train ride. A few, such as *Antique Trains of Europe*, *The Great Canadian Train Ride*, and *The Eastern and Oriental Express*, feature little else.

Travelogue Structure: The Detour

Recent work on early cinema has stressed the importance of the train in the development of film narrative (Kirby 1997). Indeed, it has been argued that the structure of classical narrative resembles the linear movement of train travel. In an article in *Film History*, I suggested that amateur movies and the automobile offer an alternative to this linearity (1991: 243-49). Most travelogues advance, halt, double back, digress, and generally meander across the landscape. If the train is the figurative engine of classical Hollywood, relentlessly moving the story forward to its inevitable conclusion, then the automobile is the figure of the peripatetic travel lecture film. The travelogue is episodic, the detour its most characteristic narrative device. Consider the printed breakdown, provided by the filmmaker, of sequences in the first twenty minutes of *Belize and Guatemala: Legacy of the Maya*: (1) "Belize City, founded by pirates in the seventeenth century," (2) "St. John's Anglican Cathedral, oldest in Central America," (3) "The largest unbroken reef in the Western Hemisphere," (4) "Ambergris Key, largest of the dozens of small islands along the reef," (5) "the ancient Maya city of Altun Ha," (6) "Belize Zoo, home of a family of jaguars," (7) "Danagriga and the largest settlement of Garifuna people," and (8) "Cocoa and chocolate processing." Jorge Luis Borges could not have dreamed up a more imaginative, nonnarrative list.

The actual focus of a travel film may not be obvious from the title. *Ukraine*, for example, opens with scenes of the newly independent country, as might be expected. But it quickly detours to tell the story of Ukrainian immigrants to Canada and Ukrainian festivals there. In addition, while in the vicinity of one such festival, the director then takes audience members to see the world's largest Easter egg, just "fifty miles away." There is a radical "because it's there" empiricism in the travelogue; links between scenes are fortuitous and seem to be governed by happenstance rather than by narrative continuity.

Along the Santa Fe Trail, despite historical associations, contains many unanticipated sequences. The viewer, perhaps accustomed to an animation of the past à la Ken Burns, through readings of letters, sumptuous landscapes, and black-and-white photographs, is instead treated to a series of visits to interpretive centers and museums in Missouri, Kansas, and farther west. The film opens in Independence, Missouri, with references to immigration in the 1800s but then shifts abruptly to the story of Harry Truman's 1948 election and subsequent administration. (Independence is Truman's birthplace.) Farther along the trail, in Abilene, Kansas, the birthplace of Dwight Eisenhower, there is a similar, digressive recapitulation of *his* political career. Although this hints at a new structural pattern, the narrative is subsequently hijacked by a sequence on tornadoes. All this in the first twelve minutes.

The producer of *Hong Kong in Transition* deliberately splits his travel documentary into two distinct parts, structured around the intermission. In the first half, the film describes the local culture, with modest restaurants, herbal medicine shops, and the like. This anthropological emphasis ends when the director, Frank Klicar, comments, "That's it for the Chinese culture of Hong Kong. What will YOU be doing when YOU get to Hong Kong? We'll discuss that when we come back after a ten-minute intermission." The second half of the film then focuses on tourism in the city, luxury hotels, a "Middle Kingdom theme park," and the Happy Valley Race Track, among other standard destinations.

The narrative arrangement of the travel lecture film has more in common with what John Fell calls the "motivated link" in early cinema (1983: 277–78) than with the question-and-answer story structure of classical narrative. Relations of space and time are not subordinated to narrative causality, as Bordwell has argued is the case with classical Hollywood film (1985: 47). Although travel lecture films usually last about eighty minutes, they could be any length. As with a music hall performance, the order of scenes could be swapped with similar results. Individual sequences do not advance a story but, instead, add layers to the original conception. Live travelogues jump from one place to another in almost random fashion. The transitions between sequences in *Belize and Guatemala*—often as little set up as "just over this mountain range" or "only ten miles down the coast"—sooner recall the chance intertitles of Luis Buñuel's *Un chien andalou* (An Andalusian Dog, 1929) than the cause and effect of Hollywood narrative.

Return to Sweden, as the title suggests, promises an exploration of the filmmaker's roots in Scandinavia. It opens with family gravestone markers in Texas. This personal angle, however, quickly disappears as the film takes on all the traits of a customary travelogue. It is only shortly before intermission—after touring Volvo and Hasselblad factories, typical villages, national parks, and an iron mine—that the director, Dale Johnson, picks up the personal thread and remarks that he wanders the seaside still not knowing the origins of his ancestors. (Small wonder, given his peregrinations.) After a visit to an immigration museum in the second reel, the filmmaker takes a classic travelogue detour: "It would be a couple of weeks before I could visit my ancestral home, so I went to film some glass blowing." Although he eventually finds distant relatives and his great-grandfather's old farmhouse, the feature-length movie includes, at most, ten minutes directly related to this family quest.

When I started this study, I assumed that, similar to many early ethnographic films, travel lecture films would magnify cultural differences by depicting bizarre and possibly inexplicable customs, a perspective that has been called "Orientalism" in other contexts. To my surprise, while this element exists, it is hardly a dominant trend. It is much more likely that audience members will hear a lecture about Martin Luther and the rise of Protestantism than they will musings about "primitives" or "the inscrutable East." Further, the travel lecture film is, as often as not, an *affirmation* of ethnicity, as the case of *Return to Sweden* implies. As noted above, *Ukraine* spends considerable time at ethnic Ukrainian festivals in

Canada. Further, it turns out that the Ukrainian footage was shot on a group tour of "Canadian Ukrainians looking for their roots" (Willis 1997: 9). John Holod's fall 1997 brochure, which includes a description of his film *Czech/Slovakia: Land of Beauty and Change*, advertises guided "Heritage Tours to Czech and Slovakia" with a company that promises "personalized visits to your ancestral home" and boasts of an 80 percent success rate at finding living relatives of tour members.

Live Performances: The Lecturer as Go-Between

As Rick Altman suggests of travelogues during the first decades of the cinema (see his essay in this volume), the film itself was a prop in a live presentation dominated by the lecturer in the hall. Travel lecture spectators evidently still enjoy this combination of human presence and moving imagery. A Florida exhibitor compared live screenings favorably with travel programs in other media: "People go up to the travel lecturers and ask 'Where should I stay?,' 'When is the best time of the year to go?,' 'How is the food?,' and that kind of thing. You don't get that on a movie screen, you don't get that on television." In-person presentation mirrors the live travelogue's emphasis on pre-industrial forms and suggests a nostalgia for the cinema before the coming of sound.

Travel lecturers always give introductions before their films. As a projectionist in Hickory, North Carolina, stated, "The spectrum of their personalities varies dramatically. Some are really low-key. They approach it as if they are showing home movies: 'This is where we went in Cozumel,' or, 'Here's an interesting beach in Portugal.' But with others, it's just show business. They come on with a ruffled shirt and a tuxedo, they tell a couple of jokes, and it's like a nightclub act." John Holod's opening monologue at the Vassar Brothers Institute screening of *Cuba* on 4 March 1998 included jokes about Fidel Castro, exploding cigars, Pope John Paul II, Bill Clinton, and Monica Lewinsky. Obviously, Holod's introduction rides the crest of current events and would quickly become dated if married to the soundtrack of his 16mm prints.

Most lecturers try to include a few references to the region where the film is being presented, a technique, common to live performers, used to foster a sense of community. Paradoxically, the filmmakers mediate the motion picture medium, rather than the other way around. They speak directly to their audiences as fellow travelers: "Those of you who have been to Hong Kong will agree with me that it has the best food in the world." At a screening in Portland, Oregon, a lecturer jokingly chastised two patrons for arriving ten minutes late. Another producer introduced his presentation with the remark, "The more I travel, the more grateful I am to be an American." And, after a pause, he added, "God bless America." Applause followed. In the past, it was not unusual for screenings to begin with the Pledge of Allegiance or the national anthem (Soule 1997: 188), as typically occurs at American sporting events.[11] The travel lecturer personalizes the anonymous, but common, "voice of God" narration that often accompanies documentaries on television (Ruoff 1992a: 222–26). In travelogue presentations, the volume varies as the speaker glances at the screen, checks his or her notes, moves toward and away from the microphone. Lecturers occasionally laugh with the audience at their own jokes. Several husband-and-wife pairs offer a novel style of tag-team narration, alternating sections of the film. Although generally using a low-tech process, lecturers have elaborate techniques for managing a live mix of sound effects and music along with the voice. Most use music and effects tracks on cassette and manipulate a portable tape recorder from the podium. Others have optical, sound-on-film prints and use a wireless transmitter that allows them to control the volume setting on the projector from the stage.

It is a convention of the travelogue that the lecturer filmed the country represented. By and large, this is so, and the rhetoric of film presentation relies on personal anecdotes, first-hand information, and eyewitness accounts (as does this chapter, I might add). However, films are occasionally narrated by lecturers who did not shoot the images. John Holod learned the technique of film presentation by accompanying veteran Dick Massey on the lecture circuit in 1989 with *New Zealand/Red Sea: Above and Below* and *Along the Mexican Border: California to Texas*. Each evening, the young apprentice learned a passage of the narration, which he read live from behind the screen, until, bit by bit, he had memorized both shows. Eventually, when Massey retired in midseason, Holod took over the presentations, paying fees for the rights to the films. Needless to say, the young lecturer then presented the films as if *he* had taken them, later splicing in footage of himself to further personalize the movies. For the rest of the season, Holod lectured about places he had never been. Though remarkable today, such a pose would not have been unusual in nineteenth-century lantern slide shows: "Sets of views accompanied by readings could be acquired from any major lantern firm and could be used by even the most untravelled to present lantern exhibitions" (Barber 1993: 69).

Lecturers rarely flaunt foreign language competency, typically presenting themselves on a trip that any audience member might easily take. Similarly, native speakers are rarely heard, as such speech is almost always filtered through the voice of the filmmaker. Although the delivery is typically quite polished, lecturers still occasionally make off-the-cuff remarks, unwittingly stumble over passages, excuse or repeat themselves, features that recall home movie screenings rather than TV programs. Many recite from memory, others consult notes. It is difficult to capture in print the charms and idiosyncrasies of live narration. Speaking of social structure in Central America, the producer of *Belize and Guatemala* stated in Portland, Oregon, that "the Mayan are on the lowest class of the rung." In the middle of a screening of *New Zealand: An Outdoor Adventure*, the speaker interrupted his narration to politely ask of the projectionist, "Could we have the focus check, please?"

Clearly, in contrast to classical Hollywood practice, the apparatus of cinema is displayed and acknowledged in the typical travelogue presentation. In some venues, such as those used by Kiwanis and Rotary clubs, the projector is visible and audible in the back of the hall. Recognizing that their audience includes many amateur photographers and would-be cinematographers, producers may explain how they obtained particularly remarkable footage. In addition, there has been a proliferation of films about travel filmmaking recently, as elderly lecturers have produced works such as *Adventure Filming the World*, *The Great American Travelogue: The Story of Travel Adventure Filmmakers*, and *The First Fifty Years*. This reflexive turn has perhaps been fueled by a growing sense of the live travelogue as a dying form. At the same time, such retrospective works also offer an opportunity for producers to recycle old footage, obtaining greater return on the initial investment.

There is a subversive, quasi-avant-garde current working in the travel film lecture field, usually under the guise of humor and parody. So, for example, "the holiest of holy pilgrimages" in William Stockdale's *Pilgrimage across Europe* turns out to be the golf course at St. Andrew's in Scotland. This anarchic spirit also appears in his macabre *Cemeteries Are Fun*. (Alan Jones, an exhibitor in Portland, Oregon, decided not to book this film, explaining, "A lot of our audience is elderly people. I don't know about having them look at gravestones for eighty minutes.") The same producer even made a film worthy of Andy Warhol, called *The Ride*, a U.S. cross-country tour shot through the windshield of his car.[12]

At the outset of the twenty-first century, the travel lecture film comprises a full-fledged industry, with filmmakers, booking agencies, exhibitors, and audiences in the millions. The industry presents intriguing parallels with early cinema, ethnographic film, avant-garde cinema, vaudeville, and home movies, all deserving of additional analysis. Delivered in person, the live travelogue is the paradigmatic form of the ever-popular illustrated lecture. Such live presentations force us to consider "cinema as event" (Altman 1990: 2–4), with the lecture as the intersection of production and reception, rather than thinking of films as autonomous texts. The live travelogue will always be with us, so we might as well start thinking about its ideological effects, its role in constructing cultural identities, and its nostalgia for pre-industrial forms.

Notes

1. The first version of this essay, "Around the World in Eighty Minutes: The Travel Lecture Film," appeared in *CineAction* 47 (1998): 2–11. I am grateful to Susan Morrison, Tom Doherty, Dirk Eitzen, and Karel Dibbets for comments on that version and to *CineAction* for permission to reprint it here. A revised version appeared in *Visual Anthropology* 15, no. 1 (2002). My thanks also to David MacDougall, Carl Plantinga, Richard Chalfen, and David Napier, who subsequently made very interesting comments on my work on live travelogues. I would like to express my gratitude to Paula Amad, Peter Bloom, Alison Griffiths, and Lauren Rabinovitz for their detailed suggestions at the 2003 Dartmouth travelogue workshop I organized. I presented a French-language version of this research at the 2003 colloquium "Voyage et cinéma" at the Université de Provence in Aix-en-Provence and am indebted to Jean-Luc Lioult and René Gardies for their insightful remarks. This essay is part of a longer manuscript "Around the World in Eighty Minutes: Notes on the Travelogue."

2. Of the over 250 feature travel lecture films now in distribution, I have seen over thirty in live performances. I have spoken with at least twenty of the lecturers currently on the circuit. Travel film lectures have a long pedigree around the world; readers familiar with the history of French and German cinema, for example, will recognize the persistence of this form. My study focuses exclusively on North America and, unfortunately, little litera-

ture exists on travel lectures in other countries for comparative purposes. This essay is based on public screenings, professional literature, fieldwork, and interviews. All quotes not otherwise attributed come from screenings I attended and interviews I conducted in Oregon, Washington, Nevada, Texas, New York, Maryland, Virginia, North Carolina, South Carolina, and Florida. I would like to thank the many filmmakers, exhibitors, and audience members who shared their passion for travelogues with me. Special thanks are due producer John Holod, who invited me into his motor home for two weeks during his 1997–98 lecture tour, and promoter Alan Jones in Portland, Oregon, who introduced me to local audience members and lent me photographs, flyers, and posters.

3. During the 1993-94 lecture season, there were numerous centennial celebrations of Burton Holmes's presentation of what these producers consider the "first travelogue" (*Travelogue* 1994: 8).

4. Annual meetings of the International Travel and Adventure Film Guild (INTRAFILM) bring together exhibitors, filmmakers, and booking agencies. INTRAFILM is the umbrella organization of the industry, comprising the Professional Travelogue Sponsors (PTS) and the International Motion Picture and Lecturers Association (IMPALA). The IMPALA film festival, which takes place at the INTRAFILM meeting, allows directors to preview new work for exhibitors. My research on live travelogues began 6–8 December 1997, at the annual INTRAFILM convention in Las Vegas.

5. While attending the 1997 INTRAFILM convention in Las Vegas, I met many travel lecturers but was most intrigued by one, John Holod, who was staying outside in the hotel parking lot in a motor home. Always joking, John seemed like a good subject for a documentary about the travelogue business, an idea he accepted with great magnanimity. The cinematographer Philippe Roques and I started shooting a portrait of Holod on 4 March 1998, in Poughkeepsie, New York, where he was presenting *Cuba at the Crossroads* at the Vassar Brothers Institute, and then we continued for a ten-day tour south that ended in Florida. The thirty-minute documentary I directed, *The Last Vaudevillian: On the Road with Travelogue Filmmaker John Holod* (1998b), presents the routine of life on tour, the hours driving, the time in-between performances, the equipment setups, and the encounters with exhibitors, audiences, and friends on the road. For information about video copies, see my website: http://www.dartmouth.edu/~jruoff.

6. The denigration of video gradually started to change in the late 1990s as several producers began to present what they call "E-Cinema travelogues," shot with small digital camcorders and transferred to 16mm for projection or, increasingly, shown directly with video projectors. Since 2000, digital video

has made significant inroads in the travel lecture industry, engendering a split between an old guard that continues to favor 16mm and innovators using digital cameras and projectors. Economies of production clearly favor digital video and indeed at the outset of the 2003–2004 season in France, Connaissance du Monde decreed that all presentations throughout the country switch to video projection equipment. My comments here, however, generally apply to the American 16mm travel lecture industry as it existed from 1950 to 2000.

7. Interestingly, only in-person appearances by the directors Michael Moore and Oliver Stone at the Portland Art Museum in Oregon in 1997 brought in large audiences comparable with those at the monthly World Cavalcade travelogue series.

8. In contrast to travel lecture films, IMAX widescreen and 3-D travelogues (like many Hollywood movies) thrive on visceral sensations of movement and sound combined with extraordinary vistas and are correspondingly aimed at a younger demographic than are live 16mm travelogues (see the essays by Lauren Rabinovitz and Alison Griffiths in this volume).

9. For the sake of this country-by-country designation, I have excluded from my sample twenty-eight thematically organized or transcontinental films, such as *Great Quotations from Great Locations* and *Christopher Columbus: The Discovery of the New World*.

10. Luis Buñuel's *Las Hurdes* (1932) parodies this encyclopedic tendency and many other aspects of live travelogues. For more on Buñuel's spoof, see Ruoff 1998a.

11. With the singing of the national anthem or other comparable gestures, these travel lecture films offer a ritual of communion through which audience members reiterate their bonds to one another before embarking on a potentially threatening imaginary engagement with another culture.

12. If, as Paul Virilio suggests, "What goes on in the windshield is cinema in the strict sense" (cited in Friedberg 1993: 203), then Bill Stockdale has made this connection literal in *The Ride*. Here is the climax of Stockdale's commentary to the feature travelogue he shot through his car's windshield: "You might think it would be boring to drive across the country and maybe some people say it is boring. And maybe you think that this film is boring. But this is America as it is, what you see is what you get. What you see is what I photographed, what isn't there, isn't in the picture. So this is everything in America, seeing it from coast to coast in just a matter of minutes. No stops for gasoline, no stops for food."

Time Traveling IMAX Style

TALES FROM THE GIANT SCREEN

Gigantism is their method as well as their style.
—Vincent Canby

ALISON GRIFFITHS

||||||||||||||||||||||||||||||||||||||||||||||||||||||||||||||||||||||||||||||||||||||||||||||||||||||||||||||||||||||||||||||||||||||||

Since its emergence more than thirty years ago, when Canadians Graeme Ferguson, Roman Kroiter, and Robert Kerr pioneered the use of a multiscreen format film for the EXPO 67 in Montreal and three years later unveiled the IMAX technology with a multiscreen system in the Fuji Pavilion at the EXPO 70 in Osaka, IMAX has latched onto the travelogue as the sine qua non of the large-screen format.[1] On one level, the symbiotic relationship between IMAX and travel makes perfect sense when we consider the early institutional venues for IMAX exhibitions, chiefly world's expositions and museums, where ideas of industrial progress, exploration, and cross-cultural encounters provided the perfect showcase for the new cinema technology. Like the artifacts severed from their contextual referents in the museum, where "objecthood is invested with the aura of fate," in the words of Didier Maleuvre, IMAX takes the world "out there" and enlarges it to gigantic proportions, heightening the sensation of virtual presence and haptic immersion (1999: 12). Ideas of travel are thus intrinsic to IMAX's genetic/generic make-up and inscribed in its promotional rhetoric and exhibition contexts.

IMAX is an eclectic derivative of a great many pre-cinematic entertainments—Gothic cathedrals, medieval tapestries, late-eighteenth- and nineteenth-century panoramas (circular paintings displayed in purpose-built rotundas) and moving panoramas, oversized canvases suspended between rollers that are moved before an audience, landscape paintings, and stereocards—and their 3-D successors in the age of cinema and post-cinema, Cinerama, Cinemascope, and 360-degree Internet-distributed technologies—which, despite their modest scale and resolution, promise immersive experiences and virtual travel in similar ways to IMAX).[2] In both a literal and chimerical sense, each of these representational forms latches on to the idea of travel undergirding a variety of nonfictional subjects delivered with heightened verisimilitude. Leery of espousing a Bazinian teleology in which IMAX appears as the culmination of a centuries-long project of perfect filmic illusionism, a more nuanced approach is required that acknowledges IMAX's complex legacy and situates it within a long history of spectacular, large-scale image making. The IMAX experience is a historically constructed one, indebted to centuries-old attempts at making illusionist and spectacular representations, with each precursor embedded in diverse and sometimes contradictory impulses.

With this in mind, my aim in this essay is to scrutinize IMAX's reliance on the travelogue as its key structuring principle. Methodologically, this essay tempers somewhat abstract ideas about IMAX, travel, and human perception derived from cultural theory with more historically grounded trade and popular-press discourses concerning the large-screen cinematic format. I'm interested here in examining how motion itself—the kinetic impulse defining travel—is textually inscribed in IMAX via the phantom ride (camera located on the front of a moving object such as a plane, train, or vehicle); the organization of our perception via shot composition, scale, and duration; and the presence (or absence) of the pan as camera movement. Through an analysis of the visual grammar of *Across the Sea of Time* (1996) and *Everest* (1998), I hope to suggest how our attention as spectators is uniquely shaped by the idiom of IMAX. As exemplary IMAX travelogues, and in the case of *Sea of Time*, a film redolent with reflexive meaning about the nature of 3-D imaging and immigration as an assimilationist journey, these films tell us a great deal about why IMAX seems so bound to the travelogue and how ideas of travel/mobility/kinesis play out on several discursive levels (Figure 1).

However, rather than make the case that IMAX simply exploits an age-old visual rhetoric and trope in a souped-up medium of ostentation (the teleological idea of IMAX films as technologically enhanced versions of eighteenth- and nineteenth-century panoramic paintings), I want to analyze sequences from *Sea of Time* and *Everest* that may advance our theoretical understanding of "panoramic perception" and how, paradoxically, it is more likely to be suppressed than showcased in IMAX films. In other words, while the popularity of the expansive IMAX screen suggests an en-

1 Cover of a teacher's resource guide to *Across the Sea of Time* (1995). Courtesy of Sony Pictures Classics.

during fascination with panoramic vision, in this case the ability to make use of our peripheral vision, giving us closer to a 250-degree (as opposed to the presumed 180-degree) visual span of the world surrounding us, most IMAX films eschew the pan's horizontality in favor of a perpendicular movement into the frame that evokes the sensation of penetrating space through depth cues. Panoramic vision no longer refers to a lateral sweep associated with the cinematic pan but functions more as a synonym for an overall view; as Sören Pold explains, "to a large extent [the panorama has] become naturalized as a general aestheticization of perception and urbanity" (2001: 54). This repression of panoramic perception is clearly linked to the absence of a classical Renaissance perspective in a great many sequences in IMAX films; iconographically, we read the IMAX image quite differently from conventional 35mm, scanning it vertically for detail and meaning rather than panoramically from left to right.

IMAX uses 15-perforation, 70mm film to shoot and project images of incredible sharpness. The 15/70 frame is ten times larger than the 35mm used in regular theaters and three times larger than standard 70mm film used in classic Hollywood epics.[3] In most IMAX films, panoramic vision is isomorphic with an omniscient gaze, a visuality of surveillance that comes from aerial cinematography and sweeping crane shots (a classic IMAX film like *To Fly* [1976] can be considered the ur-IMAX film, since its visual rhetoric is composed of little else than that simulated movement through space). A question to be explored in this essay, then, is how IMAX directors foreground depth perception in their films, a technique anticipated in nineteenth-century panorama painters' use of perspective drawing and *faux terrains* (use of props such as real grass in theatricalized, artificially arranged three-dimensional foregrounds) to underscore the illusion of depth on the grand panoramic canvases. By focusing on just two IMAX films that appropriate the travelogue as a structuring principle, I hope to generate a more theoretically informed and mutually informing body of knowledge about travel and large-format filmmaking. In the case of *Everest*, I am interested in locating ruptures in the representational architecture of IMAX, ways in which the form struggles to enunciate when dealing with the small, the fleeting, and the intimate. IMAX's complicity in constructing a monolithic, ethnocentric grand-narrative of Western supremacy is also explored in the final section here.

Journeys on the (Very) Big Screen

Imax made its mark by taking people where they couldn't go themselves. To the top of Everest or to the bottom of the ocean. — Richard Gelfond

To characterize IMAX as virtual travel or armchair tourism is something of a truism today. It is trotted out in IMAX film publicity and echoed by film critics in countless reviews. Audiences have come to expect an element of travel as a quintessential component of the entire IMAX package; for those baby-boomers old enough to remember Cinerama, "fabulous travelogues and natural-history essays that combine the earnest, predigested scholarship of a National Geographic piece with the excitement of a roller-coaster ride," in the words of one critic, IMAX simply ups the ante in terms of technological prowess and sensation delivery (Canby 1998: 18). The idea of the travelogue informs both traditional IMAX nature documentaries exploring a specific landscape and recent IMAX teen-themed films for audiences seeking a higher than usual quotient of special effects in what is increasingly a videogame-looking interface. IMAX producers now even look beyond our terrestrial world for suitable large-format subject matter, announcing a 3-D IMAX film entitled *Magnificent Desolation* that will give viewers the sensation of visiting the moon, narrated by *Apollo 13* star Tom Hanks (Dunkley 2003).

The semantics of travel thus imbues everything about the IMAX Corporation, from the imperialist overtones of its recent expansion in China, India, and Eastern Europe, to the active prepositions prevalent in its titles (Across *the Sea of Time*, Into *the Deep*, and Up *Kilimanjaro*, to cite just a few examples), to the trademark phantom ride shot mentioned earlier (Acland 1998). IMAX's interest in the travelogue has not been limited to 2- and 3-D films; they have branched out into *Back to the Future*–type simulation rides such as the IMAX Magic Carpet ride (Schwartzberg 1993: 42), which has two projectors running synchronously, one in front of the audience and the other projecting images through a transparent floor (for more on simulation rides, see Lauren Rabinovitz's essay in this collection). Some IMAX films, such as the Belgian director Ben Stassen's *Haunted Castle* (2001), make the obligatory IMAX phantom ride the centerpiece of the film, although in the absence of any character development or dramatic situations, the entire film is little more than a "special-effects demo," as one critic put it (Zoller 2001: 38). The phantom ride reached ever-dizzying speeds in spring 2004, when the co-produced IMAX/Warner Brothers film *NASCAR: The IMAX Experience*, placed spectators in the driving seat to experience speeds of more than two hundred miles per hour (*PR Newswire* 2003c).

One of the most obvious reasons that IMAX films rely so heavily on the travelogue format is the educational market that has been carved out for IMAX (or that IMAX carved out for itself): traditional nature documentaries. IMAX films are expository texts that, while not conforming exactly to John Grierson's vision of documentary film as an art/propaganda symbiosis that inculcates heightened social awareness and civic responsibility in the viewer, nevertheless contain a didactic element befitting the school-group audience that makes up a significant percentage of receipts in non-commercial venues (of the 150 or so IMAX screens in the United States, approximately half are located in science and natural history museums, while the others are in multiplexes or purpose-built venues) and in commercial venues during the day when the theaters are traditionally empty (Gardner 1999). IMAX has clearly found a niche audience in the museum, where the recent trend of blockbuster or gimmick-driven shows—the Godiva-underwritten "Chocolate" exhibit at the American Museum

of Natural History in spring 2003 is a litmus test of the current reach
of commercial interests into the museum, with free Godiva chocolates
served in the "Chocolate Factory" and a satellite shop at the end of the
exhibit full of expensive chocolate and chocolate-related kitsch including
the 1998 movie *Chocolat*—no longer seems to raise an eyebrow from the
museum-going public; in fact, demand for these shows is largely audience
driven. But as Charles Acland points out, IMAX and the museum are co-
conspirators in the discursive work performed on visitors as they enter the
museum space and are subject to the similar disciplinary regimes of the
institutional space and its motion picture corollary: "To adopt the Imax
gaze is to find oneself firmly interpellated into an epistemological pur-
view that covers both the museum and new entertainment technologies"
(1998: 435).

However, it was IMAX's legacy as a museum-based educational resource
that made Hollywood executives skeptical of the commercial appeal of
the technology, especially 3-D IMAX, which required an image make-over
with audiences who associated 3-D with gimmicky 1950s B movies. Hollywood interest in large-format films grew in the mid-1990s, especially
after the colossal success of *Everest*, which earned $91 million at the box
office. Aside from scouting out ever more lucrative locations for IMAX
theaters, the company has recently set in motion its most ambitious commercial proposal to date. In an effort to avert the feared saturation of
its traditional museum venue and nature documentary formats, IMAX is
hedging its bets on its proprietary digital remastering technology (DMR),
which allows conventionally shot 35mm "Hollywood event" films to be
converted into a 70mm format for a cost of $2–4 million. The strategy
seems to have been successful so far; 2002 was the company's first profitable year since 1999, with $11.5 million in fourth-quarter profits versus
$6.6 million in 2001; there are currently more than 225 IMAX theaters in
thirty countries. The IMAX version of *The Matrix: Reloaded* (2003) began
playing in theaters shortly after its 15 May 2003, release and the final film
in the trilogy, *The Matrix Revolutions*, was the first-ever simultaneously
released 35mm/IMAX Hollywood movie when it opened on 7 November
2003 (PR *Newswire* 2003a). Quelling fears that audiences would not pay
more for the "premium" experience—research suggests audiences will
not only pay the additional three to four dollars for IMAX versions of
films but will also travel more than twenty miles for the experience—
IMAX is hoping that a recently acquired venue at the Paris EuroDisney
will be a central showcase for IMAX films (Hernandez 2003; PR *News-*

wire 2003b). Finally, IMAX has demonstrated considerable growth in its lineup of international theater signings and installations (signings almost doubled from twelve in 2001 to twenty-one in 2003), with China slated to become the second-largest IMAX market in the world (*Toronto Ontario Star* 2003: EO6).

What is interesting about these recent developments is that they mark a shift in IMAX's conflicted identity as the purveyor of visual spectacle on the one hand and dramatic narrative on the other; as the *New York Times* critic Peter Nichols characterized it: "Large screen lends itself to the spectacle, which in turn calls for dazzling clarity and stupendous sound . . . Dramatic scenarios are often not effective with audiences conditioned to seeing roller coaster rides, bounding lions, 40ft waves and crashing avalanches" (1993: E3). Repurposing has presented IMAX with a way out of the education and museum market ghetto, which, while profitable, is a niche market that IMAX wishes to transcend. The fact that most new IMAX theaters are being constructed in shopping malls (aka "destination complexes") rather than in museums is appealing to Hollywood studios, who until recently maintained a wait-and-see attitude with regard to releasing their product in IMAX format (McDowell 1996).

But if the bond between nonfiction and the large-screen medium seems unlikely to be seriously challenged by IMAX's repurposing of standard Hollywood features, it in no small part owes to the legacy of early cinema, which not only created the conditions of possibility for large-screen projection (widescreen emerged as a way of skirting Edison's copyright patents) but created the perfect promotional vehicle for the representation of landscapes (Nichols 1993: E3; also see Cahn 1996). Viewed in this context, it is no surprise that promoters of Cinerama looked to the turn-of-the-century travelogues of Burton Holmes and Lyman Howe as models for their mid-twentieth-century enhanced cinematic technology, or that IMAX, too, should turn to the same genre, especially landscape films, as an obvious aesthetic model (see Belton 1992: 91–94). Premiering on 30 September 1952, Cinerama was a novelty few audience members had previously experienced; in Belton's words, "The frame of the theater proscenium seemed to disappear, and the audience had the uncanny sensation of entering into the events depicted on the curved screen in front and to the side of them" (1–2). *This Is Cinerama* (1952) took spectators on a virtual tour of Europe in the first half followed by the United States after the intermission; *Cinerama Holiday* (1955) juxtaposed a European couple's tour of America with an American couple's vacation to Europe

(Belton 1992: 89–90). Not surprisingly, these films were heavily nationalistic in tone, fetishizing the American landscape "as an index of technological prowess," and in the process becoming "an unlikely participant in the Cold War" (Belton 1992: 89–90). A similar nationalist fervor marks *To Fly*, among the first IMAX films ever made, produced as part of the 1976 Smithsonian Bicentennial celebrations. The film links issues of national identity to technological developments in aviation through meta-narratives of American progress and domination in flight technology. Many IMAX films address the nation as an "imagined community," hailing spectators as proud consumers of images whose verisimilitude, it would seem, could be vouched for by the putative power of the nation itself, as an invisible sponsor of these epic undertakings; *The Last Buffalo* is another good example (Johnson and Goldner 1997: 5). But in constructing this national imaginary IMAX is simply following in the footsteps of earlier large-format imaging techniques such as the panorama and nineteenth-century landscape paintings of such artists as Thomas Cole, Frederic Edwin Church, Albert Bierstadt, and Thomas Moran (Miller 1993; Wilton and Barringer 2002). As a powerful symbol and nationalist allegory, the urban landscape functions as a potent icon, as we will see in the ensuing analysis of *Across the Sea of Time*.

Seeing Time Three Dimensionally: The Man with a Stereoscope

Across the Sea of Time (1996), produced and directed by Stephen Low, son of IMAX pioneer Colin Low, is a picaresque 3-D IMAX travelogue about an eleven-year-old Russian immigrant, Tomas Minton, who—in possession of little more than a stereoscope, stereocards, and faded letters sent by his great uncle Leopold Minton to his parents back home in Russia in the second decade of the twentieth century—comes to New York City to find his uncle's surviving widow, Julia. A parable of the American dream and replete with tropes of American progress and assimilation (Neumann 2001: 113), the film is, according to the press packet, the "ultimate 'New York Experience,'" a stopping point on 68th Street and Broadway, a few blocks north of the high-cultural mecca Lincoln Center, for contemporary tourists in search of a large-screen visual orientation to the city's major sights. The tourists lining up to see *Across the Sea of Time* will doubtless identify with Leopold Minton, who, in 1908, began work-

2 Stereo photograph wx50, "Immigrants just getting off the boat," used in the IMAX movie *Across the Sea of Time*. Courtesy of the Keystone-Mast Collection, UCR/California Museum of Photography, University of California-Riverside.

ing for a commercial stereoscope company making touristic 3-D images of the city; with fist-sized digital cameras tucked away in their bags, they, too, are image-makers intent on preserving a record of the city's iconic splendor. And yet the materiality and tactility of Leopold's images contrast sharply with the digitized photographs taken by modern tourists, and while both sets of images circulate in global image markets (digital photographs e-mailed to friends and family around the world; stereographs bought, sold, and traded across international borders, winding up in parlor sitting rooms after long, sometimes circuitous journeys across time and space), they are both the products of a technologically mediated tourist gaze.

Minton's stereographs are vitally important visual elements in the film, which combines turn-of-the-century stereoscopic imagery with 1990s 70mm IMAX footage of New York City. Not only are the century-old stereographs blown up to enormous proportions on the 3-D IMAX screen but they trigger the film's syntagmatic chains; the reading of a letter or loading of a stereocard into the stereograph functions as a roadmap for the film's sequences and cues the appearance of the giant black-and-white stereocards (Figure 2). Leopold's identity as an immigrant imagemaker serves as an important metatext: he is a both a sightseer and a sightmaker, becoming a professional observer whose "new occupation extends the city beyond its physical geography, carrying it to others who can witness its scenes in commodified stereograph images" (Neumann 2001: 115). But as Mark Neumann observes, Leopold's journey is also one of assimilation, a process heightened by the ethnographer's cloak he wears in his role as a commercial documentary-maker of a burgeoning city. There is a tangible tension, then, between the voyeurism apparent in Leopold's attempts at acculturation and the transcendent ocularity of the IMAX camera, which transforms the intimacy of the private stereoscopic views into a seventy-five-foot-high spectacle. At one point he says: "I look into windows to see how Americans live" (a comment that finds symmetry in Tomas's happening upon a topless woman sunbathing on a roof). *Across the Sea of Time* thus enacts a series of interesting reversals that point up the circuitous nature of global imagemaking and exhibition: stereocards made by Leopold for mass global consumption end up as fetishized images that now evince a very private, quiet power as they promise to unlock the secret to Tomas's ancestral past. The interiority suggested by the private viewing conditions of the stereoscope is blown asunder when these same images become visual spectacle on the IMAX screen; and yet ironically, because we view them through 3-D goggles equipped with PSE's (Personal Sound Environment), we still experience them as relatively privatized images.

In similar ways to Dziga Vertov in *Man with a Movie Camera* (1929), who climbs to the top of buildings and other modern structures to better visualize the city, Tomas scales rooftops to relive the stereoscopic images created by his great uncle (there is another possible homage to Vertov in the Central Park carriage tracking shot sequence that closely resembles the carriage scene from *Man with a Movie Camera*). Vertov's kino-eye camera metaphor ironically finds new expression in the supra-mobile gaze of the IMAX camera, which in an aerial sequence sweeps down Manhattan's major arteries and flies toward the spectacularly crowned financial district from Staten Island; indeed, Vertov's belief that "I, a machine, am showing you a world, the likes of which only I can see . . . My road leads towards the creation of a fresh perception of the world . . . I decipher, in a new way, a world unknown to you" (1984: 17–18) is elegantly rehearsed for us in the aerial photography scenes of *Across the Sea of Time* (and in the iconology of much IMAX footage in general), in what James Donald calls a "utopian will to visibility" shared by Vertov and Walter Benjamin (1995: 89).

Leopold's and Tomas's shared experiences of the city suggest a trans-historical gaze, what Neumann calls the "panoramic vision of time," that is cued by the action of Tomas panning the city landscape with the stereoscope (ironically, as Neumann points out, the stereoscope is used more as a telescopic device here, since the camera does not pan to follow the movement [2001: 115]). In most instances, past and present images of iconic sites are linked via a dissolve, a formal device that serves as an apt metaphor for the blurring of subjectivities across distinct temporalities. However, the issue of whose memories are being evoked here is somewhat opaque. For example, when Tomas closes his eyes and there is a dissolve from the contemporary mise-en-scène to the same historical location (or vice versa), it is unclear whether Tomas is somehow accessing Leopold's memory of that place or whether this is what Tomas *himself* now sees. Simply being in the same physical space as Leopold, though separated by nearly a century of history, triggers a memory trace that Tomas is able to access via the stereographs and the letters; indeed, Tomas's and Leopold's subjectivities seem to merge at these moments of 3-D plenitude. The letters are double signifiers of sorts, since they represent both Leopold's memory of experiencing a particular place *and* the reactivation or mediation of these memories via Tomas's subjectivity when he reads them. Like that of any tourist, Tomas's gaze is both what John Urry calls a "socially organized and systematized gaze" and one heavily inflected by personal memory and a strong psychic investment in the outcome of the pursuit of memory. The letters and slides thus trigger a metaphorical/existential "departure" for Tomas and the IMAX audience—a vital component of any touristic act—what Urry describes as a "limited breaking with established routines and practices of everyday life and allowing one's senses to engage with a set of stimuli that contrast with the everyday and the mundane" (1990: 1–2). Sounding remarkably like an advertisement for IMAX, the idea of sensory simulation and immersion in both familiar and exotic locations clearly promises a substitute for actual tourism.

Sea of Time thus provides a fascinating metacommentary on the very idea of time travel through 3-D images, inviting spectators to step into the past in the same way as the panorama rotunda invited audiences to stand in the very middle of a vast, circular view; the use of turn-of-the-century stereoscope slides to showcase the late-twentieth-century technology of 3-D photography provides a compelling example of how the travelogue functions as a narrative glue, binding together old and new media. The stereocards provide a great deal of the emotional weight of the film, avoiding an overly sentimentalized look at the past that we often associate with *The American Experience* or Burnsian documentaries. There's a raw quality to the images, produced in part by the magnified scale and 3-D, which has a powerful visceral effect on us; while the contemporary scenes emphasize movement through space—either flying over Manhattan in a helicopter or taking a phantom ride on a Coney Island roller-coaster or NYC subway car—the stereopticon photographs "hold a quieter power," to quote Ricky Vanderknyff [n.d., unpaginated], and force us to contemplate the ontological properties of the black-and-white stereocards versus the color motion pictures. Striking in several of the black-and-white images is the return gaze of the subjects; one of the first stereocards shown in the film is of a large group of recently arrived male immigrants, many of whom are staring directly at the camera. The confrontation with history derives from several different optical effects at play in the image—the human face (each framed by a hat, worn by every single man in this stereocard) comes alive, the subjects seemingly staring back at us from a 3-D limbo. As Paul Arthur notes, this affective response comes from the scale of the projection: "With an unprecedented vividness of detail and illusion of full-bodied volume, they startle like ghosts. It is in the brief appearance of these long dead black-and-white-figures that the feeling of a shared space between screen and spectator, the impulse to reach out and make contact, is most acute" (1996: 79). Unlike the contemporary scenes that privilege motion over stasis, the stillness of the stereocards creates a heightened immersive sensation, the figures seemingly transcending the boundedness of the frame; as Vanderknyff notes, "with its immense scale . . . it's easy to feel one could walk into the scenes" (n.d., unpaginated). Unfortunately, the IMAX camera fails to linger long enough on each image to give us the necessary time to absorb the rich visual detail.

Without the stereocards, the film is, as Vanderknyff points out, "a big, moving postcard of New York" (n.d., unpaginated); but, as Arthur observes, the film "enhances its display of vertiginous postcard vistas and Coney Island roller coaster plunges with an assortment of sensory assaults . . . intent on mobilizing as wide a range of sense impressions as the urban environment will yield" (1996: 79). One of the ways the film accomplishes this is via the depth perception of the 3-D photography; the haptic quality of the image in both the stereocards and contemporary footage is enhanced through the layering of objects and the unexpected intrusion of a prop into the frontal plane, such as the sudden appearance of a huge chain in the immediate foreground in the second shot of the film in the boiler room of a Russian freighter bringing Tomas to

3 Stereo photograph x78459, "Man looking down onto Wall St.," used in the IMAX movie *Across the Sea of Time*. Courtesy of the Keystone-Mast Collection, UCR/California Museum of Photography, University of California-Riverside.

New York, a wok suddenly erupting into flame in a Chinatown restaurant, and, also in Chinatown, fish swimming in a tank. As director Low points out in the press packet, "The trick is to have layers. The more visual cues for foreground, middle ground, and background the more effective the 3-D" (1996). In the same way that the phantom ride became the trademark 2-D IMAX motif, shots that are very deep and that appear to jump out of the screen have become the stock in trade of 3-D IMAX films (Figure 3). Ensuring the maximum effectiveness of the 3-D medium and avoiding the problems besetting the representation of human figures, which in close-up appear incredibly flat, "as if they've been steamrollered into the screen," is no easy task.

The magical effect of these objects coming out of the frame into the space between spectator and screen recalls a much earlier optical illusion exploited by circular panorama painters who constructed faux terrains— the space between the viewing platform and circular canvas panoramas containing real artifacts which merged seamlessly with the painting—in order to heighten the illusionism of the image. The net effect is remarkably like viewing 3-D IMAX, an implicit parallel drawn by Vincent Canby when he wrote that "the images [in IMAX] are so brilliant and sharp that you don't feel as if you're outside looking in. In some ways, it's like attending so-called 'live' theater. The eye is free to look wherever it wants. And, as much as the eye, the mind is engaged through sheer sensation" (1998: 18). Not only does the theatricality Canby alludes to remind us of the panorama's faux terrain but the visual autonomy he speaks of perfectly describes the spectatorial coordinates of panoramic viewing. And yet, the visual autonomy he discusses is radically undercut in the contemporary footage of *Sea of Time*, which rejects horizontal movement across the frame, the direction of panoramic vision around the circumference of the painting, in favor of lateral movement into the frame.

To compensate for the stasis of the blown-up stereocards in *Sea of Time* and to mimic the action of the spectator's eyes as they scan the image for detail, the camera gently directs our attention through panning and tilting, a technique in sharp contrast to the kinetic overload of much of the film's aerial photography, phantom ride, and tracking-shot footage in its contemporary sequences. While there is very little panning in the contemporary footage, the IMAX camera compensates for this by swooping down on locations and subjects, moving through space like a mechanized eagle (the canted camera angle is a standard IMAX trope causing audience members to concomitantly tilt their bodies). But what happens when the IMAX format is transported to a topography that, while sharing some traits with *Sea of Time* (the manmade monumentality of the urban landscape with its canyons and skyscrapers is replaced by a natural phenomenon), constructs a travelogue of quite different proportions?

Screened Gigantism: IMAX on Mount Everest

Whereas we know the miniature as a spatial whole or as temporal parts, we know the gigantic only partially. — Susan Stewart

We told the story really beautifully. It was poetic; it wasn't just a male-dominated machismo testosterone drama. — Greg MacGillivray

A defining feature of early travel was the desire to survey the topography of the foreign land; as Judith Adler points out, travelers were advised to prepare for their tours by learning "something of maths, perspective, drawing, and map-making, and to carry instruments for measuring temperature, height, and distance" (1998: 15). Unquestionably male, the traveler-as-surveyor was the "monarch of all he surveyed," most often the son of an aristocrat, member of the landed gentry, or, by the end of the eighteenth century, the professional middle class (Pratt 1992: 201–27).[4] Between 1600 and 1800 the treatises on travel shifted from "a scholastic emphasis on touring as an opportunity for discourse, to travel as eyewitness observation" (Urry 1990: 4). The tourist gaze, a new way of seeing the world, coincided with the emergence of the nineteenth-century "Grand Tour," which privileged a subjective, emotionally charged, and aestheticized appreciation of scenic beauty in general, and the sublime in particular (Urry 1990: 4).

Referring to the travelogue in the context of IMAX brings into relief a set of ideas about travel, tourism, and sightseeing, ideas shaped in turn by oppositions between activity versus passivity, fake versus authentic; and the hegemony of sight versus other sensory modalities. Travel as a discursive concept has been freed of its earlier privileged connotations—everyone is pretty much on the move today, what James Clifford refers to as "dwelling-in-travel" (1997: 2).

The cultural meanings of travel are still shaped to some extent by notions of mapping and surveillance, especially the idea of looking down upon a city and tourist destination, having conquered it through ascending space. So when tourists visit Coba in the Yucatán Peninsula, Mexico, they feel obliged to make the long trek up the side of the crumbling pyramid to survey the surrounding terrain; similarly, visits to New York City and Paris are deemed incomplete without ascending the Empire State Building and the Eiffel Tower. Ascending and conquering are thus tropes associated with travel and ones most certainly co-opted by IMAX in its iconography and camera work. Ironically, this impulse to survey from above is thwarted to a large extent in *Everest*, given the enormous effort involved in transporting and using the camera at such elevations.

Released in March 1998, *Everest* set a new standard for IMAX; with a budget of $4.5 million, the film grossed $58 million in just thirty-two weeks and over $120.6 million by January 2003, making *Everest* the highest-grossing documentary and large-screen film of its time, breaking the record previously held by *To Fly*, which has netted over $115.7 million since its 1976 release. How do we account for the phenomenal success of this film? Several issues are at stake. First, the film was able to capitalize on the enormous publicity surrounding the deaths of eight climbers on the face of Everest in May 1996 (as one of twelve other expeditions assembled on the mountain that spring, the IMAX team had the foresight—or good luck—to postpone their summit attempt until the storm had passed and the near-gridlock climber back-up around Hillary's Step had dissipated). The deaths of fellow climbers imbues the IMAX film with a temporal specificity; this wasn't just *any* climbing season on Mount Everest but among the most memorable since the summit was first reached by Edmund Hillary and Tenzing Norgay Sherpa in 1953. While *Everest* conforms in many respects to a traditional travelogue, the publicity surrounding the deaths of the climbers drew into sharp relief questions about Everest's place in the political economy of Tibet, the ecological fallout from the rising numbers of summit attempts by for-profit multinational climbing organizations, and whether access to the mountain should be more tightly controlled by the Tibetan government.

Second, the film exploited a heightened public and trade-press fascination with the additional challenges of taking an IMAX camera to the "roof of the world." Even in the absence of human drama on Everest, the film was destined to generate a great deal of publicity, as Mark Singer, writing in *Sight and Sound* observed: "The sense of scale and detail large-format can offer—let alone the achievement of getting both onto the film in the first place—would be impressive even if nothing untoward happened" (1999: 26). This near-fetishizing of the IMAX process, particularly an obsession with the weight of the camera, size of the batteries, logistical challenges of filming in sub-zero temperatures, and huge support necessary to transport the equipment up the mountain, anthropomorphizes the technology, transforming the IMAX camera into a VIP that must make it up the mountain at all costs.[5] The technology in this instance is isomorphic with the subject matter; IMAX and Everest are both behemoths that swallow up their subjects, contain them, so to speak (what Susan Stewart refers to as being "enveloped by the gigantic, surrounded by it, enclosed within its shadow"; 1993: 74). There is little doubt that the IMAX screen enacts a similar enveloping process, since unlike the miniature, which can be held in a privatized, individual space, the gigantic presents "a physical world of disorder and disproportion." As a potent signifier of the gigantic, the sky is a recurring trope in tales of the gigantic, a "vast, undifferentiated space marked only by the constant movement of clouds with their amorphous forms" (Stewart 1993: 74). That the IMAX camera should take to the skies—in quite a literal sense—should come as no surprise, then, given the sky's close affinity with the vast and the sublime.

Tibetan culture in general, and the Sherpa industry in particular, is metonymically signified via Jamlin Tenzing Norgay, son of Tenzing Norgay Sherpa, following in his father's footsteps. Jamlin's spirituality and desire to climb Everest are thus motivated by a sense of destiny (and no doubt an Oedipal drive); he becomes our entry point into this "mystical" culture, and yet even his bifurcated identity is subjected to the relentless fictionalizing effects of the narration, music, and graphics used in *Everest*. In complex and contradictory ways *Everest* evokes and suppresses the cultures and identities of Nepalese people who become travelers themselves in their role as Sherpa guides. As Clifford notes, "cultures and identities reckon with both local and transnational powers to an unprecedented degree" in the twentieth (and twenty-first) centuries: "Cultural action, the making and remaking of identities, takes place in the contact zones, along the policed and transgressive intercultural frontiers of nations, peoples, locales" (1997: 7). Nepalese culture is thus reified through a heavily Orientalist gaze, reduced to a series of stylized Hollywood-influenced ethnographic vignettes such as the reenactment scene in the Buddhist temple representing Jamlin Norgay as a little boy (an image we return to at the end the film when the young Norgay is surrounded by candles). The film's attempt to evoke the spiritualism surrounding Everest is undercut by the marginalization of the Sherpa economy that supports mountaineering in the region (one is clearly more photogenic and easier to represent than the other). Not only are the Sherpas who are responsible for transporting the IMAX camera and equipment up Everest largely invisible in the film but their role in the monumental team effort necessary to make the film is marginalized. The Sherpas gain visibility only through a series of still photographs interpolated into the closing credits (the credit mentions the ten Sherpas who carried the IMAX equipment, but photographs of only four are shown). The implicit racism in this afterthought representation of the Sherpas is echoed in a comment made by the *American Cinematographer* writer Naomi Pfefferman when she reduces Sherpas to little more than necessary equipment: "As it turned out, Sherpas, camera, and batteries performed 'flawlessly' as the crew traveled up to 12 miles a day" (1995: 36). *Everest* is not the only large-format film guilty of a Eurocentric gaze; according to Acland, *Grand Canyon: The Hidden Secrets* (1984) constructs a "colonialist and orientalist story of discovery and first encounters with strange, native cultures" (1998: 437). Simplistic, teleological narratives are stock-in-trade for IMAX; this is history churned out for the tourist market that expects nothing less than "grand narratives" of conquest and (Euro-)American supremacy.

A Burksian notion of the sublime hangs heavily over *Everest*, defined as "whatever is fitted in any sort to excite the idea of pain, and danger,

that is to say, whatever is in any sort of trouble, is conversant with ter-
rible objects, or operates in a manner analogous to terror, is a source
of the *sublime*; that is, it is productive of the strongest emotion which
the mind is capable of feeling" (Burke [1792] 1925: 55). The destructive forces of nature, central features of the sublime, provide the raison
d'être of *Everest*, which has few problems ratcheting up the emotional
tempo; after all, IMAX technology has surely met its match in a subject of
such epic proportions. And yet, while the sublime qualities of the landscape are certainly evoked by the IMAX camera—the mountain's mysti-
cism is signified via repeated shots of the moon—the actual summit is
something of a cinematic anticlimax, since most of the images are photographic stills rather than IMAX-rendered breathtaking images; as Jerry
Adler writing for *Newsweek* points out: "Since the subjects were mostly
gasping for breath and barely able to lift their feet, this had the unfortunate effect of rendering the most important scenes as a series of gorgeous,
but somewhat torpid tableaux" (1998: 56). The soundtrack and photographic stills have to compensate for the absent motion picture at this
moment, a switch in tone that shifts the overall tenor of the film away
from the epic (relentlessly signified by the overbearing score) toward the
prosaic (the still photographs presented in collage fashion on the screen
unfortunately take on the look of skiing-vacation snapshots). The IMAX
camera also falls short when it comes to capturing quiet, reflective moments, including the Spanish climber Araceli Segarra's reaction to the
deaths of fellow climbers; using the frame within a frame to signify the
look of a digital camera, the scene both evinces and effaces the IMAX gaze,
which has to be recontextualized to make for a more intimate video-diary
type encounter between climber and audience.

Marking the image as "other" than IMAX reads as a metacomment on
IMAX's inability to capture the intimate, the spontaneous, the small, and
the fleeting, or at least a desire on the production team to capitalize on the
enormous success of reality TV, which relies on the iconography of video
(time-code, viewfinder, shaky camerawork) to shore up the purported
realism of this unscripted moment. Shot in the style of home video, the
expedition team's reflections on the climb and tragedy are juxtaposed
sharply with the lofty and clichéd prose of Liam Neeson's narration.
Moreover, the monstrous proportions of the human body when blown
up by the IMAX camera evoke something of Jonathan Swift's disgust at
the body—the breast in particular—in the Brobdingnag section of *Gulliver's Travels*, in which Gulliver remarks: "no Object ever disgusted me

so much as the Sight of her monstrous breasts" ([1726] 1994: 82). (One can't help but think of the monstrous size of Michael Jordan's hands in *Michael Jordan to the Max* [2000] or Mick Jagger's lips in *The Rolling Stones at the Max* [1990][Stewart 1993: 58].) The body, in medium or close-up shots at least, assumes gargantuan proportions under the magnifying lens of IMAX, especially 3-D IMAX, which not only increases the size but turns the human frame into a cardboard cutout if not carefully blocked within the mise-en-scène. Coupled with the problem of how to represent the human form in medium close-up or close-up for a sustained period is the larger issue of editing in IMAX format; as the IMAX producer Greg MacGillivray explains, "Certain things lend themselves to IMAX over and above other systems. The screen size requires a number of separate eye fixations, so shots need to be longer to allow the audience to take in the entire image. Quick cuts can be too jarring" (Heuring 1990: 42–43). If digital remastering of Hollywood films promises to imbue IMAX's grammar with new agency, the more traditional IMAX film (especially 3-D) will still be crafted with MacGillivray's considerations in mind.

The Journey's End: Final Thoughts on IMAX

In many ways IMAX has contrived to be—at least in marketing terms—our contemporary version of Homer's *Odyssey*, a form shaped by narratives of mythological import, world narratives if you like, that attempt to make sense of our place in the universe through the IMAXification (if I may coin such a neologism) of natural phenomena and a host of quasi-scientific, human-interest stories (as a tragic mnemonic of similar proportions, the 2003 IMAX release *Ghosts of the Abyss* represents a vertical penetration of space in the opposite direction to *Everest*, a voyage to the wreck of the *Titanic*). Just as the meanings of *Everest* were dramatically shaped by the climbing deaths overshadowing the IMAX ascent and will continue to shift in the wake of ever-increasing demands by climbers to make an attempt on the summit, so too does our heightened state of terrorism alert and global instability in the wake of 9/11 shape the discursive meanings of *Sea of Time*, which becomes something of an ironic and politically charged metacommentary on American identity and urbanism. Despite being Canadian in origin, IMAX is often perceived as a super-sized North American medium churned out by a super-sized culture that thrives on "bigness" and ostentation; Leopold's eagerness to assimilate and embrace the American dream thus rings a little hollow in the face of America's adventurism overseas and its troubled international reputation. Shots in which the Twin Towers fade from view as one sublime image of the Manhattan skyline dissolves into another imbue the 1996 *Sea of Time* with a pathos and nostalgia that exceeds the moving postcard genre. In addition, the image of two planes on either side of the Twin Towers in the cover art of the video release of *Sea of Time* is an ominous (and ironic) foreshadowing of the destruction of the towers and horrors that beset America on that fateful day in 2001. Moreover, as homeland security is tightened and restrictive immigration policy taints the dream of a better life in the so-called free world, the parable of Leopold Minton may ring true for far fewer immigrants in the years to come.

Sea of Time and *Everest* are travelogues that privilege spectacles of grandness and monumentality perfectly befitting a hyperbolic cinematic technology. They are calling-card films for IMAX, two very different cinematic subjects cut from the same ideological cloth. And yet as much as IMAX claims to be the *über* cinematic form, we can't help but wonder how, in an attempt to push the envelope in terms of improving the "IMAX experience" and breaking into the mainstream, IMAX faces challenges that are endemic to its ontological form. If ideas of travel and IMAX are phenomenologically bound—recall that IMAX is itself a tourist destination competing with the very same sites it represents on its screens—whether the journeys IMAX continues to offer viewers will be those they want to take is another matter entirely.

Notes

This essay was supported by a research grant from the PSC-CUNY fellowship fund and the committee for reassigned time at Baruch College, CUNY. My thanks to colleagues at the Dartmouth College workshop on the travelogue whose input helped the essay considerably: Paula Amad, Peter Bloom, Lauren Rabinovitz, and Jeffrey Ruoff. Gratitude also to William Boddy and my research assistant Maria Goldman. This essay is dedicated to Soren Boddy, who informed the work in unconventional ways.

1. The first permanent IMAX projection system was installed at Ontario Place's Cinesphere in Toronto in 1971. IMAX Dome (OMNIMAX) debuted at the Reuben H. Fleet Space Theatre in San Diego in 1973 (Acland 1998: 431).

2. For more on the relationship between IMAX, Gothic cathedrals, and

medieval tapestry, see Griffiths 2003. For a discussion of the connection between IMAX, panoramas, and iPIX (360-degree Internet technology), see Griffiths 2004.

3. Much of the technical information on IMAX is from www.imax.com and www.giantscreenbiz.com. There is also a journal devoted to large-screen film formats, entitled *LF Examiner*.

4. My thanks to Ajay Gehlawat for reminding me of this phrase in Pratt.

5. For a detailed discussion of the *Everest*'s pre-production, see Pfefferman 1995: 37. For more on the challenges of actually shooting on the mountain, see Fairweather 1998: 48–52.

||||||||||||||||||||||||||||||||||||||||||||||||||||||||||||||||||||||||||||||||||||||||||||||||||||||||||||||||||||||||||||||||||||||||||||||||||||||||||||||||

Acland, Charles R. 1998. "IMAX Technology and the Tourist Gaze." *Cultural Studies* 12, no. 3: 429–45.

Adler, Jerry. 1998. "Take it from the Top." *Newsweek*, 9 March, 56–58.

Adler, Judith. 1998. "Origins of Sightseeing." In *Travel Culture: Essays on What Makes Us Go*, ed. Carol William, 3–24. Westport, Conn.: Praeger.

Ahlheim, Karl-Heinz, ed. 1984. *Meyers Grosses Universallexikon*. Mannheim: Bibliographisches Institut.

Alloula, Malek. 1986. *The Colonial Harem*. Trans. Myrna Godzich and Wlad Godzich. Minneapolis: University of Minnesota Press.

Altick, Richard. 1978. *The Shows of London*. Cambridge, Mass.: Harvard University Press.

Altman, Rick, ed. 1990. *Sound Theory/Sound Practice*. New York: Routledge.

———. 2004a. "The Redpath Chautauqua Collection." *Cinema & Cie* 3.

———. 2004b. *Silent Film Sound*. New York: Columbia University Press.

Amad, Paula. 2001. "Cinema's 'Sanctuary': From Pre-Documentary to Documentary Film in Albert Kahn's *Archives de la Planète* (1908–1931)." *Film History* 13, no. 2: 138–59.

———. 2002. Archiving the Everyday: A Topos in French Film History, 1895–1931. PhD diss., University of Chicago.

———. 2003. "Filming the 'Face' of the World: Human Geography, Physiognomic Film Theory and Atlas Films." Paper presented at the Society for Cinema and Media Studies Conference, Minneapolis.

André, Jacques, and Marie André. 1987. *Une saison Lumière à Montpellier*. Perpignan: Institut Jean Vigo.

Antoine, E. 1915. "Mon voyage autour du monde: octobre 1912–août 1913." *Bulletin de la Société Autour du Monde*, 89–116.

Arthur, Paul. 1996. "In the Realm of the Senses: Imax 3-D and the Myth of Total Cinema." *Film Comment* 32, no. 1 (January–February): 78–81.

Association européenne inédits, eds. 1997. *Jubilee Book: Essays on Amateur Film: Recontres autour des inédits*. Brussels: Association européenne inédits.

Auster, Paul. 2002. *The Book of Illusions*. New York: Henry Holt.

Bakhtiari, Hamid Khan. 1984. Correspondence with Hamid Naficy. July 27.

Banks, Marcus, and Howard Morphy, eds. 1997. *Rethinking Visual Anthropology*. New Haven: Yale University Press.

Barbash, Ilisa, and Lucien Taylor. 1997. *Cross-Cultural Filmmaking: A Handbook for Making Documentary and Ethnographic Films and Videos*. Berkeley: University of California Press.

Barber, X. Theodore. 1993. "The Roots of Travel Cinema: John L. Stoddard, E. Burton Holmes and the Nineteenth-Century Illustrated Travel Lecture." *Film History: An International Journal* 5, no. 1: 68–84.

Bardsley, Ann. 1972. "Primitive People's Plight Irks Author." *Palm Beach Times*, 3 February, 13(A).

Barnouw, Erik. 1993. *Documentary: A History of the Non-Fiction Film*. Rev. ed. New York: Oxford University Press.

Barrillot, Bruno. 1990. *Les essais nucléaires français 1960–1996*. Lyons: Centre de Documentation et de Recherche sur la Paix et les Conflits.

Barsam, Robert Meran. 1973. *Nonfiction Film: A Critical History*. New York: Dutton.

———. 1992. *Non-Fiction Film: A Critical History*. Rev. and exp. ed. Bloomington: Indiana University Press.

Bateson, Gregory, and Margaret Mead. 1942. *Balinese Character: A Photographic Analysis*. Special Publications of the New York Academy of Sciences, vol. 2. New York: New York Academy of Sciences.

Bausinger, Hermann. 1991. "Grenzenlos . . . Ein Blick auf den modernen tourismus." In *Reisekultur: Von der Pilgerfahrt zum modernen Tourismus*, ed. Hermann Bausinger, Klaus Beyrer, and Gottfried Korff, 343–53. Munich: Beck.

Bazin, André. 1945/1967. "The Virtues and Limitations of Montage." In *What Is Cinema?* Vol. 1, 41–52. Berkeley: University of California Press.

Becker, Fridolin. 1912. *Glarnerland mit Walensee und Klausenstrasse*. Glarus: Komm. J. Baeschlin.

Behdad, Ali. 1994. *Belated Travelers: Orientalism in the Age of Colonial Dissolution*. Durham, N.C.: Duke University Press.

Belasco, Warren. 1979. *Americans on the Road: From Autocamp to Motel, 1910–1949*. Cambridge, Mass.: MIT Press.

Belton, John. 1992. *Widescreen Cinema*. Cambridge, Mass.: Harvard University Press.

Benali, Abdelkader. 1998. *Le cinéma colonial au Maghreb: L'imaginaire en trompe-l'oeil*. Paris: Éditions du Cerf.

Benjamin, Walter. 1969. "The Work of Art in the Age of Mechanical Reproduction." In *Illuminations*, trans. Harry Zohn, 217–52. New York: Schocken Books.

Benoît, Pierre. 1919/1921. *L'Atlantide*. Paris: Albin Michel.

Bergson, Henri. 1931. *Bulletin de la Société Autour du Monde*, 14 June: iii–iv.

Bernot, F. 1914. "Eloge du voyage: Discours prononcé par F. Bernot à la distribution des prix du lycée de Sens." *Bulletin de la Société Autour du Monde* 3: 231–237.

Bhabha, Homi K. 1994. *The Location of Culture*. London: Routledge.

The Billboard 1906a. 27 January, 20.

———. 1906b. 3 February, 20.

———. 1906c. "Parks." 9 June, 24.

———. 1906d. "Duluth's New Summer Park." 28 July, 28.

———. 1906e. "Riverview." 1 December, 28.

Biograph Bulletin. 1906. "Hale Tour Runs." 30 June, 73. Repr. in *Biograph Bulletins 1896–1908*, 250–52, ed. Kemp R. Niver. Los Angeles: Artisan Press, 1971.

Bitzer, G. W. 1973. *Billy Bitzer, His Story*. New York: Farrar, Straus and Giroux.

Boorstin, Daniel. 1961/1992. *The Image: A Guide to Pseudo-Events in America*. New York: Vintage Books.

Bordwell, David. 1985. "The Classical Hollywood Style, 1917–1960." In *The Classical Hollywood Cinema: Film Style and Mode of Production to 1960*, ed. David Bordwell, Janet Staiger, and Kristin Thompson, 1–84. New York: Columbia University Press.

Bouse, Derek. 2000. *Wildlife Films*. Philadelphia: University of Pennsylvania Press.

Bowser, Eileen. 1990. *The Transformation of Cinema: 1907–1915*. New York: Charles Scribner's Sons.

Brog. 1951. "Review of *Jungle Headhunters*." *Variety*, 1 May.

Brook, Harry Ellington. 1910. *Los Angeles, California, the City and County*. 23rd ed. Los Angeles: Los Angeles Chamber of Commerce.

Brown, B. S. 1916. "*Hale's Tours* and *Scenes of the World*." *Moving Picture World*. 15 July, 373.

Brown, Bill. 1997. "Reading the West: Cultural and Historical Background." In *Reading the West: An Anthology of Dime Westerns*, ed. Bill Brown, 1–40. Boston: Bedford Books.

Brownlow, Kevin. 1969–70. Interview with Ernest B. Schoedsack.

———. 1979. *The War, the West and the Wilderness*. New York: Alfred A. Knopf.

———. 1985. Correspondence with Hamid Naficy. 7 March.

Bruner, Edward. 1996. "Tourism in the Balinese Borderzone." In *Displacement, Diaspora, and Geographies of Identity*, ed. Smadar Lavie and Ted Swedenburg, 157–79. Durham, N.C.: Duke University Press.

Bruner, Edward, and Barbara Kirshenblatt-Gimblett. 1994. "Maasai on the

Lawn: Tourist Realism in East Africa." *Cultural Anthropology* 9, no. 4: 435–470.

Brunhes, Jean. 1910/1912/1920. *La géographie humaine: Essai de classification positive: Principes et exemples*. Paris: Félix Alcan.

———. 1913. "Éthnographie et géographie humaine." *L'Éthnographie: Bulletin de la Société d'Éthnographie de Paris* (15 October).

———. 1952. *Human Geography*. Abridged ed. Mariel Jean-Brunhes Delamarre and Pierre Defonatines. London: George G. Harrap.

Bruno, Giuliana. 1993. *Street Walking on a Ruined Map: City Films of Elvira Notari (Italy 1875–1946)*. Princeton, N.J.: Princeton University Press.

Buchholtz, C. W. 1976. *Man in Glacier*. West Glacier, Mont.: Glacier Natural History Association.

Bull, Bartle. 1988. *Safari: A Chronicle of Adventure*. New York: Penguin Books.

Bulletin Citroën. 1926. Paris: Édition "France."

Buñuel, Luis. 1984. *My Last Sigh*. New York: Alfred A. Knopf.

Burke, Edmund. 1792/1925. "A Philosophical Inquiry into the Origin of Our Ideas of the Sublime and the Beautiful; with an Introductory Discourse Concerning Taste." In *Works*, 1: 55–219. London: Oxford University Press.

Buscombe, Edward. 1984. "Painting the Legend: Frederic Remington and the Western." *Cinema Journal* 23, no. 4 (Summer): 12–27.

———. 1985. "Sound and Color." In *Movies and Methods, Volume 2: An Anthology*, ed. Bill Nichols, 83–92. Berkeley: University of California Press.

Buttimer, Anne. 1971. *Society and Milieu in the French Geographical Tradition*. Chicago: Rand McNally.

Cahiers de la Cinémathèque. 2002. Special Issue *Le cinéma d'Albert Kahn: quelle place dans l'histoire?* 74 (December).

Cahn, Iris. 1996. "The Changing Landscape of Modernity: Early Film and America's 'Great Picture' Tradition." *Wide Angle* 18, no. 3 (July): 85–100.

Caldwell, Genoa, ed. 1977. *Burton Holmes: The Man Who Photographed the World, 1892–1938*. New York: Harry N. Abrams.

Canby, Vincent. 1998. "Big Screen Takes on New Meaning." *New York Times*, 19 April, 18.

Chalfen, Richard. 1987. *Snapshot Versions of Life*. Bowling Green, Ohio: Bowling Green State University Popular Press.

Challaye, Félicien. 1919–20. "Les Leçons d'un Voyage autour du Monde." *Bulletin de la Société Autour du Monde* (January–December) 1919; (January–March) 1920: 51–57.

Chappell, George S. 1930. *Through the Alimentary Canal with Gun and Camera: A Fascinating Trip to the Interior, Personally Conducted by George S. Chappell*. New York: Frederick A. Stokes.

Choukri, Mohamed. 1973. *For Bread Alone*, trans. Paul Bowles. San Francisco: City Lights Books.

Citroën, André. 1923. Preface to *Le raid citroën: La première traversée du Sahara en automobile: De Touggourt à Tombouctou par l'Atlantide*, by Georges-Marie Haardt and Louis Audouin-Dubreuil. Paris: Librairie Plon.

Clarkson, Wensley. 1995. *Quentin Tarantino: Shooting from the Hip*. Woodstock, N.Y.: Overlook Press.

Clemence, Judith. 1977. "Cotlow's Calling Takes Him All Over The Globe." *Palm Beach Daily News*. 25 April, 83, 167.

Clifford, James. 1986. "On Ethnographic Allegory." In *Writing Culture: The Poetics and Politics of Ethnography*, ed. James Clifford and George Marcus, 9–121. Berkeley: University of California Press.

———. 1988. *The Predicament of Culture: Twentieth-Century Ethnography, Literature, and Art*. Cambridge: Harvard University Press.

———. 1997. *Routes: Travel and Translation in the Late Twentieth Century*. Cambridge: Harvard University Press.

Clifford, James, and George Marcus, eds. 1986. *Writing Culture: The Poetics and Politics of Ethnography*. Berkeley: University of California Press.

Cocteau, Jean. 1919. "Carte Blanche." *Paris-Midi* (28 April and 12 May): 2, repr. in *French Film Theory and Criticism: A History/Anthology, Volume I: 1907–1929*, ed. Richard Abel, 173. Princeton, N.J.: Princeton University Press, 1988.

Coissac, G.-Michel. 1925. *Histoire du cinématographe de ses origines à nos jours*. Librairie Gauthier-Villars. Paris: Éditions du "Cinéopse."

———. 1931. "Le cinéma au service de la civilisation et de la propagande." *Le Tout-Cinéma*, 7–31 August, 53–80. Paris: Publications "Filma."

Coltman, Michael M. 1989. *Introduction to Travel and Tourism: An International Approach*. New York: Van Nostrand Reinhold.

Compton, Margaret A. 2003. "Small-Gauge and Amateur Film Bibliography." *Film History* 15, no. 3: 252–71.

Conklin, Beth A. 1997. "Body Paint, Feathers and VCRS: Aesthetics and Authenticity in Amazonian Activism." *American Ethnologist* 24, no. 4: 711–37.

Cooper, Don. 1996. "Dear Coop." *Travelogue: The International Film Magazine* 19, no. 2: 36.

Cooper, Dorothy. 1984. Interview with Hamid Naficy. Coronado, Calif. July 21.

Cooper, Merian C. 1925. *Grass*. New York: G. P. Putnam's Sons.

———. 1955. *Safari beh Sarzamin-e Delavaran* (Journey to the Land of the Brave). *Grass*, trans. Amir Hosain Zafar. Tehran: Franklin Books.

Cooper, Nicola. 2001. *France in Indochina: Colonial Encounters*. New York: Berg.

Cotlow, Lewis N. 1942. *Passport to Adventure*. New York: Cornwall Press.

———. 1953. "This I Believe . . . Even Head-Hunters Are Warm and Friendly When Treated Decently, Explorer Insists." *New York Tribune*. 3 September.

———. 1954. *Amazon Head-Hunters*. London: Robert Hale Limited.

———. 1966. *In Search of the Primitive*. Boston: Little, Brown.

———. 1971. *The Twilight of the Primitive*. New York: Macmillan.

Crary, Jonathan. 1990. *Techniques of the Observer: On Vision and Modernity in the Nineteenth Century*. Cambridge, Mass.: MIT Press.

———. 1999. *Suspensions of Perception*. Cambridge, Mass.: MIT Press.

Crick, Malcolm. 1985. " 'Tracing' the Anthropological Self: Quizzical Reflections on Field Work, Tourism, and the Ludic." *Social Analysis* 17: 71–92.

The Daily Times. 1941. "University Club Hears Explorer." 17 October.

Dannenberg, Joseph, ed. 1927. *Film Year Book, 1926*. Hollywood: Film Daily.

De Grazia, Edward, and Roger K. Newman. 1982. *Banned Films: Movies, Censors and the First Amendment*. New York: R.R. Bowker.

De Kerillis, Henri. 1925. *De l'Algérie au Dahomey en automobile: Voyage effectué par la seconde Mission Gradis à travers le Sahara, le Soudan, le Territoire du Niger et le Dahomey*. Paris: Librairie Plon.

De Lauretis, Teresa. 1984. *Alice Doesn't: Feminism, Semiotics, Cinema*. Bloomington: Indiana University Press.

Delluc, Louis. 1917. "Beauty in the Cinema." *Le Film* 73 (6 August): 4–5, repr. in *French Film Theory and Criticism: A History/Anthology, Volume I: 1907–1929*, ed. Richard Abel, 137–39. Princeton, N.J.: Princeton University Press, 1988.

Depue, Oscar B. 1967. "My First Fifty Years in Motion Pictures." In *A Technological History of Motion Pictures and Television*, ed. Raymond Fielding, 60–64. Berkeley: University of California Press.

Descriptive Catalogue of Kodascope Library. 5th ed. 1932. New York: Eastman Kodak.

Dippie, Brian. 1982. *The Vanishing American: White Attitudes and U.S. Indian Policy*. Lawrence: University Press of Kansas.

Doane, Mary Ann. 1991. "When the Direction of the Force Acting on the Body Changes: The Moving Image." In *Femmes Fatales: Feminism, Film, Theory, Psychoanalysis*. New York: Routledge.

Doherty, Tom. 1994. "The Age of Exploration: The Hollywood Travelogue Film." *Cineaste* 20 (January): 36–40.

———. 1999. *Pre-Code Hollywood: Sex, Immorality, and Insurrection in American Cinema, 1930–1934*. New York: Columbia University Press.

Donald, James. 1995. "The City, the Cinema: Modern Spaces." In *Visual Culture*, ed. Chris Jenks, 77–95. London: Routledge.

Doros, Dennis (Milestone Films and Video). 2000. E-mail message to Hamid Naficy. 23 October.

———. 2003. E-mail message to Hamid Naficy. 9 January.

Dubois, Philippe. 1984–85. "Le gros plan primitif: À propos de *L'entrée d'un train en gare de La Ciotat* (L. Lumière)." *Revue belge du cinéma* 10 (Winter): 19–34.

Duluth News-Tribune. 1942. "Cotlow to Talk at Club Today." 2 February.

Dunkley, Cathy. 2003. "Warner Rides Shotgun on Imax Nascar Docu." *Daily Variety*, 19 February.

Du Tallis, Jean. 1923. *Le tourisme automobile en Algérie-Tunisie: Guide Dunlop*. Paris: Éditions des Guides du Tourisme Automobiles.

Dutertre, Albert. 1908–09. *Journal de route de mon voyage autour du monde du 13 novembre 1908 au 11 mars 1909*. Musée Albert-Kahn Archives.

Dwyer, Kevin. 2004. *M. A. Tazi and the Adventure of Moroccan Cinema*. Bloomington: Indiana University Press.

Ebert, Roger. 1996. *Wings of Courage*. www.suntimes.com/ebert/ebert_reviews/1996/03/3221.html, accessed 12 April 2004.

Eisner, Lotte. 1973. *The Haunted Screen: Expressionism in the German Cinema and the Influence of Max Reinhardt*. Berkeley: University of California Press.

Engelhardt, Tom. 1971. "Ambush at Kamikaze Pass." *Bulletin of Concerned Asian Scholars* 3, no. 1.

Enzensberger, Hans-Magnus. 1969. *Einzelheiten I: Bewusstseins-Industrie*. Frankfurt am Main: Suhrkamp.

Erb, Cynthia. 1998. *Tracking King Kong: A Hollywood Icon in World Culture*. Detroit: Wayne State University Press.

Evans, Ifor B. 1928. "Rapport (fragments)." *Bulletin de la Société Autour du Monde* (1928): 63–68.

Exhibitors Herald. 1916. 5 February.

Exhibitors Herald-World. 1930a. 10 May, 20.

———. 1930b. 2 August, 10.

———. 1930c. 23 August, 27.

Fabian, Johannes. 1983. *Time and the Other: How Anthropology Makes Its Object*. New York: Columbia University Press.

Fabian, Rainer, and Hans-Christian Adam. 1983. *Masters of Early Travel Photography*. New York: Vendome Press.

Fairweather, Kathleen. 1998. "The Towering Challenge of Everest." *American Cinematographer* 75, no. 5 (May): 8–52.

Farber, Barry. 1983. "Headhunters, Cannibals, Pygmies: Friends of Cotlow to be Protected." New York (original source unknown). Cotlow scrapbook collection, vol. 4: 108, Museum of Natural History, Cincinnati Museum Center.

Feifer, Maxine. 1985. *Going Places: The Ways of the Tourist from Imperial Rome to the Present Day*. London: Macmillan.

Fell, John. 1983. "Motive, Mischief, and Melodrama: The State of Film Narrative in 1907." In *Film before Griffith*, ed. John Fell, 272–83. Berkeley: University of California Press.

Ferrante, Maureen. 1979. "Looking Ahead to a New Season." *The Performer: The International Magazine of Stage and Screen* 2, no. 2: 40.

Ferré, Georges. 1931. *Le Sahara sur quatre roues*. Paris: Éditions de la Nouvelle Revue.

Fielding, Raymond. 1972. *The American Newsreel, 1911–1967*. Norman: University of Oklahoma Press.

———. 1978. *The March of Time, 1935–1951*. New York: Oxford University Press.

———. 1983. "Hale's Tours: Ultrarealism in the Pre-1910 Motion Picture." In *Film before Griffith*, ed. John Fell, 116–30. Berkeley: University of California Press.

Filmmuseum Landeshauptstadt Duesseldorf, ed. 2002. *Grüsse aus Viktoria. Film-Ansichten aus der Ferne*. Frankfurt am Main: Stroemfeld Verlag.

Fischer, Lucy. 1998. "Documentary Film and the Discourse of Hysterical/Historical Narrative." In *Documenting the Documentary: Close Readings of Documentary Film and Video*, ed. Barry Keith Grant and Jeannette Sloniowski, 333–43. Detroit: Wayne State University Press.

Fisher, William S. 1991. "Enthusiasm Always Shows Through." *Travelogue: The International Film Magazine* 14, no. 1: 28.

Foster, Grant. 1991. "Adventure in the East Indies, Beyond the Java Sea." *Travelogue: The International Film Magazine* 14, no. 1: 12.

Friedberg, Anne. 1993. *Window Shopping: Cinema and the Postmodern*. Berkeley: University of California Press.

Frisinger, Cathy. 2003. "Edutainment, Entertainment – or Both?" *Edmonton Journal*, 22 April, C3.

Furlough, Ellen. 2002. "Une leçon des choses: Tourism, Empire, and the Nation in Interwar France." *French Historical Studies* 25, no. 3: 441–73.

Fussell, Paul. 1980. *Abroad: British Literary Traveling Between the Wars*. New York: Oxford University Press.

Gardner, Natalie. 1999. "Museum Takes Profitable Approach to Exhibits." *Business Press* 11: 38, 15 January.

Gaudreault, André, and Germain Lacasse, eds. 1996. *Le bonimenteur de vues animées/The Moving Picture Lecturer*. Special issue *Iris* 22.

Geary, Christraud M. 1998. "Nineteenth-Century Images of the Mangbetu in Explorers' Accounts." In *The Scramble for Art in Central Africa*, ed. Enid

Schildkrout and Curtis A. Keim, 133–68. Cambridge: Cambridge University Press.

Gerhard, George. 1925. "Reel Reviews." *New York Evening World*. 3 March, n.p.

Gernsheim, Helmut, and Alison Gernsheim. 1968. *L. J. M. Daguerre: History of the Diorama and the Daguerreotype*. New York: Dover Publications.

Gilmore, John. 1983. Interview with Hamid Naficy. Santa Monica, Calif. 20 January.

Goetzmann, William H. 1966. *Exploration and Empire: The Explorer and the Scientist in the Winning of the American West*. New York: W. W. Norton.

Goldner, Orville, and George E. Turner. 1975. *The Making of* King Kong: *The Story behind a Film Classic*. South Brunswick, N.J.: A. S. Barnes.

Gradis, Gaston. 1924. *A la recherche du Grand-Axe: Contribution aux Études Transsahariennes*. Paris: Librarie Plon.

Green, Nancy L. 2002. "The Comparative Gaze: Travelers in France before the Era of Mass Tourism." *French Historical Studies* 25, no. 3: 423–40.

Green, Raphael. 1996. "Adventures of an Old China Hand." *Travelogue: The International Film Magazine* 19, no. 1: 23.

Griffiths, Alison. 1996. "Science and Spectacle: Native American Representation in Early Cinema." In *Dressing in Feathers: The Construction of the Indian in American Popular Culture*, ed. S. Elizabeth Bird, 79–95. Boulder, Colo.: Westview Press.

———. 2002. *Wondrous Difference: Cinema, Anthropology, and Turn-of-the-Century Visual Culture*. New York: Columbia University Press.

———. 2003. "Medieval Travelogues: Tapestry and Gothic Architecture as Precursors to Imax." Paper presented at the Multi-Media Histories Conference, Exeter University, UK.

———. 2004. "'The Largest Picture Ever Executed by Man': Panoramas and the Emergence of Large-Screen and 360 Degree Technologies." In *Screen Culture: History and Textuality*, ed. John Fullerton, 199–200. London: John Libbey Press.

Grimes, William. 1994. "Is 3-D Imax the Future or Another Cinerama?" *New York Times*, 13 November, H15.

Gunning, Tom. 1989. "An Aesthetic of Astonishment: Early Film and the [In]credulous Spectator." *Art and Text* (Summer): 31–45.

———. 1990. "The Cinema of Attractions: Early Film, its Spectator, and the Avant Garde." In *Early Cinema: Space, Frame, Narrative*, ed. Thomas Elsaesser, 86–94. London: British Film Institute.

———. 1998. "Early American Film." In *The Oxford Guide to Film Studies*, ed. John Hill and Pamela Church Gibson, 255–71. New York: Oxford University Press.

Gurevitch, Matthew. 2000. "The Next Wave? 3-D Could Bring on a Sea Change." *New York Times*, 2 January, 1.

Guy, Camille. 1900. *Les colonies françaises: La mise-en-valeur de notre domaine colonial*. Paris: Augustin Challamel.

Haardt, Georges-Marie. 1927. *La croisière noire: Expédition citroëncentre-afrique*. Paris: Librarie Plon.

Haardt, Georges-Marie, and Louis Audouin-Dubreuil. 1923. *Le raid citroën: La première traversée du Sahara en automobile: De Touggourt à Tombouctou par l'Atlantide*. Paris: Librairie Plon.

Haffenreffer, David. 2003. "Imax Corporation CO-COE Bradley Wechsler Guest on CNN-fn." 31 July, 12:30 p.m. EST.

Hall, Mordaunt. 1925. "A Persian Epic." *New York Times*. 31 March, n.p.

Hammond, Joyce. 2002. "Difference and the I/Eye of the Beholder: Re-visioning America through Travelogues." In "Travelogues and Travel Films," ed. Jeffrey Ruoff, *Visual Anthropology* 15, no. 1: 17–33.

Hammond, Paul. 1974. *Marvelous Méliès*. London: Gordon Fraser.

Hansen, Miriam. 1987. "Benjamin, Cinema, and Experience: The Blue Flower in the Land of Technology." *New German Critique* 40 (Winter): 179–224.

———. 1991. *Babel and Babylon: Spectatorship in American Silent Film*. Cambridge, Mass.: Harvard University Press.

Hanson, Patricia King, ed. 1988. *The American Film Institute Catalog of Motion Pictures Produced in the United States: Feature Films, 1911–1920*. Berkeley: University of California Press.

Haraway, Donna. 1989. *Primate Visions: Gender, Race and Nature in the World of Modern Science*. New York: Routledge.

Harrison, Marguerite. 1935. *There's Always Tomorrow: The Story of a Checkered Life*. New York: Farrar and Rinehart.

Hediger, Vinzenz. 1997. "Grosswildjagd." *Cinema* 42: 20–32.

———. 2002. "Hunter, Naturalist, Cameraman: A Life for Africa: Notes on the 'Gun and Camera' Topos in Natural History Films and Beyond." Paper presented at the Society for Cinema Studies Conference, Denver, Colo.

Heidegger, Martin. 1962/1977. *The Question Concerning Technology and Other Essays*. Trans. William Lovitt. New York: Harper and Row.

The Herald (Sydney, Australia). 1958. "This Man's a 'Sugar-Coated Explorer'." 14 August.

Hernandez, Greg. 2003. "Big Pictures Push IMAX to its First Profitable Year since 1999." *Daily News* (Los Angeles), 28 February.

Hertogs, Daan, and Nico De Klerk, eds. 1994. *Nonfiction from the Teens*. Amsterdam: Stichting Nederlands Filmmuseum.

————, eds. 1997. *Uncharted Territory: Essays on Early Nonfiction Film*. Amsterdam: Stichting Nederlands Filmmuseum.

Heuring, David. 1990. "IMAX Presses *to the Limit.*" *American Cinematographer* 71 (March): 34–44.

Highmore, Ben. 2002. *The Everyday Life Reader*. New York: Routledge.

Holmes, E. Burton. 1901. *The Burton Holmes Lectures, with Illustrations from Photographs by the Author*. 10 volumes. Battle Creek, Mich.: Little-Preston.

————. 1953. *The World Is Mine*. Culver City, Calif.: Murray and Gee.

Hubbard, Diane. 1977. "Explorer Criticizes Modern Technology." *Palm Beach Times*. 26 January.

Hyde, Anne Farrar. 1990. *An American Vision: Far Western Landscape and National Culture, 1820–1920*. New York: New York University Press.

Imperato, Pascal James, and Eleanor M. Imperato. 1992. *They Married Adventure: The Wandering Lives of Martin and Osa Johnson*. New Brunswick, N.J.: Rutgers University Press.

Issari, Mohammed Ali. 1982. Interview with Hamid Naficy. Los Angeles, 25 August.

Jacobs, Daniel, and Peter Morris. 2001. *The Rough Guide to Tunisia*. London: Rough Guides.

Johnson, Ted, and Diane Goldner. 1997. "Big Screens Make Mainstream Breakout Bid." *Variety*, 27 January, 5.

Johnson, Timothy W. 1982. *Grass: A Nation's Battle for Life*. In *MaGill's Survey of Cinema, Silent Films*, vol. 2, ed. Frank N. MaGill, 502–4. Englewood Cliffs, N.J.: Salem Press.

Jordan, Pierre-L. 1992. *Cinéma=Cinema=Kino*. Marseille: Musées de Marseille, Image en manoeuvres.

Kann, Maurice, ed. 1927. *Film Year Book, 1927*. New York: Film Daily.

Kaplan, Caren. 1996. *Questions of Travel: Postmodern Discourses of Displacement*. Durham, N.C.: Duke University Press.

Karsten, Rafael. 1923. *Blood Revenge, War, and Victory Feasts among the Jibaro Indians of Eastern Ecuador*. Washington, D.C.: U.S. Government Printing Office.

Kattelle, Alan D. 2003. "The Amateur Cinema League and Its Films." *Film History* 15, no. 2: 238–51.

Kaufman, Debra. 1993. "One Wild Ride: Motion-Simulation Market Picks up Speed." *In Motion*. October, 27.

Keenan, Jeremy. 1977. *The Tuareg*. London: Penguin Books.

Kirby, Lynne. 1989. Parallel Tracks: The Railroad and Silent Cinema, 1895–1929: Institutions, Aesthetics and Gender. PhD diss., University of California at Los Angeles.

————. 1997. *Parallel Tracks: The Railroad and Silent Cinema*. Durham, N.C.: Duke University Press.

Kluge, Friedrich. 1995. *Etymologisches Woerterbuch der deutschen Sprache*. 23rd expanded edition. Berlin: de Gruyter.

Kowalewski, Michael, ed. 1992. *Temperamental Journeys: Essays on the Modern Literature of Travel*. Athens: University of Georgia Press.

Kracauer, Siegfried. 1960. *Theory of Film: The Redemption of Physical Reality*. New York: Oxford University Press.

Krauss, Rosalind. 1983. *The Originality of the Avant Garde and Other Myths*. Cambridge, Mass.: Harvard University Press.

Kuepper, Heinz, ed. 1984. *Illustriertes Lexikon der deutschen Umgangssprache*. Vol. 6. Hamburg: Claassen.

Lacasse, Germain. 2000. *Le bonimenteur de vues animées: Le cinéma muet entre tradition et modernité*. Québec: Nota bene; Paris: Méridiens Klincksieck.

Lange, Hellmuth. 1930. *Filmmanuskripte und Film-Ideen*. Berlin: Photokino-Verlag.

Langer, Mark J. 1985. "*Tabu*: The Making of a Film." *Cinema Journal* 24, no. 3: 43–64.

Laux, James M. 1992. *The European Automobile Industry*. New York: Twayne Publishers.

Lawrence, Florence. 1925. " 'Grass' Thrilling Film Innovation with Big Appeal." *Los Angeles Times*. 21 May, n.p.

Lazreg, Marnia. 1994. *The Eloquence of Silence: Algerian Women in Question*. New York: Routledge.

Leblond, Marius. 1944. *L'Empire de la France: Sa grandeur, sa beauté, sa gloire, ses forces*. Paris: Éditions Alsatia.

LeProhon, Pierre. 1945. *L'Exotisme et le cinéma: Les 'chasseurs d'images' à la conquête du monde*. Paris: Éditions J. Susse.

Leutrat, Jean-Louis, and Suzanne Liandrat-Guigues. 1998. "John Ford and Monument Valley." In *Back in the Saddle Again: New Essays on the Western*, ed. Edward Buscombe and Roberta E. Pearson, 160–69. London: British Film Institute.

Lévi-Strauss, Claude. 1961. *Tristes tropiques*. New York: Criterion Books.

MacDonald, Scott. 2001. *The Garden in the Machine: A Field Guide to Independent Films about Place*. Berkeley: University of California Press.

Maleuvre, Didier. 1999. *Museum Memories: History, Technology, Art*. Stanford, Calif.: Stanford University Press.

Mast, Gerald. 1996. *A Short History of the Movies*, 6th ed. rev. Bruce F. Kawin. Boston: Allyn and Bacon.

Matos, Jacinta. 1992. "Old Journeys Revisited: Aspects of Postwar English

Travel Writing." In *Temperamental Journeys: Essays on the Modern Literature of Travel*, ed. Michael Kowalewski, 215–29. Athens: University of Georgia Press.

Mbembe, Achille. 2001. *On the Postcolony*. Berkeley: University of California Press.

McClure, Hal. 1988. "How to Start Travel Film Series." *Travelogue: The International Film Magazine* 11, no. 2: 34.

McDowell, Edwin. 1996. "America's Hot Tourist Spot: The Outlet Mall." *New York Times*, 26 May, A1.

McLuan, T. C. 1985. *Dream Tracks: The Railroad and the American Indian 1890–1930*. New York: Abrams.

Mead, Margaret. 1935. *Sex and Temperament in Three Primitive Societies*. New York: William Morrow.

Mead, Margaret, and Frances Cook MacGregor. 1951. *Growth and Culture: A Photographic Study of Balinese Childhood*. New York: G. P. Putnam's Sons.

Melville, Herman. 1846/1986. *Typee: A Peep at Polynesian Life*. New York: Viking Penguin. Originally titled *Narrative of a Four Months' Residence among the Natives of the Marquesas Islands; or, A Peep at Polynesian Life*.

Metro-Goldwyn-Mayer. 1930. *Trader Horn*, a Metro-Goldwyn-Mayer Picture. Press book, 2.

Meynier, Gilbert. 1990. "Guerre et pouvoir colonial: Continuités et adaptations." In *Histoire de la France colonial: 1914–1990*, ed. Jacques Thobie et al., 379–418. Paris: Armand Colin.

Michigan State News. 1942. "Andes Listed as Film Topic For Tonight." 24 January.

Miller, Angela L. 1993. *The Empire of the Eye: Landscape Representation and American Cultural Politics, 1825–1875*. Ithaca, N.Y.: Cornell University Press.

Mitchell, W. J. T. 1994. "Imperial Landscape." In *Landscape and Power*, ed. W. J. T. Mitchell, 5–34. Chicago: University of Chicago Press.

Mitman, Gregg. 1999. *Reel Nature: America's Romance with Wildlife on Film*. Cambridge, Mass.: Harvard University Press.

Moran, James M. 2002. *There's No Place Like Home Video*. Minneapolis: University of Minnesota Press.

Morin, Edgar. 1977. *Le cinéma: ou, L'homme imaginaire, essai d'anthropologie sociologique*. New ed. Paris: Éditions de Minuit, 1956.

Morris, Rosalind C. 1994. *New Worlds from Fragments: Film, Ethnography, and the Representation of Northwest Coast Cultures*. Boulder, Colo.: Westview Press.

Motography. 1911a. "Films to Advertize [*sic*] West." 11 April, 45.

———. 1911b. "Views of Los Angeles, Cal. [a.k.a. Seeing Los Angeles] (Imp)." 18 May, 664.

———. 1911c. "Glimpses of San Francisco (Pathé)." December, 267.

———. 1913. "Blazing Trail in Glacier National Park: Experiences with Pathe Cameraman." 20 September, 195.

———. 1914. "Yellowstone Park in Pictures." 3 October, 458.

Moving Picture News. 1911. "Educational Lectures." 11 March, 9.

Moving Picture World. 1907. 4 May, 137.

———. 1912a. "The Taos Indians at Home—New Mexico (Selig)." 10 February, 510.

———. 1912b. "Grand Canyon, Arizona (Nestor)." 24 February, 716.

———. 1912c. "Views of Los Angeles, Cal." 18 May 1912: 664.

———. 1912d. "Glacier National Park (Pathé)." 12 October, 142.

———. 1918. "Our National Parks Pictured." 2 February, 680.

Murray, Alison. 2000. "Le tourisme citroën au Sahara (1924-1925)." *Vingtième Siècle: Revue d'histoire* 68 (Octobre-Décembre): 95–107.

Musée Albert-Kahn. 1993. *Jean Brunhes: Autour du Monde, regards d'un géographe/regards de la géographie.* Boulogne: Musée Albert-Kahn.

———. 1995. *Albert Kahn: Réalités d'une utopie, 1860–1940.* Boulogne: Musée Albert-Kahn.

Musser, Charles. 1984. "The Travel Genre in 1903-1904: Moving towards Fictional Narrative." *Iris* 2, no. 1: 47–60. Repr. in *Early Cinema: Space, Frame, and Narrative*, ed. Thomas Elsaesser, 123-32. London: British Film Institute, 1990.

———, ed. 1985. *A Guide to Motion Picture Catalogs by American Producers and Distributors, 1894–1908: A Microfilm Edition.* Frederick, Md.: University Publications of America.

———. 1990. *The Emergence of Cinema: The American Screen to 1907.* Berkeley: University of California Press.

———. 1997. *Edison Motion Pictures, 1890–1900: An Annotated Filmography.* Washington, D.C.: Smithsonian Institution Press.

Musser, Charles, and Carol Nelson. 1991. *High-Class Moving Pictures: Lyman H. Howe and the Forgotten Era of Traveling Exhibition, 1980-1920.* Princeton, N.J.: Princeton University Press.

Naficy, Hamid. 1984. *Iran Media Index.* Westport, Conn.: Greenwood Press.

———. 1995. "Mediating the Other: American Pop Culture Representation of Postrevolutionary Iran." In *The U.S. Media and the Middle East: Image and Perception*, ed. Yahya R. Kamalipour, 73–90. Westport, Conn.: Greenwood Press.

———. 2001. *An Accented Cinema: Exilic and Diasporic Filmmaking.* Princeton, N.J.: Princeton University Press.

Nash, Roderick. 1973. *Wilderness and the American Mind*. Rev. ed. New Haven: Yale University Press.

Neumann, Mark. 2001. "Emigrating to New York in 3-D: Stereoscopic Vision in IMAX's Cinematic City." In *Cinema and the City*, ed. Mark Shiel and Tony Fitzmaurice, 109–21. New York: Blackwell.

New York Clipper. 1906. Edison Manufacturing Company advertisement. 28 April.

New York Times. 1923. "Climbing Mount Everest is Work for Supermen." 18 March, XII.

———. 1998. Quotation from Entertainment Design Workshop website: http://www.edesignw.com. 1 March.

Nichols, Bill. 1991. *Representing Reality: Issues and Concepts in Documentary*. Bloomington: Indiana University Press.

Nichols, Peter M. 1993. "Going beyond the 'Wow' Factor on Giant Screens." *New York Times*, 15 September, E3.

Nicholson John H. 1928. "Impressions of America." *Bulletin de la Société Autour du Monde*, 59–61.

The Nickelodeon. 1909. "Moving Pictures to Get Immigrants West." May, 130.

Nicole, Mlle. 1915. "Itinéraire aux Etats-Unis et au Canada." *Bulletin de la Société Autour du Monde* 1: 69–85.

Njoku, Daisy. 2002. "A Resource Guide to Travel Film Repositories." In "Travelogues and Travel Films," ed. Jeffrey Ruoff, *Visual Anthropology* 15, no. 1: 129–41.

Nochlin, Linda. 1989. *The Politics of Vision: Essays on Nineteenth Century Art and Society*. New York: Harper and Row.

Odin, Roger, ed. 1995. *Le film de famille: Usage privé, usage public*. Paris: Meridiens Klincksieck.

———, ed. 1999. Le cinéma en amateur. *Communications* 68.

Official Gazette of the United States Patent Office. 1904. Washington, D.C.: U.S. Government Publications 111 (August): 1577.

———. 1905. Washington, D.C.: U.S. Government Publications 118 (September): 788–89.

Olds, Elizabeth Fagg. 1985. *Women of the Four Winds*. Boston: Houghton Mifflin.

The Performer: The International Magazine for Stage and Screen. 1981. Sponsors, Artists Advise How. *The Performer* 4, no. 1: 6.

Perrigo, Lucia. 1994. "Lines by Lucia." *Travelogue: The International Film Magazine* 17, no. 2: 12.

———. 1995. "Lines by Lucia." *Travelogue: The International Film Magazine* 18, no. 2: 21, 33.

———. 1996. "Lines by Lucia." *Travelogue: The International Film Magazine* 19, no. 2: 44.

Peterson, Jennifer Lynn. 1997. " 'Truth Is Stranger than Fiction': Travelogues from the 1910s in the Netherlands Filmmuseum." In *Uncharted Territory: Essays on Early Nonfiction Film*, ed. Daan Hertogs and Nico de Klerk, 75–90. Amsterdam: Netherlands Filmmuseum.

———. 1998. "Early Travelogues, the Lure of the Exotic, and the Look at the Camera." Paper presented at Visible Evidence VI, San Francisco.

———. 2004. "Travelogues and Early Nonfiction Film: Education in the School of Dreams." In *American Cinema's Transitional Era*, ed. Shelley Stamp and Charlie Keil, 342–84. Berkeley: University of California Press.

———. Forthcoming. *Education in the School of Dreams: Travelogues and Silent Nonfiction Film*. Durham, N.C.: Duke University Press.

Pfefferman, Naomi. 1995. "On Top of the World." *American Cinematographer* 76 (August): 32–34.

Philebert, Le Général, and Georges Rolland. 1890. *La France en Afrique et le Transsaharien*. Paris: Augustin Challamel.

Pierrot, George F. 1942. "World Adventure Series" brochure. Detroit: Detroit Institute of Arts.

Pinney, Christopher. 1994. "Future Travel." In *Visualizing Theory: Selected Essays from V.A.R, 1990–1994*, ed. Lucien Taylor, 409–32. New York: Routledge.

Poirier, Léon. 1953. *Vingt-Quatre images à la second: Du studio au désert, journal d'un cinéaste pendant quarante-cinq années de voyages à travers le pays, les événements, les idées. 1907–1952*. Tours: Maison Mame.

Pold, Sören. 2001. "Panoramic Realism: An Early and Illustrative Passage from Urban Space to Media Space in Honoré Balzac's Novels *Ferragus* and *Le Père Goriot*." *Nineteenth-Century French Studies* 29, nos. 1, 2 (Fall-Winter): 47–63.

Pomeroy, Earl. 1957. *In Search of the Golden West: The Tourist in Western America*. New York: Alfred A. Knopf.

Pottier, René. 1938. *Un prince saharien méconnu: Henri Duveyrier*. Paris: Plon.

Powell, Lindsay. 2002. "Offensive Travel Documentaries on Japanese Television: *Secret Region and Japan!!* and *World Tearful Sojourn Diary*." In "Travelogues and Travel Films," ed. Jeffrey Ruoff, *Visual Anthropology* 15, no. 1: 65–90.

Pratt, Mary Louise. 1985. "Scratches on the Face of the Country; or, What Mr. Barrow Saw in the Land of the Bushmen." *Critical Inquiry* 12, no. 1: 119–43.

———. 1992. *Imperial Eyes: Travel Writing and Transculturation*. New York: Routledge.

Price, Bruce. 1968. *Into the Unknown*. New York: Platt and Munk.

PR Newswire. 2003a. "Two Imax 3D Films Reach New Box Office Milestones."
8 May.

———. 2003b. "Imax and EuroPalace to Open Imax Theatre at Disneyland
Resort Paris." 23 June.

———. 2003c. "Kiefer Sutherland Joins the Field on NASCAR 3D: The IMAX
Experience." 22 September.

Puntigam, Reinhard. 1994. Zoom In: "America" – Approaching Travel Videos Shot by Austrian Tourists in the United States. Master's thesis. Karl-
Franzens-University Graz.

Rabinovitz, Lauren. 1990. "Temptations of Pleasure: Nickelodeons, Amusement Parks, and the Sights of Female Sexuality." *Camera Obscura* 23: 71-90.

———. 1991. *Points of Resistance: Women, Power and Politics in the New York
Avant-Garde Cinema, 1943–1971*. Urbana: University of Illinois Press.

———. 2001. "'Bells and Whistles': The Sound of Meaning in Train Travel
Film Rides." In *The Sounds of Early Cinema*, ed. Richard Abel and Rick Altman, 167-80. Bloomington: Indiana University Press.

———. 2004. "More than the Movies: A History of Somatic Visual Culture
through Hale's Tours, IMAX, and Motion Simulation Rides." In *Memory
Bytes: History, Technology and Digital Culture*, ed. Lauren Rabinovitz and
Abraham Geil, 99–125. Durham, N.C.: Duke University Press.

Rahimian, Behzad. 1988. "Mazi-ye Naqli." *Mahnameh-ye Sinemai-ye Film* 63
(April-May 1988): 60-61.

Ramsey, Terry. 1926. Letter to the Editor. *Atlantic Monthly*. January: 142-43.

Ranger, Terence. 1983/1992. "The Invention of Tradition in Colonial Africa."
In *The Invention of Tradition*, ed. Eric Hobsbawm and Terence Ranger, 211–
62. Cambridge: Cambridge University Press.

Renov, Michael, ed. 1993. *Theorizing Democracy*. New York: Routledge.

Reynolds, John. 1996. *André Citroën: The Henry Ford of France*. New York: St.
Martin's Press.

Roberts, Mark. 1998. "Dream Factories: A Survey of Travel and Tourism."
The Economist, January 10, unpaginated supplement.

Rondon, Candido Mariano da Silva. 1946. *Indios do Brasil do Centro, Noroeste e
Sul do Mato Grosso*, vol. I. Rio de Janeiro: Conselho Nacional de Proteçao
aos Indios.

Rony, Fatimah Tobing. 1996. *The Third Eye: Race, Cinema and Ethnographic
Spectacle*. Durham, N.C.: Duke University Press.

Root, Nina J. 1987. *Catalog of the American Museum of Natural History Film
Archives*. New York: Garland Press.

Rosenblum, Naomi. 1984. *A World History of Photography*. New York: Abbe-
ville Press.

Rothacker, Watterson R. 1912. "Yellowstone Park on the Screen." *Motography*, April, 169.

Rubin, Judith. 1996. "Something's Wrong with Our Ship: Animated Motion Simulator Films in Theme Parks." *Animation World Magazine* 1 (November): 8. Website http://www.awn.com/mag/issue1.8/articles/rubin1.8 .html.

Ruby, Jay. 1982. *A Crack in the Mirror: Reflexive Perspectives in Anthropology*, Philadelphia: University of Pennsylvania Press.

———. 2000. *Picturing Culture: Explorations of Film and Anthropology*. Chicago: University of Chicago Press.

Runte, Alfred. 1987. *National Parks: The American Experience*. 2d rev. ed. Lincoln: University of Nebraska Press.

Ruoff, Jeffrey. 1991. "Forty Days across America: Kiyooka Eiichi's 1927 Travelogues." *Film History* 4, no. 3: 237–56.

———. 1992a. "Conventions of Sound in Documentary." In *Sound Theory/Sound Practice*, ed. Rick Altman, 217–34. New York: Routledge, Chapman, and Hall.

———. 1992b. "Home Movies of the Avant-Garde: Jonas Mekas and the New York Art World." In *To Free the Cinema: Jonas Mekas and the New York Underground*, ed. David James, 294–312. Princeton, N.J.: Princeton University Press.

———. 1998a. "An Ethnographic Surrealist Film: Luis Buñuel's *Land without Bread*." *Visual Anthropology Review* 14, no. 1: 45–57.

———. 1998b. *The Last Vaudevillian: On the Road with Travelogue Filmmaker John Holod*. Hanover, N.H.: Vaudeville Vérité.

———, ed. 2002. "Travelogues and Travel Films." Special issue of *Visual Anthropology* 15, no. 1.

Sadeqi, Khosrow Zolqadr. 1984. Interview with Hamid Naficy. Monterey, Calif. December 2.

Sadoul, Georges. 1965. *Dictionnaire des films*. Paris: Éditions du Seuil.

Said, Edward. 1979. *Orientalism*. New York: Vintage.

Saint-Amour, Paul K. 2003. "Modernist Reconnaissance." *Modernism/Modernity* 10, no. 2 (April): 349–80.

Samsam, Amir Bahman Khan. 1984. Correspondence with Hamid Naficy. July 31.

San Francisco Chronicle. 1955. "A Broker Comes Out of the Bush." 7 March.

Schenke, Eckhard. 1998. Der Amateurfilm – Gebrauchsweisen privater Filme. PhD diss. University of Goettingen.

Schivelbusch, Wolfgang. 1979. *The Railway Journey: Trains and Travel in the Nineteenth Century*. New York: Urizen Press.

Schleinitz, Egon G. 1968. *Safari-Abc: Fotografieren und Filmen in Afrika*. Winterthur: Foto & Schmalfilmverlag.

Schneider, Alexandra. 2002. " 'Mit dem Auto ins Gruene': Privater Film und private Mobilität." In *Autolust: Ein Buch ueber die Emotionen des Autofahrens*, ed. Stapferhaus Lenzburg, 51–56. Baden: Hier und Jetzt.

———. 2003. "Home Movie-Making and Swiss Expatriate Identities in the 1920s and 1930s." *Film History* 15, no. 2: 166–76.

———. 2004. *Die Stars sind wir: Heimkino als filmische Praxis*. Marburg: Schüren Verlag.

Schoedsack, Ernest B. 1971. Tape letter to Arnold Goldner, Chico State College, Chico, Calif., September.

———. 1983. "*Grass*: The Making of an Epic." *American Cinematographer*. February: 41–44, 109–14.

Schulz, Jane R. 2002. *The Romance of Small-Town Chautauquas*. Columbia: University of Missouri Press.

Schwartzberg, Schlomo. 1993. "Imax: Oscar Nominated Canadian Company on the Leading Edge of Technology." *Performing Art and Entertainment Canada* 28, no. 1: 42.

Scullin, George. 1948. "Explorers Club." *Science Illustrated*. 3, no. 5: 34–37, 80.

Sebbar, Leïla, and Jean-Michel Belorgey. 2002. *Femmes d'Afrique du Nord: Cartes postales (1885–1930)*. Saint-Juste-la-Pendue, France: Bleu Autour.

Selig Collection. 1911. Promotional flyer for *A Painter's Idyl*. Academy of Motion Picture Arts and Sciences.

———. 1912. Promotional flyer for *Seeing Spokane*. Academy of Motion Picture Arts and Sciences.

Shaffer, Marguerite S. 2001. *See America First: Tourism and National Identity, 1880–1940*. Washington, D.C.: Smithsonian Institution Press.

Shohat, Ella. 1991. "Imaging Terra Incognita: The Disciplinary Gaze of Empire." *Public Culture* 3, no. 2: 41–70.

Siegel, Kristi, ed. 2004. *Gender, Genre, and Identity in Women's Travel Writing*. New York: P. Lang.

Sierek, Karl. 1990. "Hier ist es schoen: Sich sehen im Familienkino." *In Sprung im Spiegel: Filmisches Wahrnehmen zwischen Fiktion und Wirklichkeit*, ed. Christa Bluemlinger, 147–67. Vienna: Sonderzahl.

Simmon, Scott, curator. 2000. *Treasures from American Archives: 50 Preserved Films* (DVD). San Francisco: National Film Preservation Foundation.

———. 2004. *More Treasures from American Archives, 1894–1931* (DVD). San Francisco: National Film Preservation Foundation.

Singer, Mark. 1999. "One Deadly Summit." *Sight and Sound* 9, no. 1 (January): 26.

Slavin, David H. 2001. *Colonial Cinema and Imperial France, 1919–1939: White Blind Spots, Male Fantasies, Settler Myths*. Baltimore: Johns Hopkins University Press.

Sloan, William. 1982. Correspondence with Hamid Naficy. May 12.

Slotkin, Richard. 1998. *Gunfighter Nation: The Myth of the Frontier in Twentieth-Century America*. 2d ed. Norman: University of Oklahoma Press.

Smith, Henry Nash. 1970. *Virgin Land: The American West as Symbol and Myth*. Rev. ed. Cambridge, Mass.: Harvard University Press.

Smoodin, Eric. 1993. *Animating Culture: Hollywood Cartoons from the Sound Era*. New Brunswick, N.J.: Rutgers University Press.

Snyder, Joel. 1994. "Territorial Photography." In *Landscape and Power*, ed. W. J. T. Mitchell, 176–201. Chicago: University of Chicago Press.

Sobchack, Vivian. 1995. "New Age Mutant Ninja Hackers: Reading *Mondo 2000*." In *Flame Wars: The Discourse of Cyberculture*, ed. Mark Dery, 11–28. Durham, N.C.: Duke University Press.

Solnit, Rebecca. 2003. *River of Shadows: Eadweard Muybridge and the Technological Wild West*. New York: Viking.

Sontag, Susan. 1970. "The Anthropologist as Hero." In *Claude Lévi-Strauss: The Anthropologist as Hero*, 184–96. Cambridge, Mass.: MIT Press.

———. 1977. *On Photography*, New York: Farrar, Straus and Giroux.

Soule, Thayer. 1997. *On the Road with Travelogues, 1935–1995: A 60-Year Romp*. Seattle, Wash.: Peanut Butter Publishing.

Stam, Robert, and Louise Spence. 1983. "Colonial, Racism and Representation." *Screen* 24, no. 2: 2–20.

Staples, Amy J. 2002. Safari Ethnography: Expeditionary Film, Popular Science and the Work of Adventure Tourism. PhD diss., University of California-Santa Cruz.

Stewart, Susan. 1993. *On Longing: Narratives of the Miniature, the Gigantic, the Souvenir, the Collection*. Durham, N.C.: Duke University Press.

Stirling, Matthew W. 1938. *Historical and Ethnographical Material on the Jivaro Indians*. Bulletin 117. Washington, D.C.: Smithsonian Institution, Bureau of American Ethnology.

Stoddard, John L. 1897. *John L. Stoddard's Lectures: Illustrated and Embellished with Views of the World's Famous Places and People, Being the Identical Discourses Delivered During the Past Eighteen Years Under the Title of the Stoddard Lectures*. 10 volumes. Boston: Balch Bros.

Strain, Ellen. 1996. "Exotic Bodies, Distant Landscapes: Touristic Viewing and Popularized Anthropology in the Nineteenth Century." *Wide Angle* 18, no. 2: 70–100.

———. 2003. *Public Places, Private Journeys: Ethnography, Entertainment, and the Tourist Gaze*. New Brunswick, N.J.: Rutgers University Press.

Streible, Dan. 2003. "Itinerant Filmmakers and Amateur Casts: A Home-made 'Our Gang' [1926]." *Film History* 15, no. 2: 177–92.

Sussex, Elizabeth. 1975. *The Rise and Fall of British Documentary: The Story of the Film Movement Founded by John Grierson*. Berkeley: University of California Press.

Swanson, Maxine (Maxine Logan, Maxine Howard). 1984. Interview with Hamid Naficy. Delta, Colo. August 12.

Swift, Jonathan. 1726/1994. *Gulliver's Travels*. Oxford: Oxford University Press.

Thomas, E. C. 1916. "Vancouver, B.C. Started with 'Hale's Tours.'" *Moving Picture World*. 15 July, 373.

Thompson, Kristen, and David Bordwell. 1994. *Film History: An Introduction*. New York: McGraw-Hill.

Toronto (Ontario) Star. 2003. "Coming Soon to an Imax Theatre: Stronger Profit." 28 February, EO6.

Toulet, Emmanuelle. 1991. "Cinema at the Universal Exposition, Paris 1900." *Persistence of Vision* 9: 10–37. Originally published as "Le cinéma à l'Exposition universelle de 1900" in *Revue d'histoire moderne et contemporaine* 83 (April-June 1986): 179–209.

Travelogue: The International Film Magazine. 1992. "Meet Joan Lark." 15, no. 2: 49.

———. 1994. "100 Years of Travelogues." 17, no. 2: 8.

Trebitsch, Michel. 2002. "Le Robinson juif: Un film et un texte sur l'université hébraïque de Jérusalem en 1925." *Cahiers de la Cinémathèque* 74: 99–107.

Turner, Frederick Jackson. 1920. *The Frontier in American History*. Repr. 1996, New York: Dover Publications.

Turner, Terrence. 1992. "Defiant Images: The Kayapo Appropriation of Video." *Anthropology Today* 8, no. 6: 5–16.

Urry, John. 1990. *The Tourist Gaze: Leisure and Travel in Contemporary Societies*. London: Sage.

Vanderknyff, Ricky. n.d. "See to Shining Sea." Unidentified unpaginated clipping in Billy Rose Theater Collection, New York Public Library Performing Arts Division.

Van Dooren, Ine. 1999. "Leinwandreisen um die Welt." *Kintop* 8: 31–38.

Van Dyke, II, Woodbridge Strong. 1929a. "Out to Make Trader Horn." *New York Times*, 23 June, VIII, 5.

———. 1929b. "Filming 'Trader Horn.'" *New York Times*, 30 June, VIII, 5.

———. 1929c. "Diary of a Film." *New York Times*, 7 July, VIII, 4.

———. 1929d. "More on 'Trader Horn.'" *New York Times*, 14 July, IX, 4.

———. 1929e. "Diary of a Film." *New York Times*, 21 July, VIII, 5.

———. 1929f. "Diary of a Film." *New York Times*, 28 July, VIII, 4.

———. 1929g. "Diary of a Film." *New York Times*, 4 August, VIII, 6.

———. 1929h. "Diary of a Film." *New York Times*, 1 September, VIII, 5.

———. 1929i. "Diary of a Film." *New York Times*, 22 September, IX, 8.

———. 1929j. "Diary of a Film." *New York Times*, 6 October, IX, 8.

———. 1929k. "Diary of a Film." *New York Times*, 13 October, IX, 7.

———. 1929l. "Diary of Trader Horn Film." *New York Times*, 10 November, X, 5.

Variety. 1910. "Review of *Riva, Austria and Lake Garda* (Urban-Eclipse)." 29 January, 13.

———. 1928. 20 June, 12.

———. 1930a. 13 August, 19.

———. 1930b. 27 August, 3.

———. 1930c. 27 August, 76.

———. 1930d. 1 October, 38.

———. 1931a. 7 January, 4.

———. 1931b. 28 January, 22.

Veeder, Gerry, K. 1990. "The Red Cross Bureau of Pictures, 1917–1921: World War I, the Russian Revolution and the Sultan of Turkey's Harem." *Historical Journal of Film, Radio, and Television* 10, no. 1: 47–70.

Vertov, Dziga. 1984. *Kino-Eye: The Writings of Dziga Vertov*. Trans. Kevin O'Brien. Berkeley: University of California Press.

Views and Films Index. 1907. "Hale Tour Films, Selig Polyscope 'Latest Films,' " 20 April, 5.

Vogel, Amos. 1958. "The Angry Young Film Makers." *Evergreen Review* 2: 175.

Wallace, Irving. 1947/1977. "Everybody's Rover Boy." In *Burton Holmes: The Man Who Photographed the World, 1892–1938*, ed. Genoa Caldwell, 9–22. New York: Harry N. Abrams.

Warshow, Robert. 1970. *The Immediate Experience: Movies, Comics, Theatre and Other Aspect of Popular Culture*. New York: Atheneum.

Wells, H. G. 1895/1995. *The Time Machine*. Rutland, Vt.: Everyman's Library.

Wiancko, Gene. 1996. "40 Years in Travelogues." *Travelogue: The International Film Magazine* 19, no. 2: 21.

Wiley, Ken. 1981. Correspondence with Hamid Naficy. September 6.

Williams, Carol Traynor, ed. 1998. *Travel Culture: Essays on What Makes Us Go*. Westport, Conn.: Praeger.

Williams, Linda J. 1995. "Film Bodies: Gender, Genre and Excess." In *Film Genre Reader II*, ed. Barry Keith Grant, 140–58. Austin: University of Texas Press.

Willis, Bob. 1997. "Why the Ukraine?: Filmmaker Accompanies Immigrant

Group to Homeland." *Travelogue: The International Film Magazine* 20, no. 1: 16.

Wilson, Edward L. 1874–88. *Wilson's Lantern Journeys: A Series of Descriptions of Journeys at Home and Abroad for Use with Views in the Magic Lantern or the Stereoscope.* 3 volumes. Philadelphia: Benerman and Wilson.

Wilton, Andrew, and Tim Barringer. 2002. *American Sublime: Landscape Painting in the United States 1820–1880.* London: Tate Publishing.

Wintle, Pamela, and John P. Homiak. 1995. *Guide to the Collections of the Human Studies Film Archives: 100th Anniversary of Motion Pictures: Commemorative Ethnographic Edition.* Washington, D.C.: Smithsonian Institution Press.

Wulff, Hans J. 1993. "Phatische Gemeinschaft/Phatische Funktion: Leitkonzepte einer pragmatischen Theorie des Fernsehens." *Montage/av* 2, no. 1: 143–63.

Zielinski, Siegfried. 1999. *Audiovisions: Cinema and Television as Entr'actes in History.* Trans. Gloria Custance. Amsterdam: Amsterdam University Press.

Zimmermann, Patricia. 1990. "Our Trip to Africa: Home Movies as the Eyes of the Empire." *Afterimage* (March): 2–7.

———. 1995. *Reel Families: A Social History of Amateur Film.* Bloomington: Indiana University Press.

———. 1996. "Geographies of Desire: Cartographies of Gender, Race, Nation and Empire in Amateur Film." *Film History* 8, no. 1: 85–98.

Zirinsky, Michael. 1986. "Blood, Power, and Hypocrisy: The Murder of Robert Imbrie and American Relations with Pahlavi Iran." *International Journal of Middle Eastern Studies* 18: 275–92.

Zoller, Mat. 2001. "*Haunted Castle.*" *New York Press*, 28 February, 38.

||||||||||||||||||||||||||||||||||||||||||||||||||||||||||||||||||||||||||||||||||||||||||||||||||||||||||||||||||||||||||||

RICK ALTMAN is a professor in the Department of Cinema and Comparative Literature at the University of Iowa and the author of numerous books on American cinema. Altman's *Silent Film Sound* was published by Columbia University Press in 2004.

PAULA AMAD is an assistant professor in the Department of Cinema and Comparative Literature at the University of Iowa. Amad's "Archiving the Everyday: A Topos in French Film History, 1895-1931" is forthcoming from Columbia University Press.

DANA BENELLI is an assistant professor in the Department of Theater at Illinois State University. Benelli is working on a book manuscript entitled "Jungles and National Landscapes: Documentary and the Hollywood Cinema in the 1930s."

PETER BLOOM is an assistant professor in the Department of Film Studies at the University of California, Santa Barbara. Bloom's *Mapping French Colonial Documentary* is forthcoming from the University of Minnesota Press.

ALISON GRIFFITHS is an associate professor in the Department of Communication Studies at the City University of New York. Griffiths's *Wondrous Difference: Cinema, Anthropology, and Turn-of-the-Century Visual Culture* was published by Columbia University Press in 2002.

TOM GUNNING is a professor in the Department of Art History at the University of Chicago and the author of several books on American cinema. Gunning's *The Films of Fritz Lang: Allegories of Vision and Modernity* was published by the British Film Institute in 2000.

HAMID NAFICY is a professor in the Department of Art and Art History at Rice University and the author of numerous books on Iranian cinema and television. Naficy's *An Accented Cinema: Exilic and Diasporic Filmmaking* was published by Princeton University Press in 2001.

JENNIFER LYNN PETERSON is an assistant professor in the Film Studies Program at the University of Colorado, Boulder. Peterson's *Education in the*

School of Dreams: Travelogues and Silent Nonfiction Film is forthcoming from Duke University Press.

LAUREN RABINOVITZ is a professor in the Department of American Studies and in the Department of Cinema and Comparative Literature at the University of Iowa and the author of numerous books on American cinema and television. Rabinovitz's *For the Love of Pleasure: Women, Movies, and Culture in Turn-of-the-Century Chicago* was published by Rutgers University Press in 1998.

JEFFREY RUOFF is an assistant professor in the Department of Film and Television Studies at Dartmouth College. Ruoff's *An American Family: A Televised Life* was published by the University of Minnesota Press in 2002.

ALEXANDRA SCHNEIDER is a lecturer in the Department of Film Studies at the Freie Universität in Berlin. Schneider's book on home movies, *Die Stars sind wir: Heimkino als filmische Praxis*, was published by Schüren Verlag in 2004.

AMY J. STAPLES is an archivist at the Eliot Elisofon Photographic Archives of the National Museum of African Art at the Smithsonian Institution in Washington, D.C. Staples is working on a book manuscript entitled "Safari Ethnography: Expeditionary Film, Popular Science, and the Work of Adventure Tourism."